Using

HTML

Neil Randall

with
John Jung
Greg Knauss
Tom Savola

To my mother, Katherine Randall.

Using HTML

Credits

Publisher
Roland Elgey

Associate Publisher
Stacy Hiquet

Title Manager
Jim Minatel

Acquisitions Manager
Cheryl Willoughby

Acquisitions Editors
Beverly Eppink
Doshia Stewart

Product Development Specialist
Mark Cierzniak

Editorial Services Director
Elizabeth Keaffaber

Managing Editor
Sandy Doell

Senior Series Editor
Chris Nelson

Production Editor
Kelly Oliver

Editor
Thomas Cirtin

Assistant Product Marketing Manager
Kim Margolius

Technical Editors
John W. Nelsen
Liz Reding

Acquisitions Coordinator
Ruth Slates

Operations Coordinator
Patty Brooks

Editorial Assistant
Andrea Duvall

Book Designer
Ruth Harvey

Cover Designer
Dan Armstrong

Production Team
Brian Buschkill
Jason Carr
Chad Dressler
Joan Evan
Jason Hand
Damon Jordan
Daryl Kessler
Bob LaRoche
Michelle Lee
Julie Quinn
Laura Robbins
Bobbi Satterfield
Denny Sheehan
Todd Wente
Jody York

Indexer
Jeanne Clark

About the Author

Neil Randall is the author or coauthor of several books about the Internet, including *Teach Yourself the Internet* and *The World Wide Web Unleashed*. In addition, he has written about the Internet and multimedia software in magazines such as *PC/Computing*, *PC Magazine*, *The Net*, *Internet World*, *I*Way*, *CD-ROM Today*, and *Windows*. In his real life, he's a professor at the University of Waterloo in Canada, where he forces unsuspecting English majors to develop HTML designs in his courses. He researches multimedia design and human-computer interaction, and he's a longtime fan of just about every game ever published—computerized or not.

Acknowledgments

First of all, and like everybody else who's earning money writing about the Internet these days, I owe a huge debt to Tim Berners-Lee, the man who masterminded the Web only a very short time ago. Longtime Internetter Dave Crocker put it best when he told me that Berners-Lee's brilliance lay in not inventing technology, but in taking the strengths of existing technology and putting them together so that they were accessible and easily available. HTML was part of that process, and its initial accessibility and availability made it the powerful creating tool it is today.

Next, publishers and editors. Beverly Eppink gave me this project in the first place, and I'm grateful to her for the opportunity. I'm also grateful to Mark Cierzniak for his always useful comments, and to Doshia Stewart for her patience. I'm also indebted to Paul Somerson, for his continuing support at *PC/Computing* magazine. Rich Schwerin and Deb McDonald of *PC/Computing* also get a special thanks for continuing to make my life fun. And a great many others in magazineland—you know who you are.

And then there's the University of Waterloo, where I work. I am continually grateful that a couple of years ago, when I started teaching students how to write HTML documents, nobody stepped in and told me to do something else instead. Back then, the Web wasn't anything approaching a household word, and very few people had any idea what I was actually teaching. But I was permitted to go ahead, and as a result, a number of my students gained skills they might not otherwise have picked up.

Three of these students worked on *Using HTML* with me, and their help was immeasurable. Stephanie Wunder helped me rewrite several chapters and worked extensively on the hands-on tutorials. As always, her work was superb, and as with all her projects she was 100% reliable. Celine Latulipe has worked with me on projects before this, and when I approached her about this one I had no doubt she would come through with flying colors yet again. I was completely right, and I thank her once more. Marcia Italiano, over the course of this book, developed into an extremely creative HTML designer— someone willing to push the limits continually. You can see her HTML work, as well as Stephanie's, on the *Using HTML* Web site (**http:// randall.uwaterloo.ca/UsingHTML**).

Finally, my family. If you've read any of my other books, you'll know that I keep thanking these three truly wonderful people, but that's because they keep deserving it. Heather remains willing to put up with a husband who spends most of his time in a dingy basement in front of the weird glow of a computer screen. Catherine and Michelle, my daughters, have gracefully accepted the fact that I'm not nearly as useful to them as I used to be, but they never make me feel bad about it. And besides, there's the cash… .

We'd like to hear from you!

As part of our continuing effort to produce books of the highest possible quality, Que would like to hear your comments. To stay competitive, we *really* want you, as a computer book reader and user, to let us know what you like or dislike most about this book or other Que products.

You can mail comments, ideas, or suggestions for improving future editions to the address below, or send us a fax at (317) 581-4663. For the online-inclined, Macmillan Computer Publishing has a forum on CompuServe (type **GO QUEBOOKS** at any prompt) through which our staff and authors are available for questions and comments. The address of our Internet site is **http://www.mcp.com** (World Wide Web).

In addition to exploring our forum, please feel free to contact me personally to discuss your opinions of this book: I'm **76245,476** on CompuServe, and I'm **mcierzniak@que.mcp.com** on the Internet.

Thanks in advance—your comments will help us to continue publishing the best books available on computer topics in today's market.

Mark Cierzniak
Product Development Specialist
Que Corporation
201 W. 103rd Street
Indianapolis, Indiana 46290
USA

Contents at a Glance

Show The World What You Can Do

An HTML Tool Chest

Table of Contents

Everybody's on the Web
see page 8

Your very first HTML code

see page 15

How do HTML editors work?

see page 20

Bring in the rhythm section: Including a background color
see page 31

Part III: So Far, So Good, But It's Time to Learn the Basics

Every Web page has the same basic structure

see page 46

What's so logical about logical styles?
see page 70

What graphics formats are supported on the Web?

see page 103

Putting hyperlinks to use

see page 111

Just what is an imagemap?

see page 132

Part IV: Out of the Garage and Onto the Stage: Advanced HTML

So, what are tables good for?

see page 146

The best operating system is: UNIX

*Here are
the basic
elements
of a form*

see page 163

*Some general issues of
form design*
see page 174

*What is
CGI?*

see page 182

The colorful interface— your first imagemap

see page 196

Part V: Give 'Em Something Extra

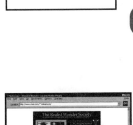

Asking your- self the right HTML questions

see page 219

Using lists for greatest effect

see page 230

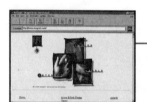

How do animated images work?

see page 252

Part VI: Show the World What You Can Do

*Finding a
Web provider*

see page 271

What-You-See-Is-What-You-Get editors

see page 295

What's a transparent image?

see page 302

Appendix A HTML Elements Reference 311

Appendix B WWW Bibliography 351

Special
HTML Tips
and Tricks

see page 359

Introduction

HTML, a hands-on tutorial, and a real live band

HTML is exciting. In fact, it might very well be the most exciting computer gig of all these days. Tell your friends you do spreadsheets, and they'll yawn. Tell 'em you write C++ code, and they'll fall fast asleep. Tell 'em you're into multimedia design, and they might say, "Cool." But tell 'em you write stuff for the World Wide Web, and then back it up with a live demonstration, and they'll think you're way out in front.

Which, of course, you are.

HTML is the language of the Web. Its real name is *HyperText Markup Language*, but nobody ever calls it that. It's simply "HTML" among friends, and that's exactly where this book will place you.

What's so cool about HTML?

HTML is nothing more than a set of codes. Every Web page in the world is done with HTML in one form or another. In fact, the magic of the World Wide Web is that everybody's Web browser—Netscape, Internet Explorer, Mosaic, Lynx, Quarterdeck Mosaic, Emissary, Mariner, MacWeb, you name it—every Web browser out there knows what to do with HTML code. That's what browsers do: they display HTML code the way it's meant to be displayed.

Using HTML takes you through the exciting process of HTML authoring. What's so great about it? First, it's not hard to do. You've seen all kinds of pages during your World Wide Web tours, and you probably already have an idea of what you want your pages to look like. To create your own pages, you only need two things: a working knowledge of HTML and access to a computer that's set up as a **Web server**.

Actually, the second of these requirements—access to a Web server—is much more difficult than the first. Part of *Using HTML* shows you how to find such a computer. Basically, you can set one up yourself, or you can rent space on someone else's machine. It's a little bit like owning a home versus renting one, except that you don't pay nearly as much.

You'll need to think about Web servers eventually, because the other truly great thing about HTML authoring is that it lets you make your point to the entire world. Everybody who has access to the World Wide Web has access to your HTML pages, and that's both thrilling and frightening. Thrilling because you can do so much with them, and frightening because you're on stage in front of a potential audience of millions.

Getting started with a hands-on tutorial

Nervous? Who isn't! It's a big stage, after all. But it's not as if you're competing against nothing but the best. The Web allows anybody on who wants on, and you don't need a degree in graphic design to put your stuff out there. Keep in mind that while your *potential* audience is in the millions, your more likely audience is a few random surfers and the people you actually tell about your site. So the best thing you can do is just get started.

That's why *Using HTML* kicks off with a hands-on tutorial. Before you even know the first thing about HTML and how it works, you'll be producing a Web page and seeing how it looks on your favorite browser. You'll work with headings, add text, emphasize main points, and create one of those great-looking lists. Then you'll try a graphic or two, and you'll even design a table and a fill-in form. By the time you've finished the hands-on tutorial, you'll know almost all the main features of HTML, and you'll be well on your way to creating a full-fledged Web site.

And the hands-on opportunities don't stop there. As you work your way through the book, you'll encounter three more hands-on tutorials. In each of these, you'll go back to your Web site and develop it further, making use of the techniques you just read about. When you reach the end of the last tutorial, you'll have on your computer a multi-page Web site with all the trimmings.

Not only that, but the hands-on tutorial is supported live on the Web itself. We've created a Web site dedicated exclusively to the readers of this book. All you have to do is fire up your browser and type the correct Web address (also known as a URL) in the Location or URL box. You'll be taken to the Web site, where you'll have to enter a specific username and password as the screen directs you. Then you're in, and you can see live-on-the-Web examples of how your pages should look.

Why did I bother with a username and password? Because if I didn't, anybody would be able to get into the site, and I honestly believe that buying a book should get you some special privileges. So while the rest of the universe is out there salivating for a chance to get inside the tutorial and create their own pages, you'll be able to look smugly satisfied that you know what's really there.

Getting into the live Web site

To enter the Web site for *Using HTML*, follow these steps:

1 Load your Web browser.

2 Type the following Web address (URL) in the Location box, the URL box, or whatever other way you can specify a particular Web location: **http://randall.uwaterloo.ca**.

3 Click on the link called *Using HTML—Private Web for Readers*.

4 You will come to a page that asks you to find two words from your *Using HTML* book. The first word will be your username, the second will be your password. This will change every time you enter the site.

5 When you get the box showing username and password, type the words in the respective boxes.

You're in. Enjoy. Once inside, feel free to look around. New hints and tips will appear regularly.

So who's the band?

To give you the experience of preparing a real Web site, I've enlisted the cooperation of Bertha's Attic, a young, up-and-coming rock band from

Canada. Bertha's Attic was thinking about putting up a Web site for a few months before I approached them, and when I suggested the possibility of doing so in conjunction with this book, they jumped at the chance. The pages you create in the hands-on tutorials will be the basis for the pages on their real Web site, which is scheduled for launch at the same time as this book.

You'll meet the members of Bertha's Attic through the course of this book. In addition, if you keep tuning into the *Using HTML* Web site, you'll find a growing amount of material about and by the band. Nobody knows, of course, if an up-and-coming band will actually make it big, or even slightly big, but from everything I've heard, this band has a solid chance. If that happens, you'll be able to say—with a completely honest face—that you were there at the beginning.

How this book is structured

You begin this book by learning a bit about HTML and authoring for the Web (Part I). Then, immediately, you launch into your HTML career, working your way through a hands-on tutorial (Part II) that takes you to the heart of the action. Here you'll begin creating a Web site for Bertha's Attic, complete with text, graphics, and even fill-in forms. At all stages of this tutorial, you can check your work by pointing your browser to the live Web site at **http:// randall.uwaterloo.ca**, and by the end of the tutorial you'll know how to construct documents that contain the most popular features on the Web.

With all these new skills at your disposal, you step back and look at HTML in detail. Part III is devoted to the basics of HTML, ranging from the simplicity of headings to the greater complexity of working with graphics and lists. Part IV builds on your increasing knowledge by launching into the more difficult but highly important features of HTML, such as tables, fill-in forms, and image maps. After each of these sections you'll go back to the Bertha's Attic Web site, adding features and elements in a short, new hands-on tutorial.

In Part V, you tackle the rest of HTML's important elements. Here you'll develop your Web site's content, use professional tricks to spice up the text on your pages, and use advanced codes to make your graphics look great. You'll even learn how to add movement to your pages, and to incorporate sound and video. At the end of this part, you'll return to the Web site for the final hands-on tutorial, and when you've finished you'll have a fully functioning Web site for the band.

So what's left? Nothing in HTML, actually. Instead, in Part VI you examine what's necessary to plan a Web site from start to finish, and how to tell the world that your personal Web site is up and running. Part VI is also about Web browsers, necessary because all of them display your Web pages slightly differently. Finally, Part VII introduces you to a variety of HTML tools available to you over the Internet itself, and the book ends with a complete HTML reference and bibliography.

Your goal in buying *Using HTML* was to learn how to write strong, effective Web pages. My goal was to give you what you needed to do exactly that. Write me—**nrandall@inforamp.net**—and let me know if I succeeded. Or, better yet, tell me where to find your personal Web site and I'll fire up my browser and check for myself.

Welcome to HTML. The excitement is just beginning.

How to use this book

This book contains a number of special elements and conventions that are designed to help you find important information quickly.

TIP   **Tips point out extra information.**

CAUTION   **Cautions serve as warning signs that you might run into trouble.**
They might also tell you how to avoid problems.

Q&A   **What are Q&A notes?**
These mainly present answers to troubleshooting questions.

Plain English, please!
If a new **term** or **concept** is introduced, it will usually be explained in a note like this one.

Another thing to note about this book: A code continuation character (➡) has been used when a code line is too long to fit within the margins of this book. This symbol simply indicates that due to page constraints, a code line has been broken that normally would appear on a single line.

1

Why Bother?

● In this chapter:

- Who's afraid of the big bad Web?

- Everybody seems to have a home page

- Jump on stage and show 'em what you can do

Everybody wants to have a Web site these days, but with so many out there, it might seem like a waste of time. What's going on? . . . . ●

Three things in life are inescapable: death, taxes, and the creation of a home page. At least, that's the way it seems as we head into the last half of the last decade of the last century of this millennium. A decade from now, home pages might be a fond memory, nothing more. But for now, they're hot, and if you're like most of the Web-surfing community, you want to put up one of your own.

Either that, or you want to work on a business's Web site because that's another thing that's happening more and more. Businesses of all shapes and sizes are appearing on the Web, some of them just for providing information and some for marketing and sales. If you're looking for a marketable skill to carry into your job search, HTML authoring is as strong a candidate as any. Even if they don't know what you're talking about, interviewers know that the Web is a major item.

Everybody's on the Web

Actually, it isn't true. Not *everybody* is on the World Wide Web. In fact, the majority of the world's population haven't even heard of it. But—and this is what matters—thousands upon thousands of companies, organizations, institutions, and individuals are looking to the Web as an important means of disseminating information. If you're not part of it, you're already somewhat behind. So *of course* you want to be on the Web. It doesn't seem like something you can avoid.

The universal stage...

Jumping onto the Web is like jumping onto the biggest stage ever designed. When you put your pages on the Web, you're inviting the world to come take a look. Most Internet users won't bother, either because they're not interested or, more likely, because they never get to know about your contribution (it's a *huge* stage). But you're putting your work on display nevertheless, and you're up there with everyone—ranging from the most amateur to the most professional. It's daunting, but exciting.

...of artists and scientists and businesses and more

So who's up on that stage with you? As it turns out, people with just about any interest you can think of—and some that you've never thought of at all—are stepping into the limelight.

The Web was begun by scientists, and it continues to be a hotbed of scientific activity. Physicists, astronomers, biologists, neurologists, research centers, and academic departments abound on the Net, as do materials for educators. You can learn a great deal by just touring around, and if you're a scientist yourself, you can instantly see how to use the Web to your advantage.

Arts communities joined the Web very early, seeing it as an inexpensive, attractive, and popular way to get the word out about their activities. They were right. People took notice, and they continue to do so. Whether you're aiming for a local audience or attempting to gain a global following, the Web makes it easy to get started. But keep in mind that quality still matters most.

Business has hopped onto the bandwagon with abandon. Thousands of large corporations and small entrepreneurships now use the Web for marketing, sales, and even customer service, and you can expect this to continue. These days you can find Web sites being advertised all over TV and radio; two years ago, that would have been impossible. If you're in business, you'll probably want your space on that bandwagon, too. And you get to hop on right beside IBM, Microsoft, Ford, Chrysler, NBC, Fox, Paramount, and all kinds of other big names.

There's more. Universities have an enormous Web presence with course catalogs and campus tours. High schools and even grade schools are getting into the act—third-graders are creating and publishing their own home pages! Social groups of all kinds have Web sites with information and publications, and an increasing number of Web-based magazines and newsletters are appearing. This is to say nothing of the hobbyists and collectors who are making their specialized interests more public than ever before.

The entertainment industry has a portion of the Web all to its own. Yes, the industry giants post Web pages, but of greater interest are the sites produced by the fans. No matter what celebrity or production you're interested in, you'll find it on the Web. It's a great way to find others with the same interest and to learn things about the topic you couldn't possibly have known.

How did the Web get so important, anyway?

The Internet began in the late 1960s, but it wasn't until the 1980s that people started to realize how powerful it could be as a communications and information medium. Scientists began to use it extensively as did researchers in the nonscientific academic disciplines. Then in the late '80s, those outside of the academic community wanted in, and they quickly realized that the Net wasn't very attractive: everything was text, and getting information was difficult.

In the late 1980s, Tim Berners-Lee and his research team at CERN (European Organization for Nuclear Research in Geneva) began to develop a hypertext system that would work over computer networks. They did it to allow researchers in high-energy physics to share their research with one another. In 1991 they released the idea to the Internet under the name WorldWideWeb, but even then the idea was restricted. Graphics were foreseen, but everything was still text-only.

1992 brought two important events. First, Marc Andreesen of the National Center for Supercomputer Activity (University of Illinois, Urbana-Champaign) developed a program that would display graphics and make navigating around hyperlinks a simple matter of pointing and clicking with a mouse. That program was Mosaic for the X Windows system, and as soon as it was released, it took the Web by storm. Macintosh and Microsoft Windows versions followed, and Mosaic became the best-known computer program on the planet besides, say, WordPerfect.

The other 1992 event of significance was the U.S. presidential election. During the campaign, the then vice presidential hopeful, Al Gore, spoke of the Information Superhighway, and when a potential presidency advocates anything, people take notice. In this case, the attention of the media turned to the Internet and specifically to the Web. The Web, after all, could be shown to the public, especially once Mosaic was in place in all its graphic splendor.

Also as a result of Gore's Internet interest, business began to take note. Suddenly, the race was on to mount bigger and better Web sites, until finally the Web became a business strategy rather than a minor experiment. All kinds of other events from 1992–95 took the Web from a minor convenience to a major communications tool, but it's safe to say that the interest by business has been the driving force. Once businesses get fascinated, they get *really* fascinated. And they want us to get fascinated as well.

It's not too late to carve your own niche

With everybody on the Web already, you might be wondering what you could possibly add. That would be a worthwhile thought if, in fact, the Web was limited. But it's not. It has a virtually unlimited audience, it has all the room you could want, and there's a crying need out there for material worth paying attention to.

The fact is, a substantial percentage of the Web is junk even if the Web sites themselves are well designed. You can surf your brains out for hours at a time and find nothing worth stopping to visit, and that's why it's a good time now to have your say.

Simply put, there's room for you in cyberspace. If you have a reason for putting up a Web page, by all means, put one up. Even if you don't have a reason and you just want to try your hand at designing one, go ahead. If your site becomes popular, more and more people will take notice. If not, you'll have design experience at your fingertips.

But what will make you truly popular is if you offer something valuable. Think about that as you're carving your niche. Make it a niche that people want to visit.

What's HTML got to do with it?

HTML (HyperText Markup Language) is at the core of the World Wide Web. It's nothing but a coding language—one that tells your Web browser how to display the information—but how you handle it will go a long way to determining your success as a Web author.

Used well, HTML can produce extremely appealing results. Used badly, it can be worse than turning rank amateurs loose with desktop publishing software. You'll find plenty of both kinds of designs all over the Web.

When you load your Web browser—Netscape, Internet Explorer, Mosaic, whatever—and click a hyperlink, you are telling your browser to use the Internet to download the file associated with that hyperlink. It's just like loading a file from a hard drive, except that this hard drive might be an entire hemisphere away.

Once the download takes place, the HTML document is displayed in your browser. Because the document has been coded in HTML, your browser knows how to make it look: headings will look like headings, fill-in forms will have their special appearance, graphics will be shining brightly, and so on. It's all possible because of HTML.

In Chapter 2, you'll learn a bit more about HTML. For the rest of the book, you'll put this popular coding language to work. Enjoy.

HTML: What's It All About?

● **In this chapter:**

- **HTML is all about playing tag**

- **Can I just borrow someone else's ideas?**

- **How a good editor can simplify your life**

You bought this book to learn how to write HTML, and that's what you'll do. But first, you'll have to learn basically how HTML works, and that's what you'll do here . . . . **>**

HTML isn't difficult. But it *is* demanding. Keep in mind as you're working through this book that, in essence, an HTML document is a piece of programming. It's not hard programming—not nearly as involved as C++ or even Basic—but it's programming of a sort nevertheless. You're **coding** actually, but in principle, it's much the same thing.

You want your Web pages to look right. To make that happen, you have to instruct Web browsers to display them correctly. That's what your HTML codes do: they tell your reader's Web browser what your page is supposed to look like on-screen. Fortunately, all browsers display most HTML codes the same way, so once you have it right for one browser, you're fairly sure of having it right for all of them.

Fairly sure? Yep. Some browsers never advanced past their preliminary development, and they don't display well at all. Others are older and don't incorporate the latest HTML advances. Still others, such as the widely used Netscape Navigator and the soon-to-be-widely used Microsoft Internet Explorer, allow authors to write special codes that only those browsers display.

You'll learn about these specialty codes as you work through this book. For the most part, though, HTML code is standard, and the basics are the same for everybody.

What do I use to write HTML code?

If you were setting out to write a letter, you'd probably use a word processor. If you wanted to create a newsletter, you'd load some kind of desktop publishing software. For financial tables, you'd probably turn to a spreadsheet program.

To write HTML code, you don't need a high-powered program at all. All you need, in fact, is a lowly text editor. If you're a Microsoft Windows user, good old Notepad (WordPad in Windows 95) or DOS's Edit will do just fine. UNIX people can turn to vi or pico. Macintosh owners have their share of text editors as well.

Text editors save files in ASCII format. This is the most basic format computers know about, and many programs allow you to save in ASCII format as an option. All word processors will let you do so, for example, usually through the Save As feature. Choose File, Save As, then in the File Type box (or File Format box or whatever), select ASCII or text. That does the job. So you can use your word processor to create your HTML files, but only if you remember to save your work as an ASCII file.

Because HTML is so popular, software devoted to producing HTML code has begun to appear. These programs, called HTML editors, automate some of the more tedious procedures and in some cases even hide the ugliness of the plain ASCII code. You'll learn about HTML editors in this book, starting, in fact, in the very next chapter. For a full look at HTML editors and tools, see Chapter 24.

For now, just fire up a simple text editor or your favorite word processor, and jump in.

Playing tag for fun and profit

You'll encounter the word **tag** in the HTML world—even in this book. The tag is the basic coding unit in the HTML system. Everything in HTML depends on the tags.

Tags are enclosed in angle brackets (< and >). For example, the paragraph tag is <P> and the horizontal line tag is <HR>. You can write the tags in either uppercase or lowercase letters. Just remember—you need both the opening bracket (<) and the closing bracket (>) to complete the tag. Don't forget to include both. (Normally, Shift+comma gets you the left angle bracket, and Shift+period gets you the right one.)

You'll learn more about tags soon. Right now, let's get going.

Your very first HTML code

Ready? First, create a folder or directory to store your HTML files. That'll help you find them as you go along.

Now, in a brand new document in your text editor, type the following:

```
Hello!<HR>
```

That's it. Nothing else. Just the word *hello*, an exclamation point, and HR enclosed in angle brackets (the H and R may be lowercase if you prefer). No carriage return is necessary, but if you want one, go ahead. HTML pays no attention to standard returns.

Next, save the file. Call it FIRST.HTML or FIRST.HTM (DOS and Windows 3.x users *must* use the three-character .HTM extension). If you're working in a word processor, be sure to select ASCII or text format before saving.

There, you're done. You've created your first HTML file. Tough, huh?

Now for the fun part: load your Web browser. If you have to log on first, do so (some browsers let you work offline). What you want to do now is load your FIRST.HTML (or FIRST.HTM) file into your browser. This procedure differs from browser to browser, but the idea is to open a **local** file instead of a Web location.

In Netscape, for example, choose File, Open File, then select FIRST.HTML from the directory where you stored it. In Internet Explorer, choose File, Open, and then click the Open File button in the Open Internet Address box. Other browsers may require different steps.

With FIRST.HTML selected, click Okay. Presto! You have your first Web page staring at you. All you have is "Hello!" with a long line underneath, but it's a start. Essentially, the rest of this book shows you how to make that first page more attractive.

Note the following:

- "Hello" needs no coding at all. It's simply a piece of default text, and browsers will display it in whatever font their users have configured for default text. Usually, this is Times New Roman 12 point or something similar, but users can change it.

- The silly looking <hr> tag, which stands for horizontal rule, became a screenwide line in your browser. That's because the <hr> tag is interpreted by the browser and displayed accordingly. Virtually all browsers know what to do with <hr>.

- You *must* give your HTML document an extension of .HTML or .HTM if you want it displayed properly. If you let your text editor give it an extension of .TXT or .ASC, your browser won't do its job.

Your second HTML code

In Chapter 4, you'll produce some fairly elaborate HTML code. Right now, just dress up FIRST.HTML a wee bit to see how things work.

Open FIRST.HTML in your text editor (it's probably already open). Now, type **<H1>** in front of Hello! and type **</H1>** directly after it (that's the numeral 1 after the H). Leave the <HR> tag as the last element in the line. Your document should look like this:

```
<H1>Hello!</H1><HR>
```

Now save the file again. Make sure it's saved as FIRST.HTML. Reload it into your browser. You'll see that "Hello!" is now much bigger and bolder, but apart from that, nothing has changed.

So what happened? With those two small additions, <H1> and </H1>, you transformed "Hello!" from default text to a level-1 heading. You'll learn all about headings in Chapter 5, but you've already created one. Your browser interpreted the <H1></H1> code as a heading and assigned it the font for level-1 headings. Usually, this is a much larger font than for default text, but again your readers will be able to configure their browsers to display it as they want.

What you just did to this document was easy, but it was one of the most important tasks in HTML coding. You created a **container.** Good work!

Most of HTML involves placing items inside containers, which have an **opening** tag and a **closing** tag. Notice that <HR> has only one tag—it's not a container. But the heading tag, in this case <H1>, needs an </H1> on the other side of the item to end the formatting code. The text item "Hello!" is inside this <H1></H1> container, and that tells the browser to make it appear with the level-1 heading font.

Keep the following three points in mind:

- For HTML containers, every opening tag must have a corresponding closing tag. Closing tags are the same as opening tags, except that they have a forward slash (/) in front of them. The opening tag for *italics* is <I>, for example, while the closing tag is </I>.

- You don't have to put spaces between HTML codes, nor do you have to use carriage returns. Browsers know how to display your text just fine. They'll put a carriage return after a heading container (add some text after the heading and before the horizontal rule and see what happens), and another one before the horizontal line. If you want to specify your own spacing, you need to know some further HTML codes. For now, let the browser do its work.

- Once you've begun an HTML document, you can keep adding to it and revising it to your heart's content. Just hit the reload key of your browser and monitor your changes.

Welcome to HTML. You've already done the basics. Now it's on to Part II where you'll create the first pages of a real Web site.

Hands-on Step 1: Download an Editor

● **In this chapter:**

● **Your HTML editor can be your very best friend**

● **Where can I find an HTML editor?**

● **Downloading and installing your editor**

The most helpful tool you can possibly have as an HTML author is a full-featured HTML editor. In your first hands-on tutorial, you'll find one on the Web itself. . . . . . ➤

The only tool you actually *need* to author HTML documents is a text editor. Any text editor will do, as will any word processor that lets you save your file in **text** or **ASCII** format. If you're a Windows user, Notepad (WordPad in Windows 95) will do just fine. UNIX users can use vi or pico. Mac users have access to an equal number of excellent editors, and MacWrite—which many people still have—certainly does the job.

Author, meet your editor

Nonetheless, there's a category of software tools out there designed to make the HTML authoring process much easier than text editors: HTML editors. They remove some of the pain of typing HTML tags and containers and putting in all the little minutiae (without which your HTML documents won't work right).

And not only do they make it easier, they help with accuracy as well. Type a hyperlink from scratch—with all of its angle brackets and quotation marks and seemingly endless Web addresses—and you'll know how easy it is to make a simple mistake. HTML editors help you keep your coding correct.

How do HTML editors work?

Simply put, HTML editors hide HTML code. For example, with a text editor you must type the following typical initial code:

```
<HTML>
<HEAD>
<TITLE>My First HTML Document</TITLE>
</HEAD>
```

But with an HTML editor, you can just type your title, highlight it, and select the Title tag from the menu. The editor fills in the ugly stuff on its own.

In this way, editors work much like word processors. Anyone familiar with WordPerfect's old Reveal Codes feature knows what word processing codes look like, and they're not pretty. WordPerfect and Word for the Macintosh or Windows look much nicer, but the codes are still there working in the background. They're just hidden from your view, that's all.

HTML editors haven't reached the same level of sophistication, but they're getting there. By the time you read this, there will likely be three or four fully graphical HTML editors available for use. There are already a couple now, and one of them, Live Markup for Windows, is the editor you'll see throughout the hands-on steps in this book (Chapters 4, 10, 16, and 21). Several others are in the works as of this writing. One of the most promising is Netscape Navigator Gold, which will let you edit and create HTML code right inside the Netscape browser.

So I just need one good HTML editor, right?

It's a nice thought, but it isn't realistic yet. The next few months might see the perfect, it-does-everything HTML editor, but so far there isn't one.

The best suggestion I have is to download a few of them and try them out, choosing the one you like best for your main editing tool. Keep in mind that a different editor might handle a different feature in a better fashion, and you should turn to it for the functions you need. For example, I use Live Markup for my main HTML work; however, it doesn't (yet) do forms or tables, so I switch to different editors for those functions. WebForms does a nice job on forms, and HotDog Professional is pretty good with tables. I create the HTML code using these tools, and then copy and paste it across to Live Markup. It works fine.

Downloading your HTML editor

The good news about HTML editors is that they're available as freeware or shareware on the Internet itself. You can buy commercial editors, but before doing so why not try out some free (or cheap) ones? In many cases, in fact, the commercial ones are available with somewhat lesser capabilities on the Net, so you can try before you buy.

The editor used in the hands-on steps in this book, Live Markup, is available at the following Web site:

http://www.digimark.com/mediatech

The editor you'll see throughout the other chapters in this book is HotDog Professional, which is available at the following URL:

http://www.sausage.com

Use your Web browser—Netscape, Mosaic, Internet Explorer, Web Explorer, whatever—to go to that site. Click the download link (it's different in each case), and let your browser download the file.

Many other HTML editors are available. Turn to Chapter 24 to learn more about them and their differences. For now, here are several Web sites to visit where editors are in abundance. In all cases, go to the site with your Web browser, and then follow the links to the download instructions. Click the link leading to the actual file, and save the file directly to your hard disk from inside your browser.

Sites for Microsoft Windows users:

The Ultimate Collection of Winsock Software (**http://www.tucows.com/softhtm.html**)

Shase Virtual Shareware Library (**http://vsl.cnet.com/**)

Mag's Big List of HTML Editors (**http://union.ncsa.uiuc.edu/ HyperNews/get/www/html/editors.html**)

Yahoo (**http://www.yahoo.com/Computers_and_Internet/ Internet/World_Wide_Web/HTML_Editors/MS_Windows/**)

W3 and HTML Tools (**http://www.w3.org/hypertext/WWW/Tools/**)

Sites for Macintosh users:

Shase Virtual Shareware Library (**http://vsl.cnet.com/**)

Yahoo Macintosh HTML editors (**http://www.yahoo.com/ Computers_and_Internet/Internet/ World_Wide_Web/HTML_Editors/Macintosh/**)

Utexas Mac Archive (**http://www.yahoo.com/ Computers_and_Internet/Internet/ World_Wide_Web/HTML_Editors/Macintosh/**)

Info-Mac HyperArchive Root (**http://hyperarchive.lcs.mit.edu/ HyperArchive.html**)

Mag's Big List of HTML Editors (**http://union.ncsa.uiuc.edu/ HyperNews/get/www/html/editors.html**)

W3 and HTML Tools (**http://www.w3.org/hypertext/WWW/Tools/**)

Sites for UNIX users:

Shase Virtual Shareware Library (**http://vsl.cnet.com/**)

Mag's Big List of HTML Editors (**http://union.ncsa.uiuc.edu/ HyperNews/get/www/html/editors.html**)

Yahoo (**http://www.yahoo.com/Computers_and_Internet/ Internet/World_Wide_Web/HTML_Editors/X_Window_System/**)

W3 and HTML Tools (**http://www.w3.org/hypertext/WWW/Tools/**)

See Chapter 24 for a more detailed listing and description of HTML editors available to download.

Installing your editor

There's no way for this book to cover all the installation quirks of all the HTML editors out there. Suffice it to say that a basic knowledge of your operating system is necessary to get the installation started—once you've **extracted** the files, that is.

Because nobody likes to download great big files, almost every program you come across, including HTML editors, will be compressed in one form or another. For Windows users, the usual method is PKZIP, which yields files with a .ZIP extension. You must have an unzipping program. Several are available including WinZip and PKZip, which can be downloaded as shareware.

Files for the Macintosh often download as self-extracting archives (SEA files), and the Mac is much smoother at handling compressed files than Windows or UNIX. UNIX users must get used to a number of different compression programs, and if you're a regular UNIX user, you probably know about them anyway.

In fact, if you've used the Internet to download software, including your Web browser, this procedure is probably second nature by now: extract, find the SETUP or INSTALL file, double-click, and do the installation. Then you're ready to go.

Hands-on Step 2: Let's Do a Quick Couple of Pages

● **In this chapter:**

● **Design titles and headings for your document**

● **Link to external sites**

● **Save and preview WWW documents**

● **Give your pages life with some graphics**

● **Create unordered lists**

● **Meet the band!**

The fundamental purpose of all HTML documents is to force Web junkies to sit up, click, and take notice of the display you've placed before them. In this set of tutorials, you'll start learning how to make that happen . . . . ➤

L ike all the "Hands-on" chapters in this book (3, 10, 16, and 21 are the others), this chapter gets you working at building Web pages. Specifically, you'll be creating pages about Bertha's Attic, the band I told you about in the Introduction. They're dying to hear from you, by the way. In fact, you'll create a link in these pages that will let you send e-mail directly to them.

And don't think that you're only getting the basics here. The HTML elements you'll work with over the next few pages are fundamental to almost all Web pages you design. By the time you've finished this chapter, you'll be ready to work your way through the rest of the book.

If you read Chapter 3 (if not, you might want to do that now), you should have an HTML editor. Load it up, and then follow the steps outlined below. You'll also need your browser because that's where you'll display your work.

There are two ways of checking what you've done. First, there are several screen shots in this chapter that help guide you. Second, as you go through the tutorials, you'll be given instructions to go to the *Using HTML* Web site. To get there, type the Web address in the Open Location or Go to box of your Web browser. All these addresses begin with **http://randall.uwaterloo.ca/**.

At any point, feel free to add your own HTML elements. Your pages won't look the same as those in the book, but if you're comfortable experimenting, go right ahead. That's what learning HTML is all about.

I've chosen Live Markup Version 32b11a to compose all the Bertha's Attic HTML documents (for many reasons that you will discover when you read the chapters following this one), but any HTML editor will do the trick. The text-only code is also shown in this chapter, for those who want to write HTML code in a text editor.

Fire up your personal Web editor and watch while Bertha's Attic becomes an international World Wide Web star. Oh, and by the way, if you send them a message, I won't be the one answering it. They will—for better or for worse.

Sound check: Getting the HTML editor up and going

Each Web editor has its own specific method of opening a new HTML document, but the most common is to select the New command from your editor's menu or toolbar—similar to opening a new file in a word processor.

Live Markup will be the editor of choice here, and all examples will pertain to it. You can get it from the Web (**http://www.digimark.net/mediatech/**).

If you're using Live Markup, go to the File menu at the top of the screen and select New. Live Markup will then prompt you to choose between opening an HTML file or a text file. You'll see the screen shown in figure 4.1.

Fig. 4.1
Live Markup's interface allows users to create text or HTML files, and it saves the documents in the appropriate format (.TXT or .HTM/.HTML).

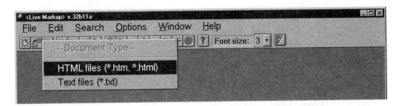

Choose the HTML formatting option. You will now be given a blank screen called Document1.

The very first thing you should do, as an organized WWW author, is save your file under an appropriate name. All HTML files must be saved before you can preview them on a browser, and now is as good a time as any.

Select the Save As command from the File menu and insert the file name, type, and directory (see fig. 4.2). I named my file ba1.htm and saved it in my Website Htdocs directory. You can put it in whatever directory you want. In fact, why not create a new directory just for your HTML pages?

CAUTION **All files saved from a WWW editor—ASCII and WYSIWYG alike—** must be saved with an .HTM or .HTML extension. If you're using DOS or Windows 3.x, .HTM is your only choice. Win95, WinNT, Mac, or UNIX users can use .HTML instead.

Fig. 4.2
The Save dialog box
may vary according
to your editor and
operating system, but
the essentials of saving
remain the same.

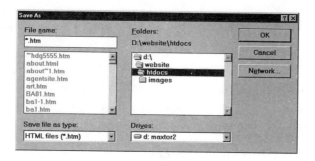

First chord: The title

Next we will add a title. Suffice it to say that titles must be both descriptive and revealing because your document's title is the name that all other documents link to throughout the Web. A detailed discussion of titles appears in Chapter 5.

From the Elements menu, select Document Information. In Live Markup, the information box shown in figure 4.3 appears.

Fig. 4.3
The Title element is
not mandatory but it
helps to create order
and descriptive appeal
on the Net. Insert a
title that accurately
describes your
document's content
but also catches your
reader's eye.

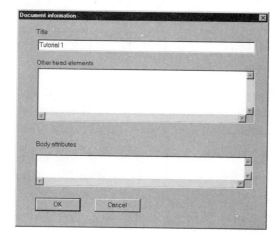

Erase the word "untitled" that appears in Live Markup's dialog box and name your file. I called mine Tutorial 1.

Save your HTML document once again and preview your document. Your title will appear in your browser window, not as a part of your new page.

TIP **To preview your document with a standard HTML editor, fire up** your browser and select the File Location or Open File command (or a command with a similar name) from the File menu. Specify the file by entering its directory location or file name, and then click OK.

For code-only authors...

In the hands-on chapters, you'll see sections called "For code-only authors." These let you construct your HTML code in ASCII text instead of through an HTML editor. Any text editor will do for this job.

The HTML tags that control the TITLE element are <TITLE> and </TITLE>. The Title element is always inserted in the HEAD of your document, indicated by the <HEAD> and </HEAD> commands. The first few lines of your HTML code will not appear in your actual document; they act as supplementary material. Actual content is inserted in the BODY of the file.

To insert the title for this document, type the following in your text editor:

```
<HTML>
<HEAD>
<TITLE>Tutorial 1</TITLE>
</HEAD>
<BODY>We'll get to this in a minute</BODY>
</HTML>
```

Great riff—Your first heading

The first item you'll actually put on the HTML page is a heading. Live Markup offers three ways of inserting headers.

One option is to go to the Elements menu, and click Header. Live Markup will display a rectangle on the first line of your document indicating where to insert the heading information.

The second way of inserting headers is to select the blue Hx button from the toolbar.

To produce a similar result, click the red, blue, and yellow 3-D cube contained in the toolbar. A smaller text rectangle will appear. Now right-click the text square and choose the Header option from the pop-up menu.

The 3-D color cube on Live Markup's toolbar symbolizes the Text Block command listed under the Element menu. Insert this block when you want to type physical text in your Web pages. The small square that appears on your document screen with the text block command acts as a marker that holds the text you insert. Deleting the text block deletes all the information it holds.

Fig. 4.4

Selecting Header from the pop-up menu (produced by right-clicking the Text icon in Live Markup) has the same result as using the toolbar or menu methods of header insertion.

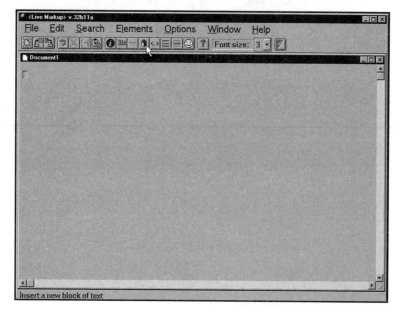

Headings range in size, H1 being the largest and H6 the smallest. Right-click the Heading rectangle on your document screen and select H1 for the first heading in your document.

Type **Bertha's Attic**. That's your first heading. Now save the file and pre-view your document. Your site will look pretty bland at this point in its construction but don't worry—things are about to get better.

Most people seem to like centered headings. No problem—let's center it. In Live Markup, right-click the heading insertion rectangle and select the Center option. Other WYSIWYG editors simply require users to select the heading material and click a center button on the toolbar.

Compare your page with mine to see how they match up, by typing **http://http://randall.uwaterloo.ca/ba1.htm** in your browser's location box (or Open Location or Go to command).

For code-only authors...

Because your heading will be the first thing to appear on your Web page, it is also the first thing you insert in the BODY of your document. After the first body tag (<BODY>) type the following code:

```
<H1>Bertha's Attic</H1>
```

This code will produce the largest size heading (but numbers from 1-6 may be substituted for alternative fonts).

The center feature in code-only editors is more complex than the WYSIWYG format because it requires the **nesting** of elements. Nesting means that certain elements are inserted within other element containers. You have to put the <CENTER> and </CENTER> opening and closing tags around the whole header. Here's the code:

```
<CENTER><H1>Bertha's Attic</H1></CENTER>
```

If you have entered all the correct HTML codes, your page should look like the first tutorial page found at **http://randall.uwaterloo.ca/ba1.htm.** Check out this site by typing the URL in your browser's location box (or the Open Location or Go to command—I'm going to stop referring you to this alternative, okay?).

Bring in the rhythm section: Including a background color

You're probably used to seeing nice background colors out there on the Web. Let's put one in, to make our page more... well, spiffy. There are two ways of choosing a background in Live Markup. The easiest is to click the Options menu. To create a page with a solid color as a background, choose Colors, and then Background. You receive a color palette similar to figure 4.5.

Fig. 4.5
Live Markup allows you to choose a color directly off the standard color palette or to select a more precise background color from the customized palette.

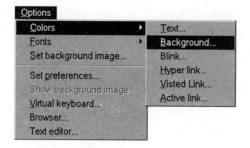

From here simply click a color block and then click OK. Save your file, and go take a look. Your page should resemble the document you find at **http://randall.uwaterloo.ca/ba2.htm** (although your background colors may be different).

For code-only authors...

Setting the background color using a tagged editor is no simple process. You have to insert a hexadecimal "red-green-blue" value in the form #rrggbb that corresponds to a specific color scheme. Thankfully, coded Web editors often provide a color table that displays colors along with their corresponding numerals.

Inserting a specific color requires the following code (in which the # sign is followed by a color label taken from the chart). In this case, you'll get a bright green:

```
<BGCOLOR="#80FF00" LINK = "#00FFFF">
```

Preview your document. It should resemble the page you receive when you type **http://randall.uwaterloo.ca/ba2.htm** in your browser's location box.

We're cookin' now—Setting a background image

Background images are even snazzier than background colors. To insert an image for your background, go to the Options menu of Live Markup and choose Set Background Image. The screen shown in figure 4.6 appears.

Fig. 4.6
Most Web editors allow you to insert any graphic file that you have saved on your system as the background image for your Web page.

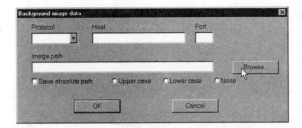

Q&A *Where can I find graphics to download and use as backgrounds in my World Wide Web pages?*

For variety among pages check out some of the downloadable background files on the Net:

- Netscape Backgrounds: **http://www.netscape.com/assist/ net_sites/bg/backgrounds.html**
- The Background Sampler: **http://www2.netscape.com/assist/ net_sites/bg/backgrounds.html**
- The Virtual Background Museum: **http://www.teleport.com/~laj/ VBM/**
- Sample Backgrounds: **http://128.200.162.20/backgrnd.html**
- Carol's Background Clipart Collection: **http://www.rmii.com/ bugsy/clip3/**

Before downloading anything, though, check for copyright notices on the sites. Many sites make their materials available to the public domain, but others want some kind of acknowledgment. Remember, copyright laws apply, even on the wild and wooly Internet.

Now download or copy a background image into a directory on your hard drive.

TIP **Internet Explorer users can, uh... "borrow" the background used** in the Bertha's Attic site by right-clicking on the background and then selecting the Save Background Image as option.

In the box below Image Path, fill in the location of the graphic; then click OK.

Save your file, and take a look! See if it looks like **http://randall.uwaterloo. ca/ba3.htm**; it should.

For code-only authors...

Inserting a background image in tagged editors requires the following HTML coding:

```
<BODY BACKGROUND="URL or path/filename.gif">
```

In your case, let's assume you've saved your background image file in your HTML directory as backgrd.gif. Your code will look like this:

```
<BODY BACKGROUND="html/backgrd.gif">
```

Of course, you'll have to make the path match your particular machine. For DOS/Windows users, it might be something like c:/html/backgrd.gif—notice that the slashes aren't backslashes, they're forward slashes.

Background color and image tags usually appear as the first item inserted after the <BODY> tag, but they will be applied as long as they are inserted among the text between the <BODY> and </BODY> containers.

Compare your results with the page I created at **http://randall.uwaterloo. ca/ba3.htm**. Remember that your background image will be different, but the page's essential elements will remain the same.

Hey, the lyrics matter—It's text time!

Now comes the easy part: text. You probably want to limit the amount of text in your HTML documents; after all, no one wants to stare at paragraphs and paragraphs of information when there are so many other creative ways to present material. However, some text is always necessary to clarify and describe the functions of your pages.

To add text using the Live Markup Web editor, simply click the colored 3-D cube (or select Text Block from the Elements menu) and start typing.

You can type text in the standard font size, but right-clicking Live Markup's text icon reveals numerous other options, shown in the following table. Most good HTML editors offer the same options; just look around the menus.

Text Type	HTML effects
Paragraph	Blank line inserted before text
Extended Quote	Italic font
Preformatted	All characters receive the same screen space
Address	Italic font for author's Internet address
Header	Header fonts from H1-H6

Choose the appropriate styles and type—it's as simple as that. Once you have created the paragraphs or blocks of text that explain the function and expectations of your Web page, you can dress your text up with some of the physical and logical styles discussed in Chapter 6.

Using Live Markup, you can emphasize your text with bold, italic, definition, or citation fonts, or create blinking text, relative font sizes, typewriter texts, and underlined fragments. Highlight the text you wish to alter and right-click the chosen text. The menu shown in figure 4.7 appears.

Fig. 4.7
Live Markup's physical and logical styles are displayed in lengthy pull-down menus. Almost all Web editors provide these same textual elements in varying design methods.

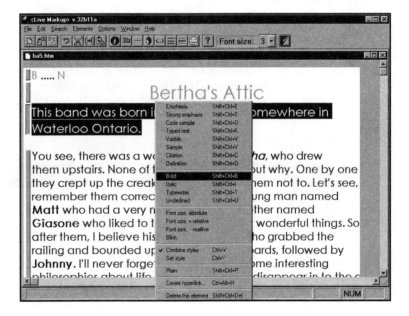

The standard Bertha's Attic page, found at **http://randall.uwaterloo.ca/ba4.htm**, provides a brief history of the band and cues the Web pages that follow. Without the manipulation of font styles and physical appearance, this page would seem rather *blah*. Fonts and styles can do a lot for your pages, so practice the text elements offered by your personal Web editor until you are comfortable with their use.

To get this text, fire up **http://randall.uwaterloo.ca/ba4.htm** and select View Source (or View Document Source) in your Web browser. From there, you can copy the text and paste it into your HTML document.

For code-only authors...

There are just as many text styles available for code-only Web authors as there are for WYSIWYG users; unfortunately, codes are harder to write. One thing is easy, though: to insert text blocks using a code-only Web editor, all you do is fire up the editor and start typing. No worrying about menus or strange icons.

The following table shows some of the most useful HTML elements for text formatting.

CAUTION **Be careful when you type large blocks of information in code-only** editors. Although the editor may display your text with the line breaks and paragraphs that you have inserted using the carriage return, the Web browser will not. Text blocks in code-only editors must be contained within the appropriate line break and paragraph tags for the browser to recognize the elements.

Format Element	HTML Container
Line Break	<HR></HR>
Paragraph	<P></P>
Italic	<I></I>
Emphasis	<EM></EM>
Bold	<B></B>
Strong	<STRONG></STRONG>
Preformatted	<PRE></PRE>

All text inserted between these element containers is affected by the tags that surround it. For example, the following code would place the words "Bertha's Attic" in what is commonly known as bold, italic font:

```
<EM><STRONG>Bertha's Attic</STRONG></EM>
```

The difference between italic and emphasis, and bold and strong, is discussed in Chapter 6. For now, use EMPHASIS and STRONG when combining elements and italic or bold when the element stands alone.

To get the text for this page (including all the codes), go to **http://randall.uwaterloo.ca/ba4.htm**. Then select View Source (or View Document Source) in your browser. Now copy the text and paste it into your HTML document. It will look like this:

```
<H4>This band was born in a dusty attic somewhere in
Waterloo, Ontario.</H4><P>You see, there was a woman named
<B><I>Bertha</I></B> who drew them upstairs. None of them
could figure out why. One by one, they crept up the creaky
old stairs. I told them not to. Let's see, if I remember them
correctly, there was a young man named <B>Matt</B> who had a
very nice smile, and another named <B>Giasone</B> who liked
to talk about the most wonderful things. Soon after them
came another young man, I believe his name was <B>Tim</B>,
who grabbed the railing and bounded up those wooden boards,
followed by <B>Johnny</B>. I'll never forget Johnny; he had
some interesting philosophies about life. The last one I saw
disappear into the attic was <B>John-Marc</B>, slowly creep-
ing up there with curiosity. Yup, that was the last I saw of
them. Of course, it was not the last I heard of them...</
P><CENTER><H2><B><I>They certainly made a racket up there!
</I></B></H2></CENTER>
```

Experiment with these element styles until you are comfortable with their use. Save and preview your work to see the effects.

Your page should look something like the page I created for Bertha's Attic at **http://randall.uwaterloo.ca/ba4.htm**.

Now we're simply flyin'—Your very first hyperlink

Hyperlinks are probably the first thing you discovered when you fired up your browser, and they remain the most important element of any World Wide Web page. Used correctly, hyperlinks transport users to new, interesting, and related sites. Used incorrectly, hyperlinks arrive at dead ends and frustrate users.

WWW editors support many different kinds of hypertext links, most of which you will master in the following tutorial. But to get you acquainted with links—their purpose and creation—we'll first examine external connections. External hypertext links move users to a new WWW location (already established on the Web) when they click a highlighted word in your WWW page.

To construct a link using Live Markup, you must first select the word or words that you want to appear as highlighted, clickable text on the World Wide Web. Right-click the selected text to reveal your menu of options. Select the Create Hyperlink option near the bottom of the command menu, and you receive the screen shown in figure 4.8.

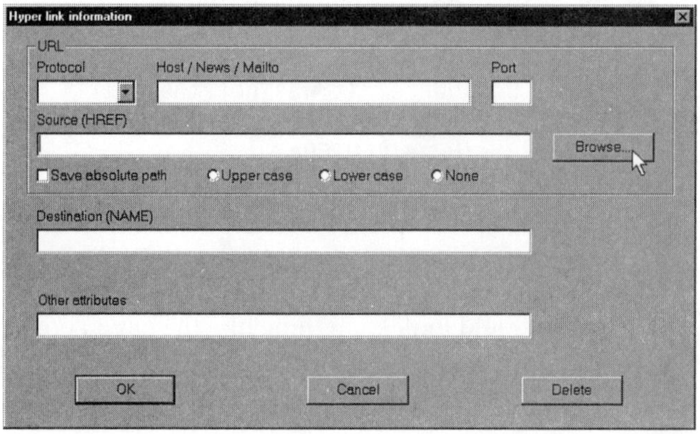

Fig. 4.8

This dialog box, or one similar to it, prompts users to insert the URL or destination name of the site they are linking to.

In the Protocol box, type **http**. Or, choose the http option from the pull-down menu.

In the Host/News/Mailto column, insert the address of the site you link to. If you do not have a site to link to and would like to practice the external link, insert **http://randall.uwaterloo.ca/UsingHTML.htm** in the host column. This address will transport you to the support page for this book.

After you have inserted the address of your destination site, click the OK button. Save and preview your work to display the results. From your Web browser, click the hypertext link you have created to make sure it actually works. If your link malfunctions, return to the Hyperlink dialog box (which will now be represented by the Edit Hyperlink command) and verify your address.

To verify, type **http://randall.uwaterloo.ca/ba5.htm** in your browser's location box. I highlighted the title of my document and linked it to the *Using HTML* home page. See figure 4.9 to see how the page looks.

For code-only authors...

Composing external links in HTML code is complex, but once you get used to it, it's pretty easy. Basically, it's just a matter of enclosing the Web address inside an <A></A> container (the anchor container).

The HTML code that links the words "Using HTML" to the book's home page looks like this:

```
<A HREF="http://randall.uwaterloo.ca/Using_HTML.htm">Using HTML</A>
```

The Internet Address of Bertha's Attic home page is enclosed in quotations and framed by the HREF component. The entire tag string is enclosed by the <A></A> tags. To create any additional external links, just copy this format and substitute the appropriate URL and text selections.

After you have constructed your external link, save the HTML file and preview your document. Test the link from your browser to ensure its accuracy, and compare your results to the page found at **http://randall.uwaterloo.ca/ba5.htm**.

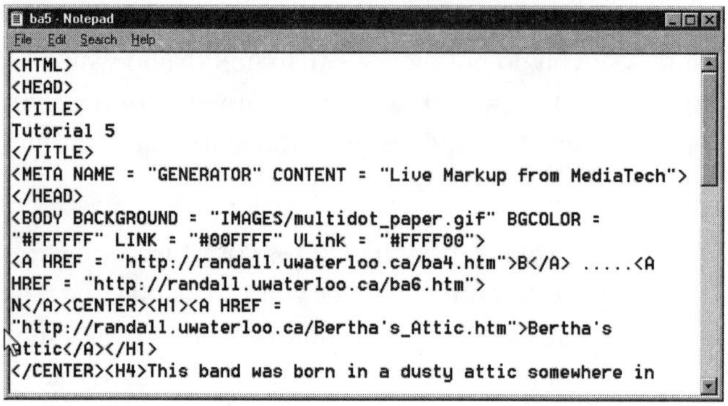

Fig. 4.9
Although Hotdog
is a tagged (or non-
WYSIWYG) Web editor,
its advanced linking
functions resemble the
WYSIWYG method of
incorporating external
links.

```
ba5 - Notepad
File  Edit  Search  Help
<HTML>
<HEAD>
<TITLE>
Tutorial 5
</TITLE>
<META NAME = "GENERATOR" CONTENT = "Live Markup from MediaTech">
</HEAD>
<BODY BACKGROUND = "IMAGES/multidot_paper.gif" BGCOLOR =
"#FFFFFF" LINK = "#00FFFF" ULink = "#FFFF00">
<A HREF = "http://randall.uwaterloo.ca/ba4.htm">B</A> .....<A
HREF = "http://randall.uwaterloo.ca/ba6.htm">
N</A><CENTER><H1><A HREF =
"http://randall.uwaterloo.ca/Bertha's_Attic.htm">Bertha's
Attic</A></H1>
</CENTER><H4>This band was born in a dusty attic somewhere in
```

Now let's put in a graphic

Now that our Bertha's Attic biography is complete we'll move on to the next page in our band archive—pictures of our rock 'n' roll Web stars.

Let's leave the first page as it is and start a new one. This will simplify things a bit, and it will allow us room to experiment with both pages as we go along.

Fire up your Web editor and open a new HTML document. Be sure to save the document and give it a descriptive title.

Now, using any combination of the Heading, Text, Background, and Hyperlink techniques discussed above, design a page that introduces and describes the graphics you intend to insert. Call it "Pictures from the Attic." Don't worry about the graphics themselves (we'll get to them).

Let's make this page display Bertha's Attic's band members, concert shots, and music memorabilia. In my case, I took the negatives of some band photos and had a camera store develop them on a CD-ROM. That way, I could work with them in my computer.

You don't have to do all that. To get the photos, load your Web browser and go to **http://randall.uwaterloo.ca/atticpix.htm**. Once you get there, right-click any of the pictures and save the graphic to your hard disk with the name attic1.gif. Put it in your HTML directory so you can work with it.

Once you've downloaded the images and have set up your new HTML document with headings and text, it's time to insert the images.

Using Live Markup, you must first click the text icon in the toolbar or select the text block command from the Elements menu.

Next, click Live Markup's yellow happy face graphic on the toolbar, or select the Image command from the Elements menu. This step will insert the happy face icon into the text block space you have created on your working screen.

Position your mouse over the Live Markup icon and right-click. Your screen should look like the one shown in figure 4.10.

Fig. 4.10
Live Markup uses handy graphical icons to display the space reserved for pictures throughout your HTML document.

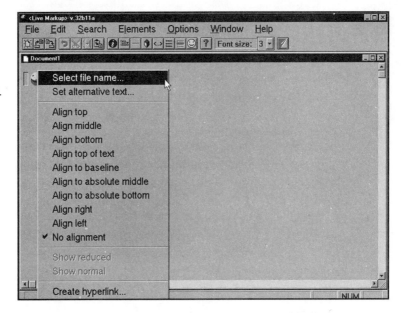

Choose the Select file name option from the Graphics menu. In the "Image Path" column, fill in the location of the graphic **attic1.gif**. Your image path will resemble the following location directions:

```
C:\HTML\attic1.gif
```

Or, you can also just click the Browse button and locate the graphic that way.

When you have filled in the dialog box, click OK. Live Markup displays the image directly on your document's screen.

Save your file and preview the document using your Web browser. Then compare your document with the one I created at **http:// randall.uwaterloo.ca/ba6.htm**.

For code-only users...

The HTML code that inserts graphics in your World Wide Web documents looks like this:

```
<IMG SRC="html/attic1.jpg">
```

Now save the document and preview the results. Now compare your page with the one I created at **http://randall.uwaterloo.ca/ba6**.

Toss in a list

You're just about done. The last basic element that you will learn in this tutorial involves one of the World Wide Web's most popular features: bulleted lists. There's much more on lists in Chapter 7.

Creating lists in Live Markup may seem confusing at first glance, but the steps involved have been established with more complex operations in mind. For now, follow the steps outlined in this tutorial. You will be acquainted with nested, ordered, and definition lists in the next "Hands-on" chapter.

To create a list in Live Markup, select the List icon from the toolbar or choose the List command from the Elements menu. Live Markup inserts a small, square container at the edge of a new line on your page.

Next, select the Insert new list item icon from the toolbar or choose the List Item command from the Elements menu. A small black dot now appears beside the List container.

Now insert a text block and type the first item that will appear in your bulleted list. Here it is:

```
John-Marc Desmarais - Bass Guitar, (one vocal)
```

To insert additional list items, simply click the Insert new list item, add a text block, and type the data. For this band list, add the following items:

```
Matt Devine - Rhythym Guitar, Vocals
Tim Devine - Keyboards, Background Vocals
Giasone Italiano - Lead Guitar, Vocals
Johnny Jacklitch - Drums, (one harmonica)
```

On-screen, your file should look something like the one shown in figure 4.11.

Fig. 4.11
Live Markup's listing
format allows for
nesting among lists. See
Chapters 7 and 10 for
nesting, numbered,
and definition list
details.

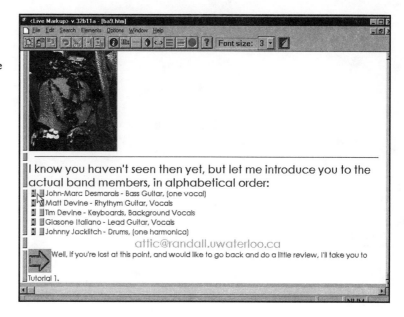

Save your file and preview the document to see what it will look like for your readers. Now compare your page to the Bertha's Attic application at **http://randall.uwaterloo.ca/ba7.htm**.

For code-only authors...

Copy the following HTML code to create the unordered lists for the band.

```
<UL>
<LI>John-Marc Desmarais - Bass Guitar, (one vocal)
<LI>Matt Devine - Rhythym Guitar, Vocals
<LI>Tim Devine - Keyboards, Background Vocals
<LI>Giasone Italiano - Lead Guitar, Vocals
<LI>Johnny Jacklitch - Drums, (one harmonica)</UL>
```

Save your file and preview the document, and then compare it to my page at **http://randall.uwaterloo.ca/ba7.htm**.

Well you've done it! You've created your first WWW page with some of the most important HTML elements. Chapters 10, 16, and 21 will expand on the concepts outlined in this chapter. By the time you're done all the Hands-on Steps, you'll have a small but rich Web site.

And you'll know the band pretty well, too.

In the Beginning: Up Front with Titles and Heads

● **In this chapter:**

- **Make a habit of using the <HTML> tag**

- **How much can you do with the <HEAD> element anyway?**

- **Tags that offer information about the document**

- **Titles are more than just titles**

- **Do titles have to be so static?**

Titles and heads might not seem important, but they help you get started thinking about your overall design . . . . ●

You already know how to get started. But that was just two pages, and now you're about to embark on the whole enchilada (to thoroughly mix a metaphor). It's a bit intimidating. After all, this is programming we're talking about, and programming is for the advanced, the experts, the geeks—right?

Wrong! HTML authoring is programming, but it's fun programming and reasonably easy. HTML focuses on artistic invention and visual display, and the coding and tagging functions are simply means to an end. So take a deep breath, fire up your Web editor, and take that first step.

All HTML pages must begin with specific labels that make the purpose and location of the document clear to anyone who accesses them. Because HTML is a hierarchical language, markup tags and elements are best analyzed from the outside working in—like Chinese boxes. The outermost element—<HTML>—contains the whole document.

The next element is the <HEAD> tag, which acts like a smaller container to separate information *about* the document from the body of the file. Inside the head tags lies the <TITLE> element, which gives users a hint of the kind of information the document contains and provides a descriptive phrase for linking to other pages.

 TIP Most Web editors make all of this very easy: to insert the tags, just fill in the blanks or click an icon. Also, these editors are very good at reminding you to include the <HTML> start and end tags.

Every Web page has the same basic structure

Okay, folks. Here's the first and most basic rule of HTML design. Every page you create must contain the same overall structure, and that structure looks like the following:

```
<HTML>
<HEAD>
<TITLE>The Title of Your Page</TITLE>
</HEAD>
<BODY>*The guts of the Web page--text, graphics, links, and so on.
</BODY>*
</HTML>**
```

* *The opening and closing <BODY></BODY> tags are covered in Chapter 10.*
** *The closing </HTML> tag occurs at the very end of the whole document.*

As you browse through the Web and check out how various pages have been written, you'll notice that consistency isn't always there. That's because Web browsers display some elements even if they're not actually specified. This is especially true of the <HTML> element itself, which is optional. But it won't always be, which is why you should always use <HTML>.

Don't forget the HTML element

The World Wide Web was originally designed as a **platform-independent** technology? Platform independence simply means that Web pages can be read by *any* browser on *any* computer system, regardless of what editor was used for their creation.

Q&A *How is this different from reading any computer document?*

Have you ever changed word processors? Maybe you started out using WordPerfect, but then you bought Word for Windows? Word could load those WordPerfect documents, but the reverse wasn't true.

Every document created with a word processor, spreadsheet, and desktop publishing package has a file structure that only the creating program can read. That's why, in the DOS world, they all have different extensions (.DOC, .XLS, and so on). The only way that one program can read a document created with a different program is by using a **filter** that converts the file.

Web browsers are different. They're all designed for one purpose only: to read documents that contain HTML tags. That's why the Web is so powerful. The Web browser on *your* computer can read documents that are stored on *any* computer. The only requirement is that the documents must be written in HTML.

Written properly (that is, using correct HTML terms), Web pages may be moved from server to server or accessed by any regular WWW browser with only slight, often insignificant variations. This saves you innumerable amounts of editing time and increases the availability of your documents.

Can you imagine constructing the same page dozens of times in order to accommodate the preferences of different viewing mechanisms? Hardly a good time.

CAUTION **Although WWW pages boast platform independence, experimentation with alternative browsers may reveal some slight variations in textual or graphical reproduction. The most common differences include color shading, clarity, and font reproduction, so if the purity of these elements is essential to your document, you may want to proof the effects among varying browsers. Most browsers choose an appropriate default substitution in cases where exact replication is not possible.**

The HTML element tags (<HTML>,</HTML>) contain all other text and tags within the document. The opening tag, <HTML>, is the first thing typed, and the closing tag, </HTML>, is the last, coming at the very end of the document. Most browsers are programmed to ignore any text that appears outside of these two tags.

Q&A *Hey, wait a minute! Didn't word processors used to have tags?*

They sure did. Think back; think way, way back to the days of WordStar and other such coded word processing programs when devoted users were forced to insert tags (called dot-commands in WordStar) to indicate where text, tabs, or margins occurred. WordPerfect for DOS users still get involved with tags whenever they use the Reveal Codes feature. In fact, all word processing and document creation software include these tags. You just don't see them any more—at least on PCs and Macs. Head for a UNIX machine, however, and play around with LaTEX and troff documents, and you're right back to those seemingly primitive days. Primitive, many would argue, but very powerful. When you see the codes, you have full control over your document. That's why some people see the advent of graphical HTML editors as a step backward rather than forward. That's not a viewpoint you'll see in this book very often.

Here's a quick HTML example, taken from the UCLA home page (**http://www.ucla.edu/**). As always, the <HTML> tag opens the page, followed by the <HEAD></HEAD> element, which encloses the <TITLE></TITLE> element. After that comes the <BODY>.

```
<HTML>
<HEAD>
<TITLE>UCLA WWW Home Page</TITLE>
</HEAD>

<BODY>
```

Because the <HTML></HTML> tags are optional, you might well be wondering why to include them at all. The reason is quite simple: HTML is a fairly new language, and you don't know what will happen in the future. Someday, HTML might split into two or more subsets, and these tags will then be essential. Furthermore, Web browsers could be programmed to display other types of documents, in which case the <HTML> tags will let the browser know what to do. They're a good habit to get into, and if you're using a Web editor, it probably inserts them anyway.

Stories need titles, and so do Web pages

It's as simple as it sounds—the **TITLE** element names your document, like the title of this book, its chapters, or even the section headers. Every HTML document you create should include a title—and only one title—within the <HEAD> element. Effective use of the <TITLE> and </TITLE> attributes results in a descriptive and stimulating sentence that sums up the document content in a concise manner.

 TIP **The title of any HTML document should label the text screen,** serve as a recording mechanism of documents already viewed, and allow quick document indexing. The title does not, however, assign a file name to a document; this function is performed by the Save As command found in the File menu of your HTML editor. One of the best examples of title applications is as an indexing function among **hotlists** (see the shaded box on the next page) or bookmark catalogs.

Figure 5.1 shows the title on the home page for Compaq Computer Corporation (**http://www.compaq.com/**). The <TITLE> of the document is written in HTML as follows:

```
<TITLE>Compaq Computer Corporation, Graphics path</TITLE
```

You can see this title in Netscape's title bar (the dark strip at the top of the screen) in figure 5.1.

Title

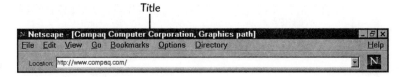

Fig. 5.1
Netscape's title bar
shows what the authors
of this page chose to
call it, and although
it's not particularly
helpful, it's better
than not having a
title at all.

Functional titles

Creating an effective title for your HTML document is more of a rhetorical and stylistic process than a technical skill, but weighs heavily on the success of your page on the World Wide Web. You construct an HTML document to send a message to the world, but this solitary message is competing for attention with millions and millions of other pages. The title of your document is one of several elements responsible for attracting an audience and should be given some serious consideration.

On the other hand, the last thing you want to do is take several hours to come up with a good title, especially when the time would be better spent creating effective headers instead. See Chapter 10 for headers and other useful attractors.

TI**P**   **Your title should be two things: descriptive and functional.**
It should describe your page's content as closely as possible and should also serve a purpose. If someone decides to add a bookmark or hotlist entry for your page, a properly constructed title will remind him of the exact type of information that your page has to offer—there's nothing more frustrating than a bookmark called "Page 2" or "My Home Page!"

Consider the good and not-so-good titles that you might come across when surfing the Net. The following four figures show some typical examples.

As shown in figure 5.2, Netscape 2.0 displays the title of this page—2025 Introduction—in the widow box at the top of the screen. Notice that this generic title does not indicate that the page is devoted to a study of air and space capabilities for the future, nor does it reveal that the study is interactive.

The title in figure 5.3, again displayed at the top left corner of the screen, reveals both the name and the nature of the site (commercial) in a descriptive and inclusive phrase.

Fig. 5.2

A generic title in Netscape 2.0.

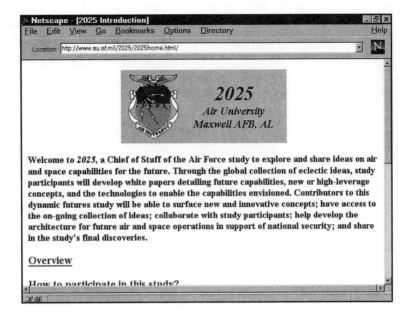

Avoid using the catchy slogans and company names that you have created for your Web page or service as the title of your document. In figure 5.4, notice that "CandleWeb" does not indicate the nature of the service (animation software for HTML coding) or the purpose of the page.

Fig. 5.3

After the Stork's title.

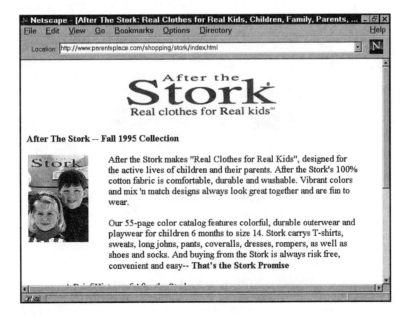

Fig. 5.4
The CandleWeb title does not give enough information about the page.

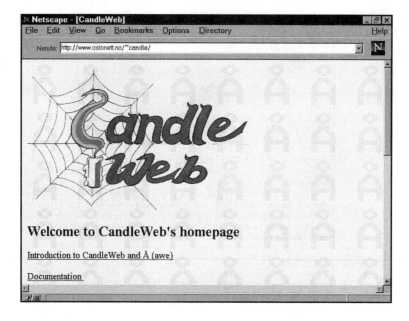

The title in figure 5.5, Wingspread: Art of New Mexico and Southwest, provides users with an inventive solution to the problem encountered in the previous example. To clarify the purpose and content of your document while being creative and descriptive, use the site name (Wingspread) followed by an explanatory sentence or phrase.

Fig. 5.5
An example of a creative and descriptive title.

HTML does not limit the length of the TITLE element. However, before you rush off to give your Web pages endlessly descriptive names, keep in mind that the space where the title is displayed (either the viewer's title bar or window label) is limited. A good rule of thumb for the length of a title is no more than a single phrase or no longer than 60 characters.

Getting a head

Like people, HTML documents have heads and bodies. Also like people, the body of an HTML document is larger than the head. Of course, the analogy ends right there because the HTML bodies are more significant by a long shot than HTML heads, and that's not supposed to be true with human beings. But still… .

As the name implies, the head section of any HTML document precedes the main information (or the "body") of the Web page. The tag <HEAD> and closing tag </HEAD> surround the contents of the head section. Text contained between the <HEAD> and </HEAD> tags points to general information about the file and is not displayed as part of the document text itself.

 CAUTION **Although the <HEAD> element and its contents are not displayed** as part of the actual Web page's text, one significant component of the header, the <TITLE>, does appear when the page is accessed. The title given to a page can usually be seen at the top corner of the browser screen and indicates the name that the author has given to the HTML document.

The HEAD element may contain any number of six possible commands:

- **TITLE**   Describes the document's name
- **ISINDEX**   Indicates that the document can be searched
- **BASE**   Reveals the original URL of the document
- **NEXTID**   Creates unique document identifiers
- **LINK**   Displays relationships to other documents
- **META**   Embeds any additional information

Only the TITLE element is required. The rest are optional and often do not appear in basic HTML constructions. In fact, even complex pages require only the TITLE bar for full World Wide Web functioning. But it's important to know how all of these function because they can help you produce a richer, more sophisticated Web site. And you want to be prepared if browsers start to demand them.

Search the world over...

If you have a database that you want your readers to be able to search, you need to let them know that searching is possible. This is the function of the <ISINDEX> tag, which prompts your Web browser to display a search box. To make this box work, you have to link it to a "searchable" item, such as a database, through a CGI program (see Chapter 18).

 Plain English, please!

CGI stands for Common Gateway Interface, but nobody calls it that. It's the means by which Web documents collect information from outside the Web.

The <ISINDEX> tag begins a chain of communication. When a browser connects to an HTML page containing the <ISINDEX> element in its header, a series of messages are transmitted from page to browser to viewer. First, the <ISINDEX> command informs the browser that the document may be examined using a keyword search. This information prompts the browser to display a search query or string that informs the user that the database can be searched.

 CAUTION **<ISINDEX> does *not* indicate that you may conduct a search of the** text you are actually reading. Instead, server-side gateway programs designed for full database searches usually send documents containing the <ISINDEX> element to a client. <ISINDEX> automatically inserts a Search box, but it doesn't make the Web site searchable.

The ISINDEX element is empty (contains no text other than the element name itself), optional, and should be placed in the HEAD portion of any HTML document.

 TIP **Because many older HTML documents included the <ISINDEX>** element within the body of the Web page, current HTML definition recognizes this format. There is no need to alter any existing documents that place the <ISINDEX> command in the body, but all new HTML constructions should feature the element in the <HEAD>.

Here's an example of <ISINDEX> as taken from the Web itself. The location is **http://forth.emwac.ed.ac.uk/**, a UK-based Microsoft page. Near the bottom of the HTML code, the following appears:

```
Our search engine supports
 <A HREF="/pages/kb/indexes/booleandefs.htm">Boolean</A>
searches. Here are some <A HREF="/pages/kb/hints.htm">hints</A>
on using our search engine to find what you are looking for.<P>
<ISINDEX>
<P>
<I><B>Notice to Lynx users:</B> This page contains
 the &lt;isindex&gt;
tag, which tells your browser to display some type of searching
mechanism. If you do not see this mechanism, contact your local
network administrator to correct this problem. For now, press
the &quot;s&quot; key to perform a search. Thank You.</I>
```

The actual <ISINDEX> tag appears in the middle of the code. Below it is an explanation for Lynx users; users of older Lynx versions might not see the search box. Figure 5.6 shows this HTML code as it appears on the Web.

 Plain English, please!

Lynx is a World Wide Web browser designed for text-only displays. It's extremely powerful, but it doesn't show graphics. It's available for DOS, but the most popular implementation is for UNIX. **99**

Fig. 5.6
This fill-in dialog box indicates that a keyword search may be performed on the database of material presented by Microsoft.

> Netscape - [Microsoft Corporation World-Wide-Web Server]
> File   Edit   View   Go   Bookmarks   Options   Directory   Help
>
> Location: http://forth.emwac.ed.ac.uk/
>
> *We invite you to use our new search feature from the home page!*
>
> Our search engine supports <u>Boolean</u> searches. Here are some <u>hints</u> on using our search engine to find what you are looking for.
>
> This is a searchable index. Enter search keywords: [_____]
>
> **Notice to Lynx users:** *This page contains the <isindex> tag, which tells your browser to display some type of searching mechanism. If you do not see this mechanism, contact your local network administrator to correct this problem. For now, press the "s" key to perform a search. Thank You.*
>
> If you have any problems connecting to or getting information from this server, please contact www@microsoft.com . Individual replies to email may not be possible, but all mail will be read and all possible problems will be looked into. © Microsoft Corporation 1995.
>
> **Thank you for using Microsoft products!**

Go back to the base ...ics

Sometimes, a document is moved from a location where it has established relationships with surrounding documents and is inserted in a new location. In this new environment, the previously related URLs are no longer valid. However, if the document is altered to include the <BASE> element and base URL in its <HEAD>, the previously related (linked) documents will once again be found. This element functions to maintain the effectiveness of links and connections throughout the World Wide Web.

 Plain English, please!

> **<BASE>** tells a Web browser where to find other Web documents in the Web site. It isn't of much use unless you've moved the document to a new directory or machine. **"**

If included in the <HEAD>, the <BASE> element contains only the HREF attribute that holds the base URL of the document. The base URL provides users with the address of the HTML document's original location, indicating that the site has been moved.

If Web authors decide not to include the <BASE> element in their HTML documents, browsers assume the base URL to be the URL used to access the page.

 CAUTION **Although the BASE command is effective for moving pages, be** aware that many browsers, such as MacWeb and Lynx, do not recognize the command and use the default exclusively.

What's NEXTID?

The <NEXTID> command is not used by humans, WWW browsers, or hypertext servers. Sounds easy so far, right? Instead, <NEXTID> is used by HTML editing programs to label pages with specific identifying numbers.

The <NEXTID> command contains a single internal element, N, which gives each page its numeric label. For example, a page with the sequence <NEXTID N=132> is page number 132 to HTML editing programs. The following is an example of what the <HEAD> portion of a document looks like using the <NEXTID> command:

```
<HTML>
<HEAD>
<NEXTID N=132>
<TITLE>title of document</TITLE>
</HEAD>
<BODY>body of document</BODY>
</HTML>
```

TIP **In all likelihood, you'll never have to use the <NEXTID> tag.**
On the other hand, your HTML editor might well add an ID number on
its own. Generally speaking, you can safely ignore it.

Lookin' for links

This is probably the easiest of all the optional <HEAD> elements! The
<LINK> command simply displays the relationships your document main-
tains with other documents on the Net. <LINK> can give directions to related
indices and glossaries or to different versions of your current document
(graphic and textual drafts). The <LINK> element contains all of the same
attributes as the anchor element (A) in HTML construction.

Note that <LINK> has nothing to do with "hyperlink," the very common
HTML term that's discussed in Chapter 9.

TIP **Some Web artists use the <LINK> element to point to preceding or**
following documents in a series—such as a *next* or *previous* button. No
browsers are yet advanced enough to handle such demands, and <LINK>
remains largely unsupported and rarely used throughout HTML invention.

Use the following <LINK> format to point to documents related to your page:

```
<HTML>
<HEAD>
<TITLE>title of document</TITLE>
<LINK HREF="file1.htm" TITLE="Title of related document">
</HEAD>
<BODY>body of document</BODY>
</HTML>
```

What's a META for?

Put simply, the <META> element takes care of everything else you could ever
want to say about your document, including indexing and cataloging information. If present, the <META> option must include the CONTENT attribute as
well as either the NAME or HTTP-EQUIV attribute—but never both.

- The **NAME** attribute ("name") specifies name for the client server.

- The **HTTP-EQUIV** attribute ("string") can be used in place of the NAME element, but causes the META elements to be parsed by the HTTP server and converted to HTTP response headers.

- The **CONTENT** attribute ("string") is mandatory and indicates all content associated with the META element.

66 *Plain English, please!*

Some practical examples might clear this whole META issue up for you, but if they don't, hang in there! There's more to HTML than META, and some browsers insert this information for you.

```
<META NAME="Document Branch" CONTENT="Volume 1_Branch_4X3">
```

This example uses the NAME and CONTENT attributes to tell the client that the document is a derivative (of some sort) of Volume 1 of a master text. From here, it's up to the indexing program to understand the meanings behind these names.

```
<META HTTP-EQUIV="Last Modified" CONTENT="23-Feb-95 13:28:44 GMT">
```

This command line instructs the client server to include the CONTENT string (23-Feb-95 13:28:44 GMT) as part of the *Last Modified* header field that is sent with the HTTP response header that precedes the document in a standard HTTP transaction. HTTP response headers normally contain information about the document and the server, but can also include descriptive information about the file. 99

Well, there it is—everything you could ever want to know about headers (and probably a lot more than you really care to know). If you understand the basics of header design, you are ready to construct a title. Any additional, more advanced material comes with experience and expertise—two of the fastest growing commodities among Internet users.

Where the Content Is: The Document Body

● **In this chapter:**

- **The function of a Web page's body section**

- **Tips on how to use text headings**

- **Breaking up your text by paragraph or line**

- **Choosing text styles for your pages**

- **Using the horizontal rule**

*The main part of a Web page—where you put everything your readers will actually see—is called the **body**. It can be big or it can be small, but the body had better be right! . . . .* ⊘

No matter what you want to use the World Wide Web for—advertising a business or service, posting weekly results for your softball league games, or publishing the latest family information for relatives in other parts of the world—you'll quickly discover that a Web page is, quite literally, nothing without its body section.

Similar to an artist's canvas, the body of a document displays the results of your creative energies and artistic inspirations. However, keep in mind while painting your "portrait" that HTML is merely a tool for organizing and distributing the information you have already established: what the body contains will always remain a product of your own imagination and labor.

What actually is inside the body section?

The body section of all WWW documents is defined by the <BODY> element. It has both an opening tag, <BODY>, to show where your information starts and a closing tag, </BODY>, that indicates where the data ends. Inside the body you'll find text, hyperlinks, headings, graphics, image maps, forms, tables, and everything else your users actually see. Figure 6.1 shows how the body tags look in a Web page.

Fig. 6.1
Many Web editors, such as HotDog, automatically display the <BODY> tags in new documents to save you from having to write them.

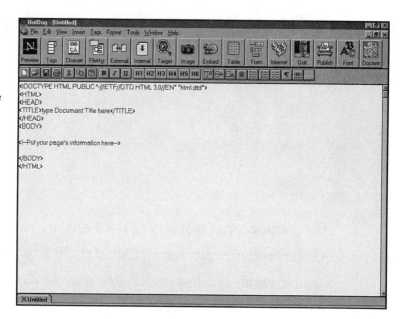

TIP **Although most Web browsers can handle Web pages without the** <BODY> element, you really should use it. As HTML progresses, <BODY> tags will matter a lot more. Using the <BODY> tags is a good way to save work later when codes become crucial to your documents.

The HTML code in listing 6.1 (from **http://www.yahoo.com/**) shows where the body fits in the overall Web page structure. Note that it's embedded inside the <HTML> opening and closing tags, which means it's a substructure of <HTML> itself. Almost everything else in your document is a substructure of <BODY> and thus fits inside the <BODY></BODY> tags.

Listing 6.1   HTML Code from the Yahoo Page

```
<HTML>
<HEAD>
<TITLE>Yahoo
</TITLE>
<base href="http://www.yahoo.com/">
</HEAD>
<BODY>
...actual content of page...
</BODY>
</HTML>
```

Headings help the reader find what's there

Headings are pretty much the first thing HTML authors learn how to write. There are six **levels** of headings, and browsers generally show a different font size for each level. That means you can use the varied heading sizes to create a hierarchy of information. The idea is to keep information of equal importance inside headings of equal size, to give larger headings to larger categories, and so on. Figure 6.2 demonstrates this idea.

The current HTML standards (1.0, 2.0, and the ever advancing 3.0), support six levels of headings: H1, H2, H3, H4, H5, and H6. Each browser has a different definition for each heading level, so that a heading of H1 will look very different from an H4 heading (see fig. 6.3 to see how the various levels are displayed). But keep in mind that users of some Web browsers can display headings in whatever font they want, so it might be wise not to spend an inordinate amount of time on heading creation.

Fig. 6.2
Headings work like
levels in an outline,
giving you a simple
reference to the
structure of your
information.

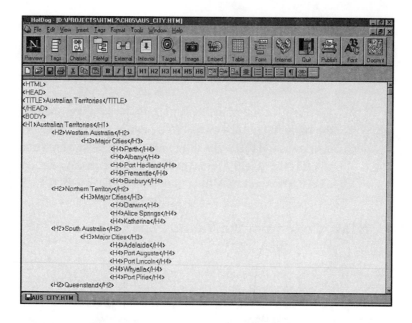

Fig. 6.3
Microsoft Internet
Explorer and Netscape
Navigator format the
various headings simi-
larly; other browsers
vary in how they
display them.

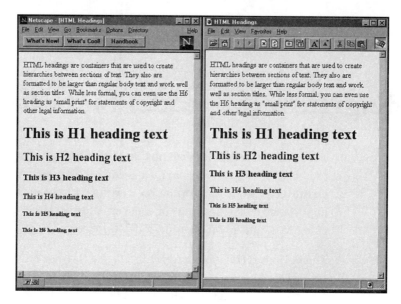

TIP **HTML does not allow more than one space in a row; it ignores any** additional blank lines. You may still use spacing to make your pages easier to read and edit when using your HTML editor. Just remember that empty space will not appear on the Web itself.

Inserting breaks in your text

Most people don't like reading dense paragraphs on a computer screen. Instead, they like their on-screen information presented in bite-size chunks along with headings, graphics, separation lines, and so forth. One method of separating and chunking information is through paragraph breaks and line breaks. The <P> and <BR> elements let you add white spaces in your documents to keep information separated.

To construct paragraph breaks <P>, you must tell the browser to end the current paragraph and insert a double space before proceeding with the next cluster of information. To construct line breaks <BR>, you must tell the browser to end the current text *here*—wherever the line happens to be at the time—and continue the information on the very next line.

TIP **If you're trying to replicate the Return or Enter key of your word** processor, use <BR> rather than <P>. It gives you more direct control over the spacing on your page.

Using paragraph breaks

The <P> tag separates text into paragraphs for easy reading and visual appeal. While HTML 3 defines the paragraph tag as a container—requiring both <P> and </P> tags—browsers still recognize the older HTML standard, which requires only the opening <P> tag on its own and will start a new paragraph anyway. But it's a good idea to use the container format: first, because it's becoming essential, and second, because it offers some strong formatting benefits.

 Plain English, please!

Containers are HTML elements that consist of both an opening tag and a closing tag (the latter usually indicated by a /). They're called containers because the text they define is *contained* between these two commands. **"**

If you want to create white space in your document, you might be tempted to insert consecutive paragraph containers. Good idea, except they don't work. Browsers won't take the hint and separate your text further. Instead, try using an empty preformatted container with two blank spaces between the <PRE> and </PRE> tags (covered shortly). Most Web browsers will read this as acceptable content and generate a blank line. The HTML for creating white space using the preformatted containers is shown in listing 6.2.

Listing 6.2   Example of Preformatted Text

```
<BODY>
...insert body of document and end paragraph...
<PRE>

</PRE>
...continue body of document with new paragraph...
</BODY>
```

Figure 6.4 shows how the paragraph tag is used in Web pages.

Fig. 6.4

Enclose text and other elements and objects (such as graphics) between the <P> and </P> tags to group them into a single paragraph.

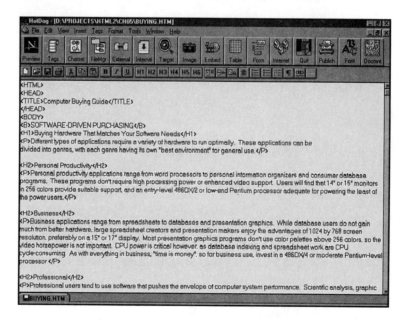

Line breaks are often your best HTML friend

Sometimes you want your text flow to end at a certain point and begin on a new line without separating spaces. The HTML tag that creates these textual breaks is represented by <BR>. This tag is not a container—wherever you put it in a document, it will tell the browser to interrupt the content and place the information that follows at the beginning of the next line.

The effect is the same as single spacing (as opposed to paragraph tags, which double space after the container). You can place as many <BR> tags as you want consecutively, and you'll get as many new lines. This is the surest way of controlling the number of "carriage returns" you put in your document.

Figure 6.5 and figure 6.6 show how line breaks can be used to create various text layouts.

Fig. 6.5
These text effects all use forced line breaks to make the text wrap automatically to the next line for an effect.

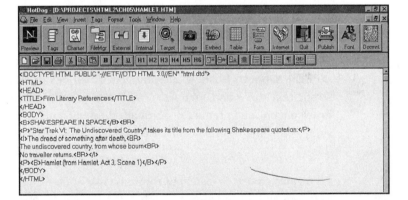

Fig. 6.6
Browsers like Netscape break the line at the <BR> tag regardless of where the break takes place on-screen.

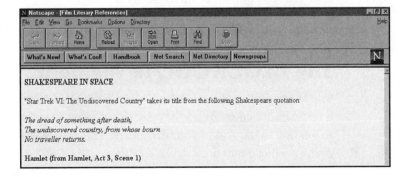

CAUTION **Browsers follow whatever HTML orders you give them—even if the** on-screen output is less than pretty. A line break can look ugly if the text has wrapped because the browser's window is too narrow for your intended line length. The shorter you keep lines of text between <BR> tags, the better your chances of exact spacing and visual replication in the browser window.

Why not save your fingers with preformatted text?

If you want to put information on the Web and you already have it in a non-HTML document, you don't have to spend your time retyping. Instead, you can use HTML's preformatted text containers <PRE></PRE>. These containers let you keep the original formatting of the text. Some even let you use regular line breaks, even without the <BR> tag.

The PRE element

The preformatted text element, represented by the containers <PRE> and </PRE>, supports blank spaces and lets other tags or links (like the bold and strong text styles and anchors) modify the text. The one catch is that WWW browsers normally render preformatted text in a plain, monospaced font, such as the unattractive Courier (although some browsers let you change this).

Preformatted text is excellent for items like code examples, which you want to indent and format appropriately. <PRE></PRE> tags also enable you to align text by padding it with spaces for table creation. However, because those tables will appear in monospaced font, you may prefer to spend the extra time constructing standard HTML table blocks.

The BLOCKQUOTE element

You might find, in the creation of your Web pages, that you need to show a bibliographical reference or want to set apart a section of text indented in relation to the rest of your document. The <BLOCKQUOTE> container performs these functions. Unlike <PRE>, <BLOCKQUOTE> does not keep any line feeds already present in your text nor does it allow consecutive blank spaces. What it does provide is a uniform indented format.

The <BLOCKQUOTE> tags may contain other HTML codes, such as text styles and line breaks. Figure 6.7 shows how you use <BLOCKQUOTE> in a Web page, and figure 6.8 shows how Netscape displays this information.

Fig. 6.7
The format your text already has inside the <BLOCKQUOTE> container is ignored unless you add the same formatting using HTML commands.

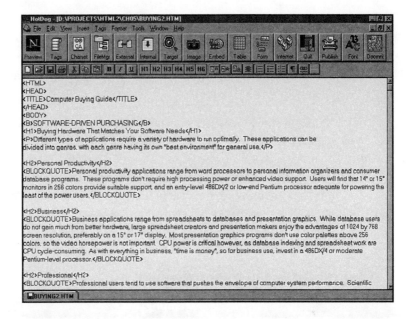

Fig. 6.8
<BLOCKQUOTE> text uses the regular body text font (the same style featured through-out the rest of your HTML document) as well as an even indentation from the left-hand margin.

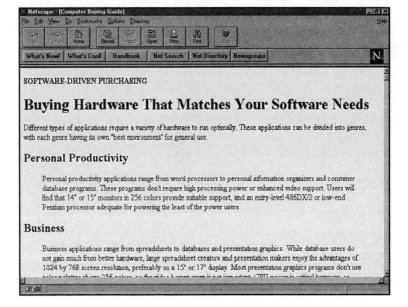

Physical text styles give you complete control over appearance

If you've used any word processor of merit, you'll instantly recognize HTML's physical style elements. Physical styles emphasize your Web page's plain text with boldface, italic, and underlining. These container tags are absolute— meaning that every Web browser will display the physical style elements in exactly the same manner.

Although some browsers may have limitations on how they can display logical text styles—such as Lynx, which is a text-only browser—there is no other way for a browser to interpret a physical style. Bold is bold. Italic is italic. Logical styles (covered in the next section) may be flexible, but physical ones are not. Table 6.1 gives you some descriptions of physical styles. Figure 6.9 shows how physical style tags are used, and figure 6.10 shows how Web browsers display them.

Table 6.1 Physical styles and their meanings

Style	Meaning
B	Boldface (where possible)
I	Italics
TT	Monospaced typewriter font
U	Underlined (HTML 2.0)

Styles Available Only with the Proposed HTML+

Style	Meaning
S	Strike-through
SUB	Subscript
SUP	Superscript

Fig. 6.9
Physical style containers affect all of the text between their opening and closing tags.

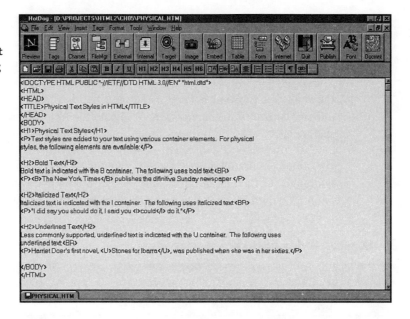

Fig. 6.10
Browsers do not vary in how they display physical styles, and physical styles can be combined for additional effects.

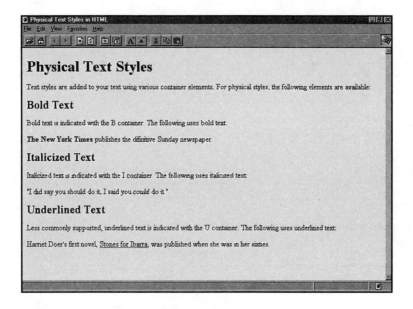

What's so logical about logical styles?

Logical style tags indicate how the Web editor uses the applied text, not how Web browsers should display the document. Just as paragraph and heading tags indicate how a passage is to be used within the document, logical styles allow the browser to decide how to format the text to best fit the rest of your Web page.

Each logical character style has an opening and a closing tag that form a container for the inserted text and restrict the logical application to the contained data. Table 6.2 shows descriptions of logical styles.

Table 6.2 Logical styles and their meanings

Style	Description
EM	Emphasized text
STRONG	Strongly emphasized text
CITE	Text in a citation
CODE	Text representing an HTML element sample
DFN	Text in a definition
SAMP	Text in an output sample, similar to code
KBD	Text representing a keyboard key
VAR	Text defining a variable or value
STRIKE	(proposed HTML 2.0) Struck out text

Proposed Additional Elements for HTML+

ARG	Command argument
ABBREV	Abbreviation
CMD	Command name
ACRONYM	Acronym
PERSON	Proper name
Q	Short quotation

Q&A *What is the difference between EM and Italics?*

The creation of logical elements such as <EM> and <STRONG> may seem repetitive because the physical styles italic and boldface produce similar effects. The difference between the two lies in their nesting abilities. Logical highlighting elements may be nested inside of one another, but this is often insensible given the fairly specific meanings assigned to each. Nesting of logical elements is also confused by some browsers that produce inappropriate renditions. Physical styles, on the other hand, can be nested appropriately, and formatting text to appear as underlined, bold, or italic is not an unreasonable request.

One of the interesting points about logical styles is that, no matter how you use them, your readers can view them more or less the way they want. All they have to do is configure their browsers to display each logical style in a particular way. For instance, if someone likes emphasized text to be in a 24 point Times Roman font, all of the text in <EM> containers will be displayed as 24 point Times Roman regardless of what the rest of the Web page looks like. And the readers know that every Web page that uses logical styles will conform to their own preferences. Figure 6.11 shows how logical styles are written, and figure 6.12 shows how Internet Explorer's default settings shows them.

Fig. 6.11
Unlike physical styles, logical styles can't be used in combinations.

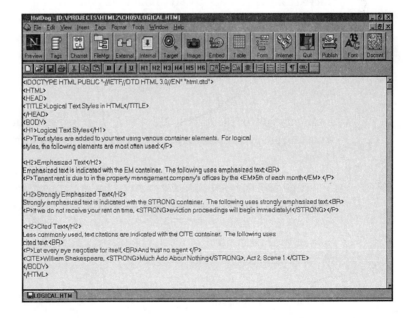

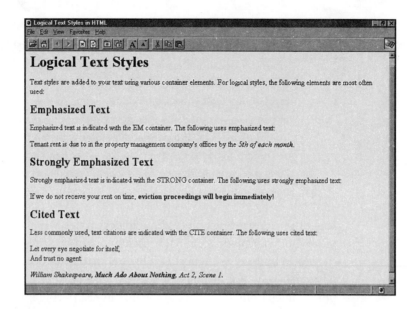

Horizontal lines keep the parts of your page separate

There really isn't much to say about horizontal lines except that they're popular. The <HR> tag places a shadowed line across the width of the Web browser's window. If the reader changes the size of the window, the line resizes to match. The <HR> tag is an empty tag and does not require a closing element for functioning. Horizontal rules insert a paragraph break before and after the line.

As an example of the use of <HR>, load your browser and go to **http://www.corpserv.nrc.ca/corpserv/nrc.html** (Canada's National Research Council).

Netscape provides additional functions for horizontal rules. These give you control over the weight of the line, its length, and the location of the hard rule within the browser's window. Netscape also lets you drop the "etched" look of the line in favor of a solid black rule. Table 6.3 lists the Netscape parameters and what they do.

Table 6.3 Netscape Extension to <HR>

Extension	Description
SIZE	Set thickness of horizontal line
WIDTH	Set width as a measure of pixels or percentage of viewer window's width
ALIGN	Allows line to be justified for left, center, or right within the viewer window
NOSHADE	Changes appearance of horizontal line to be solid black with no "etched" effect

Figure 6.13 shows how you can use these extensions to the <HR> element in your Web pages.

Fig. 6.13

If a browser does not recognize the Netscape extensions, it will ignore them.

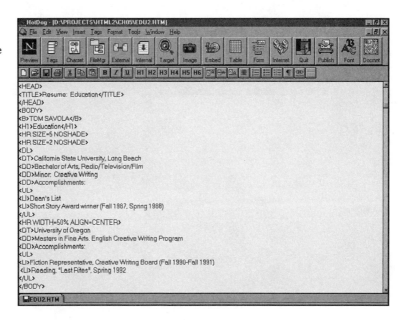

Figure 6.14 shows how Netscape displays the extensions.

Fig. 6.14
Controlling the
appearance of your
lines adds a creative
touch to Web pages.

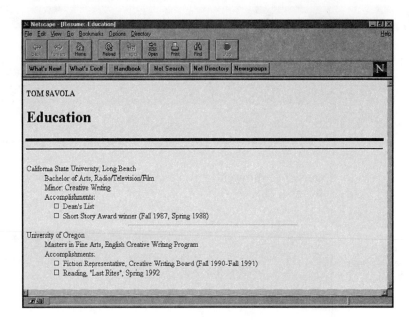

7

I Have This List, See...

● **In this chapter:**

- Hit the mark with bulleted lists

- You can count on your numbered lists

- The versatility of definition lists

- Can lists be combined?

I do lists. You do lists. Letterman does lists. So does Guinness. The Web does lists, and it's your job to put them there. . . . ➤

Want a challenge? Try to get through two hours of your waking life without encountering a list. Any kind of list. Sure you could avoid watching Letterman. Or at least avoid the Top Ten segment. But that's late at night, and by that time you'll have run into all sorts of lists. Pick up the newspaper, and you'll see lists of stories and editorials. Read the ads, and you'll see lists of components, prices, and store locations. Grab a can of spaghetti sauce, and you'll find a list of ingredients. And then there are your own lists: groceries, phone numbers, things to do, and things *not* to do.

Lists are popular because they work. Bulleted lists add pizzazz to a presentation and prove to the audience that you actually have several points to make. Numbered lists set things in order and are superb for offering a process of instructions. Lists cut to the chase, eliminating unnecessary verbiage while organizing things into categories and hierarchies. It's hard to imagine getting through life—or even a single day—without them.

Blessed is the list maker?

Lists aren't the be-all and end-all of civilization. Yes, they're everywhere, but they're often misused. The purpose of lists is to present specific points of information quickly and clearly. Bulleted lists of three items work well; bulleted lists of 15 items don't. And a numbered list of 35 instructions has little value.

Keep these things in mind when you're thinking about creating your Web lists. The Web is filled with useless lists designed by HTML authors who just didn't think and certainly didn't test. Make sure your readers know that you understand the important functions of lists of all kinds.

One other point: A page with nothing but lists is a page with no intelligence. For a list to be effective, it must be short, to the point, and chunked. What does **chunked** mean? Your readers can only take in so much information at a time (and on the Web, it's even more important because users whip through these pages), and it's your responsibility to offer it to them in digestible "chunks." Small lists, logical categories, and headings all make a very real difference.

In HTML, you have five kinds of lists

Think about the lists you see every day: DOs and DON'Ts, instructions and warnings, to-do and to-buy, topics and arguments. Lots of lists look the same, but the range of formats is extensive. On any given day, you'll see lists with items separated by bullets, numbers, or just plain spaces. You'll see annotated lists (in which each item contains a paragraph or so of explanation), indexes, tables of contents, menus, and so on.

The Web lets you create five different kinds of lists, and although you can't use them to re-create all the lists you'll find in the world, you'll find them immensely useful nevertheless. The list types are:

- **ordered lists** <OL>, a.k.a. numbered lists
- **unordered lists** <UL>, a.k.a. bulleted lists
- **definition lists** <DL>, a.k.a. glossary lists
- **menu lists** <MENU>
- **directory lists** <DIR>

In fact, you don't need to learn all five types. Only three list types are regularly found on the Web: ordered, unordered, and definition. Menu and directory lists are specialized types of unordered lists, and whether they display differently from normal unordered lists depends on your Web browser.

As a result, I'll cover only the three main types in this book—ordered lists, unordered lists, and definition lists.

Lists by the number: *ordered* lists

 TIP Use numbered/ordered lists when you want to emphasize the ordering. In a set of instructions, for instance, step 1 must be done before step 2, and the numbers help your reader follow along. The same holds true for rankings: you want to show them in order beginning with the best.

The HTML element for ordered lists (or more easily remembered as **numbered lists**) follows the basic rules for all HTML lists: it is a container element using the beginning and closing tags <OL> and </OL>. Each item within the list is identified by the item tag <LI> (which stands for **list item**).

The syntax for numbered lists is:

```
<ol>
<li>
<li>
</ol>
```

Each `<li>` represents a single item within the list.

Figure 7.1 shows a numbered list—in this case, a list of the top ten computer viruses as compiled by Symantec Corporation (**http://www.symantec.com/virus/hot/hot.html**).

Fig. 7.1

Symantec's numbered list of computer viruses sorts the viruses in order of how often they've been reported.

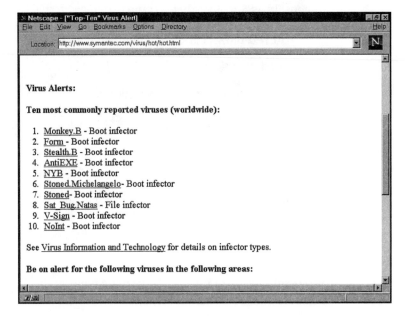

The HTML code for the numbered list in figure 7.1 is as follows:

```
<ol><li><a href="/virus/specific/boot/monkey.html">
➥Monkey.B</a> - Boot infector<li><a
href="/virus/specific/boot/form.html">Form </a>
➥- Boot infector<li><a
href="/virus/specific/boot/stealthb.html">Stealth.B</a>
➥- Boot infector<li><a
href="/virus/specific/boot/antiexe.html">AntiEXE</a>
➥- Boot infector<li><a
href="/virus/specific/boot/nyb.html">NYB</a>
➥- Boot infector<li><a
href="/virus/specific/boot/mich1.html">
```

```
➥Stoned.Michelangelo</a>
➥- Boot infector<li><a
href="/virus/specific/boot/stoned.html">Stoned</a>
➥- Boot infector<li><a
href="/virus/specific/file/natas.html">Sat_Bug.Natas</a>
➥- File infector<li><a
href="/virus/specific/boot/v-sign.html">V-Sign</a>
➥- Boot infector<li><a
href="/virus/specific/boot/noint.html">NoInt</a>
➥- Boot infector</ol>
```

Notice that each element within the list starts with the <LI> tag (there's no corresponding </LI> tag). The entire list is surrounded by the <OL> and </OL> container tags. This list looks complex because each element is a hyperlink (and let's face it, hyperlinks look pretty ugly in ASCII code), but it could just as easily be a simple list of colors. What's important here is that the list items themselves can contain just about whatever HTML code you can dream up.

These lists work much the same as the numbered lists in your word processor. You don't number each item manually; you just put in the information and your browser adds the numbers for you. If you add a list item, the browser will renumber the entire list.

HTML editors such as HTML Assistant and HotDog, in fact, offer a button on the toolbar that makes creating numbered lists easy. Just type the list items (on separate lines), highlight them all, and then click the numbered list button. Again, it's just like using your word processor (well, one that has a numbered list button, anyway).

Each <LI> tag signals the browser software to start a new line for the item.

 TIP **You can use almost all of the formatting HTML tags inside lists.** One of the most useful is the paragraph tag <p>, which allows you to separate text within a list item.

 CAUTION **Avoid using headings in your list items; they don't look very good,** and they don't really serve the function headings are supposed to serve. Also, pay attention to your closing tags in lists, especially when you use nested lists (lists inside of lists). Forgetting a tag can do amazingly horrible things to the appearance of the page.

Take advantage of Netscape enhancements

As you've come to expect by now, Netscape offers additional help when it comes to producing numbered lists. This help is in the form of <OL> enhancements, and they let you control the following two key elements:

- You can set the numbering style, ranging from Arabic numbers (1, 2, 3, 4) to letters (a, b, c, d; or A, B, C, D) or even Roman numerals (i, ii, iii, iv; or I, II, III, IV).

- You can set the first number in the sequence so that it's not necessary to start with 1.

Table 7.1 shows the enhancements to ordered lists that are possible when designing for Netscape.

Table 7.1   Netscape extensions to ordered (numbered) lists

Attribute	Description
TYPE=A	Set markers to uppercase letters
TYPE=a	Set markers to lowercase letters
TYPE=I	Set markers to uppercase Roman numerals
TYPE=i	Set markers to lowercase Roman numerals
TYPE=1	Set markers to numbers
START	Set beginning value of item markers in the current list

These attributes are written just like ordinary tag attributes, placed directly after the main tag itself. For example:

- **<OL TYPE=A>** produces a lettered list with items "numbered" A, B, C, D, and so on.

- **<OL TYPE=I>** yields a list that uses Roman numerals; items will be numbered I, II, III, IV, and so on.

- **<OL TYPE=i START=4>** displays a list with a lowercase Roman numeral in front of each list item starting with iv (the Roman numeral for 4).

Obviously, these extensions give you more options for displaying items in lists. It's a good thing, too: numbered lists are unexciting by their very nature, and they need all the help they can get.

When you're creating multiple lists, consider using a mix of list styles. By doing so, you can help users easily distinguish between different types of information. Figure 7.2 shows a source page that includes a list using mixed markers, and figure 7.3 shows the final product as it appears in Netscape.

Fig. 7.2

You can put lists with different types of markers inside other lists (even if the list is not the same type, such as an ordered list inside a bulleted list).

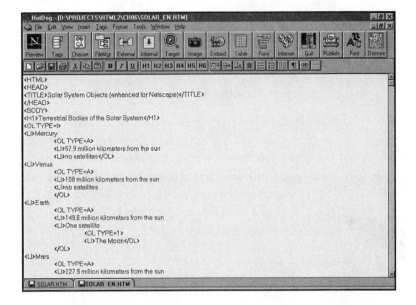

Fig. 7.3

Mixing list types can provide a nice looking list as well as keep different lists separate from each other.

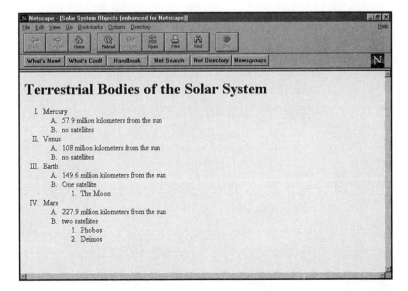

Number one with a bullet: *unordered* lists

By far the most common type of list on the Web is the unordered list. But almost nobody actually calls these things **unordered** lists; instead, they call them **bulleted** lists. Why? Because the items in an unordered list are separated by **bullets**—big black circles that have become a staple of overhead transparencies, PowerPoint presentations, and books like this one.

Unlike numbered lists, bulleted lists don't have an obvious order to them. That is, the second bulleted item isn't necessarily more significant than the fifth—unlike numbered lists, in which item two is almost always more important than item five. In fact, this lack of order tells you why they're called **unordered.** It's not because the items aren't put in some kind of order, it's just that the order doesn't matter.

Most Web page designers use bulleted lists rather than numbered lists because they look better. In fact, there are so few numbered lists on the Web that you might never actually put one in place. Nonetheless, they're good to know about because a well-designed numbered list can help present information to your reader more usefully. In reality, though, bulleted lists are often just as ordered as numbered lists are, but numbers aren't used because they would destroy the aesthetic effect.

The tags for bulleted lists are <UL> and </UL>. As with numbered lists, each list item begins with the <LI> tag. Also like numbered lists, each item can include other HTML elements, including additional sublists (nested lists). And don't worry about line breaks—your browser will insert line breaks whenever it finds a new <LI> item tag.

Each browser will use its own internal bullet icons for these list items. You can't control these. As an example, figure 7.4 shows Netscape Navigator and Internet Explorer displaying the same lists. Despite the difference in bullet styles, the HTML code is exactly the same.

Fig. 7.4
Bullets display differently in different browsers, depending on the browser's built-in bullet styles.

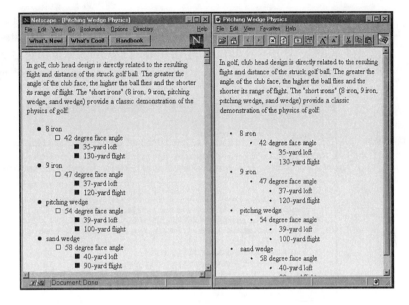

Except for the change in container tags from <OL></OL> to <UL></UL>, writing the HTML code for bulleted lists is exactly the same as writing the code for numbered lists. You can even put bulleted lists within bulleted lists, as seen in the following code (it's in Spanish, and it's taken from **http://www.nafta.net/indexesp.htm**):

```
NAFTAnet, Inc. es una empresa interesada en brindarle las
mejores oprtunidades del Tratado de Libre Comercio de
América del Norte <A href="naftaesp.htm">(NAFTA)</A>
y el resto del <A HREF = "naftacos.htm">continiente
americano.</A>
Nuestros servicios le permitirán:
<UL>
<LI>Enlazar electrónicamente con socios comerciales
y especialistas en comercio internacional a través
de la más avanzada tecnología en telecomunicaciones,
<LI>Obtener lo mejor en <A href="newsesp.htm">
información</A>y <A HREF="analysis.htm"">análisis</A>
sobre NAFTA.
<LI>Promover el comercio electrónico entrenuestros socios
a través de nuestro
<A HREF = "market.htm">Centro de Negocios NAFTAnet.</A>
<LI>Tener acceso a fuentes de información sobre:
<UL><LI><A HREF = "ecediesp.htm">Comercio electrónico
e intercambio electrónico de datos</A>,
<LI><A HREF = "bizdirs.htm">Directorios de negocios</A>,
<LI><A HREF = "ecat.htm">Catálogos, escaparates y centros
comerciales electrónicos</A>,
<LI>Listas de oportunidades y mucho más.</UL></UL>
```

Figure 7.5 shows what this code looks like in Netscape. The first four items on the page constitute the main list, with each item denoted by a round black bullet. Attached to the fourth item is a sublist, which is also a bulleted list but has square bullets. This system of bullet styles is the default in Netscape.

Fig. 7.5
This HTML page contains two bulleted lists: the main list (solid circles) and the sublist (squares).

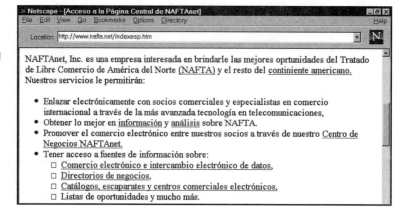

Use Netscape extensions for different bullet styles

Netscape, as always, refuses to take defaults lying down. Netscape gave you Roman numerals and other extensions for numbered lists, so it only makes sense that Netscape would offer enhancements for bulleted lists.

Remember all that stuff about the browser (not the Web author) controlling what the bullets in a bulleted list actually look like? Well, if you write for the Netscape browser, you can choose the bullet styles yourself—as if you hadn't guessed.

The new bullet styles are as follows:

- **filled circles** <UL TYPE=disc>

- **filled squares** <UL TYPE=square>

- **open squares** <UL TYPE=circle>

Hardly a cornucopia of bullet varieties, but a little better than a measly little black dot. How do they look? Pretty much as you'd expect. Figure 7.6 demonstrates how to use these bullet types in your lists, and figure 7.7 shows you what a Netscape user sees when he views Web pages with these special markers.

Notice from the previous bulleted list that the TYPE designation for open squares is "circle." You have to wonder who dreamed this one up.

Fig. 7.6
Mixing bullet types will help readers distinguish different types of information.

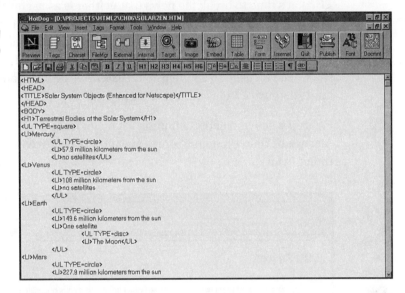

Fig. 7.7
Three bullet types are displayed here: open squares, filled squares, and filled circles.

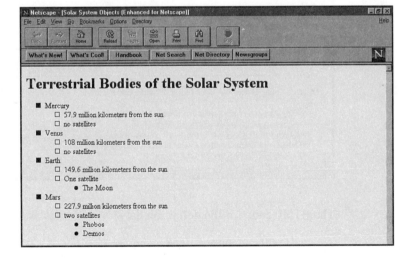

Faster than a speeding bullet—*definition lists*

Now that you know how to construct numbered lists <OL> and bulleted lists <UL>, it's time to break the news that neither is as useful or as powerful as **definition** lists <DL>. Sometimes called **glossary** lists, definition lists are used to create lists that look like glossary entries in which a term or phrase is accompanied by an indented definition text paragraph. This is a great tool to use when you need to list items with extensive descriptions (such as real estate listings or items in a retail catalog).

Figure 7.8 shows a short definition list taken from the home page of the Alliance of Ohio Community Arts Agencies (**http://www.aok.ohio.gov/aok/index.html**).

Fig. 7.8

The definition list is at the top of this screen. At the bottom, the bulleted list is comprised of custom-made bullets.

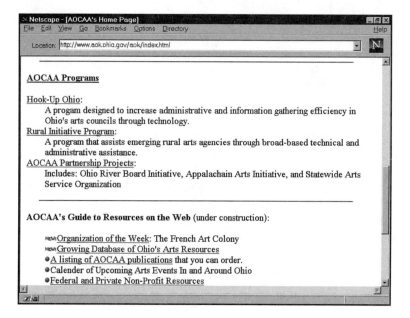

The HTML code for the definition list shown here is as follows:

```
<dl><dt><a href="/aok/program.html#Hook-Up">Hook-Up Ohio</a>:
<dd>A program designed to increase administrative and
information gathering efficiency in Ohio's arts councils
through technology.
```

```
<dt><a href="/aok/program.html#Peer">Rural Initiative Pro-
gram</a>:
<dd>A program that assists emerging rural arts agencies
through broad-based technical and administrative assistance.
<dt><a href="/aok/program.html#Other">AOCAA Partnership
Projects</a>:
<dd>Includes: Ohio River Board Initiative, Appalachian Arts
Initiative,and Statewide Arts Service Organization</dl>
```

As you can see from this code, definition lists do not follow the same format as either numbered or bulleted lists (or any other HTML elements, for that matter). The definition list is enclosed inside a container labeled <DL> and </DL>. Inside the definition list, a <DT> tag is used to indicate the header for the item or items (the <DT> can include a URL reference), and the <DD> tags indicate each separate list item. Both DT and DD are open tags—they don't need closing tags to contain their information.

The important point about definition lists is that they make your information appear very attractive and very well organized. You can have one <DD> item for each <DT> heading, or you can have several. This heading-item feature gives definition lists a professional appearance right from the start.

In other words, definition lists have three elements—<DL>, <DT>, and <DD>—rather than two. <DT> presents the headline, while <DD>s make up the actual items.

In the previous HTML code, there are three headings, each with one item. To be more technical, each <DT> has one corresponding <DD>. It's entirely possible to include several <DD>s with each <DT>, and you can have numbered or bulleted lists inside the <DT> listing. You have a great deal of design flexibility with definition lists, which is why they're so great.

CAUTION **Make sure your heading is short enough to fit on a single line; if** it's too long, it will wrap down onto the next line without indenting, and it will look pretty ghastly.

Figure 7.9 shows how a definition list can be used to create an online catalog with HTML. Figure 7.10 shows how Netscape displays these text lists on-screen.

Browsers can vary in how definition lists look in the Web pages they display. For instance, Mosaic has a tendency to use a double-space between terms, but Netscape does not. All this means is that readers may be able to read Mosaic definition lists easier, but Netscape users will be able to see more of the definition list information on-screen at any given time.

Fig. 7.9
Some HTML editors indent list items to make it clear which items belong to which list portions.

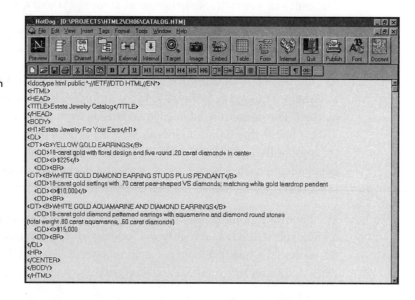

Fig. 7.10
This is how the definition list looks in a browser.

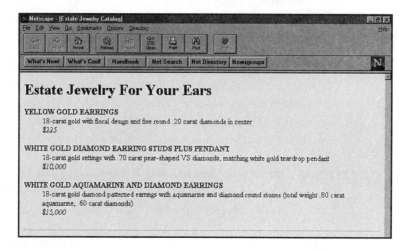

Combining similar and different lists

If you think of HTML elements as the rules of Web authoring, then it stands to reason that sometimes you've just got to break the rules. Not all of your information is going to fall into neat categories and packages. Unless you're the writer for David Letterman's "Top Ten List," your world is not so tidy.

Combining types of containers and elements goes a long way to making your Web pages dynamic and interesting. Instead of forcing your content into a narrow form (like a bulleted list), experiment with combinations of lists that work together to deliver your message.

If you have a numbered list, and one of the list items is a list itself with no specific order to it, insert a bulleted list. Browsers are smart enough to indent the bulleted list within the numbered list, giving your Web page a smart look and better communication capability. Figure 7.11 gives you a look at how easy it is to put containers into containers, letting different lists work for you. Figure 7.12 shows how Internet Explorer displays this mix of containers.

Fig. 7.11
You can indent your code to make it easier to read as plain text, but browsers don't take their on-screen formatting cues from these indentations—they are smart enough to do it themselves.

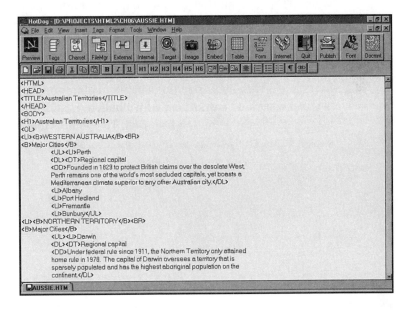

Fig. 7.12
Lists embedded in other containers may "inherit" certain style and formatting characteristics. Again, it's up to the browser to determine what the list looks like on-screen.

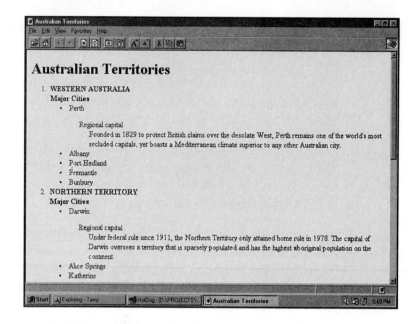

When HTML first started, lists were the most important organizational tool available. To a large degree, they still are. While you certainly don't want to overuse them, lists offer you the possibility of categorizing your material and setting it down on the page so that anyone can find what he wants.

Experiment with lists. Find out what kind of information needs a numbered list, and what kind works best with a bulleted list. If you want sophisticated list designs, learn definition lists well. The point is that your readers will expect lists to help them navigate your site, and for that reason alone they're worth the time you spend on them.

Without Graphics, Your Web Pages Are Nothin'

● **In this chapter:**

- Keep those images inline

- How do you combine text and graphics?

- Supported graphic file formats

- What happens if a browser can't display an inline graphic?

- Using other graphic file formats

Dazzle your readers with full-color graphics inserted right into the text of your Web pages . . . . ❯

Back in the old days (like two years ago), graphics and the Internet just didn't get along. The Net was text, text, and more text. To see a graphic you had to know all about file transfers, download protocols, and image viewing software. The Net was as graphically rich as your phone book's white pages.

Now the Web *is* graphics. More and more Web pages rely primarily, or even exclusively, on attractive, colorful graphics to the extent that many pages have nothing at all to offer users of non-graphics browsers. Turning off your browser's graphics option these days is a little like watching TV with only the sound on: you might get by, but you'd hardly be impressed.

> ### " *Plain English, please!*
>
> What's a **graphic**? Graphics are pictures. They can be drawings, photographs, or computer paintings. They can even be pictures of text. In computer talk, graphics are files of a specific kind. They're **binary** files as opposed to **text** or **ASCII** files. This means that your favorite text editor won't be able to read them properly, and you'll need a graphics viewing program instead. The best-known graphics types are GIF, JPEG, TIFF, PCX, and BMP. There are several others as well. "

You can create Web pages without graphics. They'll work, and some people will thank you. Then again, when was the last time you saw a Calvin Klein ad without graphics? Or a billboard? Or a top-flight magazine? Or a tapestry? Even the staid old *New York Times* has beefed up its graphics component because its publisher realizes that even the steadiest reputation in the world won't keep readers for long. For better or for worse, we live in an age of images, and if you hope to attract Internetters to your Web site, you'd better learn how to use graphics.

"Inline" is in

You don't see many professional documents without graphics. There's a reason for this: designed properly, a picture really *can* be worth a thousand words. Through television and magazines, we've come to expect graphical presentation of information, and your Web readers will expect this as well.

Graphics help your Web pages

Here are a few of the enhancements your graphics will provide:

- They break text into digestible "chunks," making the page easier to read.

- They separate content so that the reader knows when a new subject has been started (or when a transition has been made).

- They provide content that is not available via text, such as a picture of your pet or your latest watercolor masterpiece.

- They add color, humor, and excitement to the medium.

- They demonstrate the author's creativity.

 CAUTION **Keep in mind, at all times, that these are enhancements for your** reader, not for you as designer (even the last point). As with everything else, only the customer matters. Badly designed graphical Web pages are almost always the result of the author not considering the reader's point of view.

Now that you're convinced—well, pretend you are anyway—it's time to move on to the production of graphics in HTML. By the end of this chapter, you'll be well on your way to producing your own—and very effectively, as well.

The IMG element lets you insert graphics files

Let's start with a picture. Figure 8.1 (**http://www.atitech.ca/**) contains several graphics created with the IMG (image) element of HTML. They're called **inline images.**

When you want to insert a graphic file into a Web page, you create inline images. These are attached to a document using an **URL** (Uniform Resource Locator) reference. The URL is the specific location on the Internet where the graphic file is located. It can be on the same Web host computer that your Web pages are on, or it can be on a host somewhere else on the Internet.

Fig. 8.1
How many inline images can you spot? Obviously, there are three. The fancy line is also a graphic, and it's not so obvious.

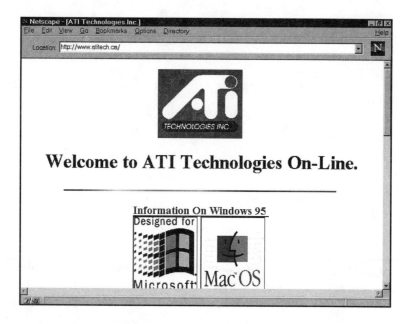

> **Plain English, please!**
>
> **Inline** images are graphics files that appear on a Web document. As a Web author, you put them there by referencing that file in your HTML document.

To create the URL pointer for your image, use the IMG element. This element acts as a placeholder in your text where the browser will put the graphic. The IMG is an empty container with the following syntax:

```
<IMG SRC=image_URL>
```

IMG is the HTML image tag; it appears with all inline images. SRC means **source** and refers to the location of the image (it's on some hard drive somewhere in the world), and this location is shown as the **image_URL**.

The image_URL can be a full URL with full machine name (e.g., **http://randall.uwaterloo.ca/mystman.gif**—try it). Alternatively, it can refer to the graphics file's *relative* URL; in this case, you refer to the file's location relative to the directory where the Web page is.

The following is the HTML code for the ATI Technologies page shown in figure 8.1:

Important— Please answer these questions:

Please check any that apply: I own a

☐ DVD Player (55)   ☐ CD-ROM Drive (56)

Your
Age (09)

Email Address _____

What is your
Telephone Number? (05)   [Area code]

My main music interest is: (Check one, but you are always free to choose from any

☐ **Hard Rock**
Tom Petty
Third Eye Blind

☐ **Soft Rock**
Mariah Carey
Elton John

☐ **Alternative**
Kid Rock
Blink 182

☐ **Hard Music**
Ozzy Osbourne
Korn

☐ **Rap/Hip Hop**
Will Smith
NAS

☐ **Country**
Shania Twain
Dixie Chicks

☐ **Contemporary Christian†**
Point Of Grace
Steven Curtis
Chapman

☐ **Dance/Pop**
98 Degrees
Britney Spears

PLAY from Columbia House
1400 N. Fruitridge Avenue
Terre Haute, IN 47811
play.columbiahouse.com
AOL Keyword: CHMUSIC

Note: We reserve the right to request additional
information, reject any application or cancel any
membership. Applicable tax added to all orders.

```
<center>
<IMG src="gif/ati2.gif" alt="[ATI LOGO]">
<H1>Welcome to ATI Technologies On-Line.</H1>
<img src="/gif/byline.gif">
</center>
<center>
<h3>
<a href="/Win95/index.html"> Information On Windows 95 </a>
<br>
<a href="/Win95/index.html"><img src="/gif/w95logo.gif" ></a>
<a href="/MAC/index.html"><img src="/gif/mac.gif" ></a>
```

Lines 2, 4, 10, and 11 of this code use the IMG tag. All four use relative URLs as the image_URL component. The ATI logo (line 2) is a file called ati2.gif, and is found in the /gif/ directory of the machine that holds ATI's Web server software. Also found there is the colored horizontal line (byline.gif) found in line 4. These two examples show a straightforward use of the IMG tag.

Lines 10 and 11 are more ambitious. These graphics, representing the Windows and Mac boxes shown in figure 8.1, are hyperlinks as well as inline images. Notice that creating them is identical to creating a standard hyperlink, except that in place of text, you place the IMG SRC tag for the graphics file.

In line 11, <img src="/gif/w95logo.gif"> calls up the w95logo.gif file from ATI's /gif/directory and displays it as a clickable hyperlink. The hyperlink is shown in the code as <a href="/Win95/index.html"> followed by </a> after the image reference.

Q&A My inline graphic is too big. Don't browsers automatically resize graphics files according to the width of the window the way they wrap text?

No. In fact, be careful when you create wide graphics; many people do not run their browsers full-screen (or can't set their screen size larger than VGA or 640 by 480), and graphics wider than five or six inches may get cut off by the side of the browser window.

The IMG tag will be a constant companion during your HTML authoring. Work with it often because it'll keep coming back.

Why are all my graphics pushed against the left margin?

On their own, Web browsers don't do much to help text and graphics share space on a Web page. The text in figure 8.2, for example, looks tiny when lined up along the bottom of the image. It's not very attractive, partly because the white space beside the graphic is simply an empty blob.

Fig. 8.2
Web browsers treat images like a character in the line of text and don't wrap text along side the graphic.

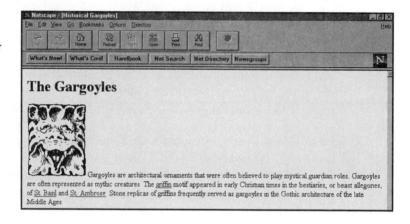

Fortunately, you can do something about this. IMG comes with an attribute called ALIGN. ALIGN determines how text and images interact with one another on a Web page. Specifically, ALIGN controls how text that's placed in your HTML code on the same line as an image will line itself up along the vertical sides of the image.

The ALIGN attribute is written as:

```
<IMG ALIGN=value SRC=image_URL>
```

The possible values for ALIGN are shown in table 8.1:

Table 8.1 Standard ALIGN values

Value	Effect on text
TOP	Aligns the top of the text to top of the image
MIDDLE	Aligns the middle of the text to the middle of the image
BOTTOM	Aligns the bottom of the text to the bottom of the image

The BOTTOM value is the default for IMG and does not need to be specified if it's what you want to use. When using any of the standard values, Web browsers leave white space around the text on the line, and the text wraps down to the next line beneath the bottom of the image. Figure 8.3 shows how each standard alignment includes a variety of image alignments used in HTML code.

Fig. 8.3

Do not mix ALIGN values on the same line of text in a browser window, as there is no common Web browser interpretation for mixed alignments.

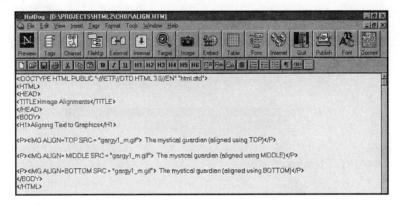

Figure 8.4 shows how Internet Explorer handles each of these attribute values.

Fig. 8.4

Only the text on the current line will follow the selected ALIGN option. Text on the next line in the browser drops underneath the inline image.

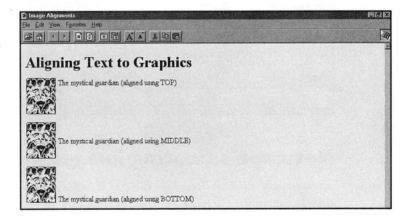

How Netscape extends your alignments

Netscape provides a few more tools for controlling how text and graphics work together on-screen. These nonstandard extensions are really the first true desktop publishing controls for inline images. Netscape's ALIGN values are shown in table 8.2.

Table 8.2   Netscape ALIGN values

Value	Effect on text
TEXTTOP	Aligns the top of the tallest text on the line with the top of the image
ABSMIDDLE	Aligns the bottom of the text with the middle of the image
ABSBOTTOM	Aligns the bottom of the text with the bottom of the image
BASELINE	Aligns the bottom of the text with the bottom of the image

Figure 8.5 shows how Netscape displays the different alignment options.

Fig. 8.5
Each ALIGN value provides a different layout of white space around the text.

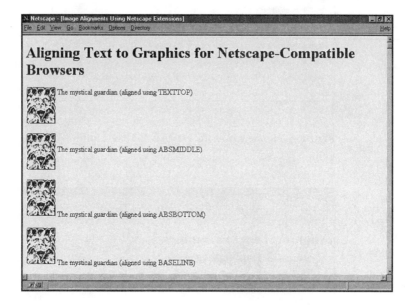

Netscape's floating images

Netscape provides more ALIGN values for a new type of inline image called a **floating graphic**. No longer tied to one line of text (with all of that awkward white space), these graphics "float" against one of the margins, and text wraps along the entire height of the image.

The two ALIGN values are LEFT and RIGHT, and they specify which margin the image will float against. Figure 8.6 shows how easy it is to use these extensions in your Web page IMG links.

Fig. 8.6
The LEFT and RIGHT values also change the function of inline images and not just the function of the surrounding text.

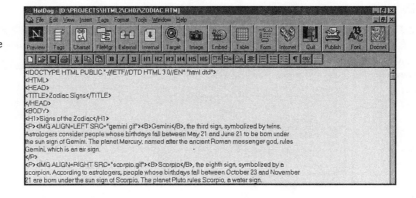

In figure 8.7, you see how Netscape displays floating images.

Fig. 8.7
Floating images are detached from the surrounding text and act just like frames in desktop publishing programs.

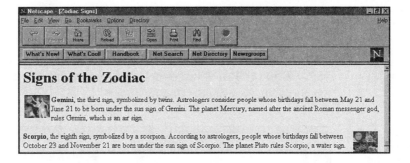

Two other design attributes are available for Netscape pages. To control the amount of spacing between text and floating images and between the edge of the window and the images, use the attributes **VSPACE** and **HSPACE**. VSPACE defines the space (or gutter size for those of you familiar with page layout) above and below a floating image, and HSPACE controls the space to the right and left of a floating image. Figure 8.8 shows the VSPACE and HSPACE attributes at work in an HTML document.

 Plain English, please!

Sometimes the blizzard of cryptic abbreviations in a coding language makes you forget that they actually make some sense (well, now and then). **VSPACE** means *vertical space,* **HSPACE** means *horizontal space.* So <IMG ALIGN=LEFT HSPACE=10> simply means, "Align this image and put 10 globs of space to the left of it." That's it.

Fig. 8.8
The values of VSPACE and HSPACE are relative; a good gutter value is somewhere around five.

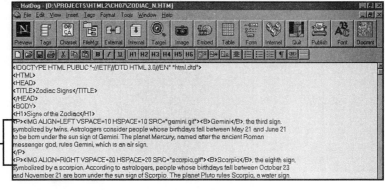

To see the results of VSPACE and HSPACE, compare figure 8.7 with figure 8.9. In figure 8.7, no gutters have been provided around the image (i.e., no VSPACE/HSPACE attributes).

In figure 8.7, the images are noticeably off the left and right edges, and the text does not jut up right against them. It is an example of how to add VSPACE and HSPACE values in HTML. Figure 8.9 shows how Netscape puts the gutter space around a floating image.

Fig. 8.9
VSPACE and HSPACE always control both sides of an image—you can't give a side more or less space than its opposite.

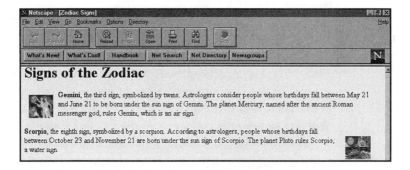

Not everyone in your audience can see those wonderful graphics

Odd though it may seem, not everyone on the Internet has access to Netscape, Mosaic, Internet Explorer, or any other graphical browser. Of the twenty million plus audience available to you on the Net, a sizable percentage still use browsers like UNIX's Lynx, which is extremely capable but which doesn't display graphics. Other users keep the graphics feature of their browser turned off. But these people want access to your Web pages as much as anyone else. And if your Web site is about information, you won't want to disappoint them.

So how can you accommodate these users when you use graphics in your Web pages? HTML provides a simple solution: IMG's ALT attribute (ALT means **alternative**). ALT defines a text string that replaces your images in browsers without graphics support. This text generally is often displayed in a box (to separate it from the surrounding body text), and is clickable if your image was a hyperlink.

There is no real limit to how long your ALT text can be, but a variant on the KISS principle—Keep It Short and Simple—is as good a rule as any. Figure 8.10 shows what Internet Explorer shows with its graphics turned off.

Fig. 8.10
In HTML 3-compatible browsers, ALT text supports HTML elements, such as text styles and anchors.

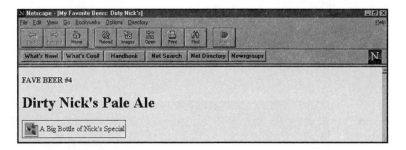

IMG ain't done yet—it has more to offer

Netscape provides three final extensions for the IMG element. The first pair, **WIDTH** and **HEIGHT**, are designed to make your Web site faster reading. The third, **BORDER**, is used primarily for looks.

WIDTH and HEIGHT help solve one of the Web's continually nagging problems. When people click a link to your Web pages, their browsers generally wait until all the inline images are loaded before going back and filling in the text around them. The WIDTH and HEIGHT attributes alleviate this wait.

By telling the browser the pixel dimensions of the images in your Web page, it can then mock up the layout and lay in the text *before* starting to retrieve the images. If you are the reader and want to click a text link before the images finish loading, you're free to do it. Figure 8.11 shows a Web page with the dimension attributes.

Fig. 8.11
WIDTH and HEIGHT values are arbitrary, but should match your image's actual measurements so it looks right on-screen.

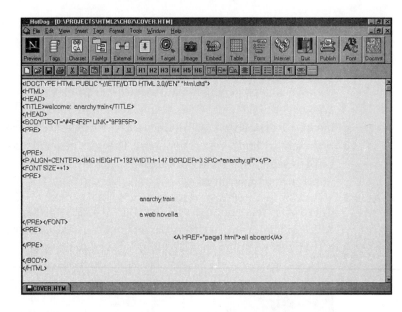

Figure 8.12 shows Netscape's interpretation with a graphic partially displayed.

Fig. 8.12
The black border is a placemarker where the inline graphic will load.

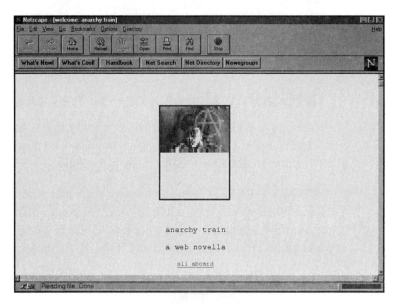

Much less useful is the BORDER attribute. Its purpose is to let you change or remove the border that appears around inline images that are also clickable hyperlinks. Increasing the border will make it more obvious that the image is a link, while decreasing it makes it less obvious. Not many Web authors use it because, to be quite frank, it doesn't do much.

To use BORDER, add it to your IMG statement and give it a numerical value. Figure 8.13 shows how Netscape displays these different BORDER values.

Fig. 8.13
A high BORDER value practically invites your reader to click the image and see where it leads.

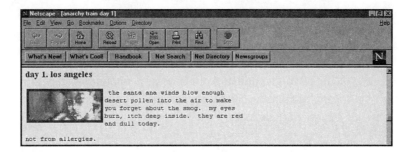

 Q&A **If I remove the border, won't that make it look just like an ordinary inline image?**

Yes, exactly. The value, BORDER=0, removes the telltale border around the image and, as a result, potentially confuses your readers. If you want to remove the border for aesthetic reasons, be sure to include text inside the <A HREF> anchor so people will know they can click it.

A potential design reason for removing the border would be to offer a bonus for any reader who takes the time to move the mouse around and figure out that the graphic is actually a link. But are you sure you want them to work that hard?

What graphics formats are supported on the Web?

As explained near the beginning of this chapter, images are stored on computers as graphics files. But that's not all. They can be stored in many different file formats, and all formats have their particular advantages and disadvantages.

This situation is much the same as with any other type of program. Your word processor saves files in specific formats, and these are incompatible with other word processors. Microsoft Word needs special filters to read WordPerfect files and vice versa, and Microsoft Excel and Lotus 1-2-3 files have always had trouble getting along.

In theory, the World Wide Web supports every graphic format possible. Because of the limits of Web clients such as browsers that can handle only certain file types by themselves, the number of supported formats is, in practice, limited to the most popular and versatile.

Most browsers support only two graphics formats: JPEG and GIF. To view others, you need a "helper" application: a separate program that you configure to run whenever your browser encounters a specific type of file. Helper applications are available on many FTP sites on the Web and on disks of shareware as well.

 Plain English, please!

Helper applications are completely separate programs from your Web browser. A paint program, a word processor, a video player, a MIDI player—any or all of these might be useful helper applications. They're covered in more detail at the end of this chapter.

Table 8.3 lists the most commonly used graphic file formats.

Table 8.3   Graphic file formats supported by WWW browsers

Format	Extension	Support
Graphics Interchange Format	GIF	Browser
Joint Photographic Experts Group	JPEG, JPG	Browser or Helper program
Bitmap	BMP, XBMP, XBM	Browser or Helper program
Device Independent Bitmap	DIB	Browser or Helper program
Tagged Image File Format	TIFF, TIF	Helper program
PC Paintbrush	PCX	Helper program

Not every browser supports all of these file types; most only handle two (GIF and JPEG). If you want to use other graphic files, make sure that your audience knows how to handle them in your Web pages. This means that they need to configure their software to recognize the file type and run a software program that can load it automatically when they click the graphic's hyperlink in your Web page. You can specify this on the Web page itself.

The graphics duel of the century: GIF or JPEG?

When you're designing your Web pages, you should usually keep your graphics in a consistent format. This means deciding between GIF and JPEG, the two most popular formats. But is one better than the other for different purposes or reasons? The easy answer is yes. The hard part is choosing the right format for the right use. At times, you might well need both.

Why have more than one "standard" graphic format? Each brings its inherent strengths and weaknesses to the WWW. The following table (8.4) shows how GIF and JPEG compare.

Table 8.4 GIF versus JPEG: The match-up

Format	Image type	Colors	Compression type	Creator
GIF	Bitmap	Up to 256 colors	LZW	CompuServe, Inc.
JPEG	Bitmap	Up to 16.7 million colors	JPEG	Joint Photographic Experts Group

Which to choose: GIF or JPEG? That depends on what the graphic is going to be used for and what it will contain. Each format has its own strengths and weaknesses:

Advantages of GIF files

- Universally accepted graphic file standard on the Web

- Multimedia extensions for multi-image GIF files and sound file (MIDI) extensions

- Fast decompression so it can be displayed quickly when in Web pages

- Better for computer-generated images using fewer than 256 colors

Advantages of JPEG files

- Smaller file size, which makes Web pages faster

- Supports "true color" images (such as photographs)

- Compression level can be controlled to increase or decrease file size and image quality

Disadvantages of GIF files

- Has to use dithering for colors outside the image's 256 colors

- Images can conflict with each other if they do not have the same color palettes

- Compression is not as high, so file sizes tend to be larger

Disadvantages of JPEG files

- Lossy compression scheme affects the quality of images with high compression

- Slower decompression takes more time to display images on-screen

- Not every graphical browser can show JPEG images

Make big graphics into little graphics to keep users happy

Not all graphics are necessary. Some are just nice to have. "Eye candy" (graphics that have no real function) has its very definite place, but don't force it on users who don't want it. If you must include photos of your children, portraits of your dog, and a life-sized image of your five latest traffic tickets, consider using **thumbnail** images instead.

Thumbnails are miniature versions of the real thing, just big enough to see what the picture is about but small enough that browsers can retrieve them in seconds. Use the anchor element to link the thumbnails to the full-sized image; if readers want to see the original picture, one click brings it to their desktop.

Getting by with a little help from your browser's friends

Just because Web browsers are pretty limited in the graphic formats that they can display on-screen doesn't mean you can't use your favorite files in your Web pages. For instance, TIFF is a popular file format for both color and black and white images. Unfortunately, TIFF is also an uncompressed format, so file sizes are enormous compared to GIF and JPEG.

If you want to make use of your TIFF files without converting them to GIFs or JPEGs, put links in your Web pages that lead the reader to the TIFF files, as in figure 8.14. Then, readers can download them one at a time and view them outside the browser (which wouldn't support them).

Fig. 8.14
Anchor links can use either text or graphics as their "clickable" component.

Links to TIFF files ⏤

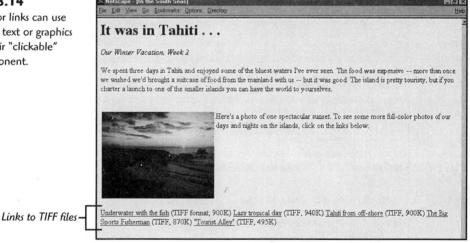

Once your readers have downloaded a TIFF file, they need some way to see it. How? By telling their browsers to use a helper program (explained above). Through a browser's preferences feature, users can configure the browser to *automatically* launch a specific helper application whenever their browser encounters a particular type of file. Windows' Paint, for instance, can be configured to launch whenever a PCX file is encountered, and a favorite Zip program can be chosen to launch when a compressed ZIP file is downloaded.

To view the TIFF graphic, your user will need a program that supports this graphics format. Programs like LView Pro or Paint Shop Pro do the job admirably, and are available as shareware over the Net. By configuring their browsers to launch LView Pro, for example, whenever a TIFF file is downloaded, viewing these files is painless.

Helping your readers with helper applications

If you include file types that browsers don't normally handle by themselves, be sure to offer instructions on your Web page. Or direct them to a site where they can find out all they need to know to view the file. This is the approach taken by CBC Radio in Canada who want people to hear their programs through the RealAudio sound player. Figure 8.15 displays the link as the RealAudio logo near the top of the page.

Fig. 8.15
The CBC Radio page tells you why you'll need the RealAudio sound player and gives you a link to a download site.

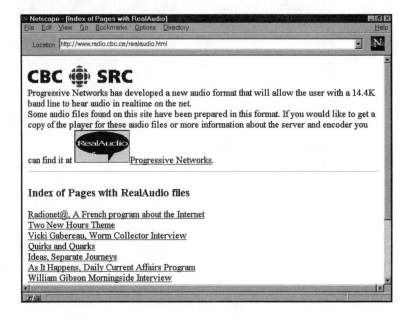

Graphics have become the mainstay of the World Wide Web. They're extremely important for your page design, and mastering the numerous graphic effects is time well spent. By all means, experiment. But be sure to test your graphics-driven pages to make sure they display properly, their links work as designed, and they don't take forever to download.

Linking Web Pages to Other Internet Services

● **In this chapter:**

● **Dissect the URL—the Internet's ZIP code system**

● **Create hypertext links and anchors**

● **Link other Internet services into a page**

The Web is based on the concept of hypertext, and virtually all Web documents contain hyperlinks to other Web documents. It's the hyperlinks that make the Web so easy to use . . . . . ➤

Hyperlinks are the basis of the World Wide Web. They should also be at the core of your Web pages. By clicking on these links, your readers can move within your own web or transport instantly to any other part of the Web. In fact, they can go to just about any part of the Internet itself, even to those resources that aren't part of the Web. Hyperlinks make the "world-wide" part of the Web possible, and they're what every Web user looks for.

Before you learn about hyperlinks, though, you need to learn about URLs.

The Uniform Resource Locator (and what that means)

Every hyperlink contains a Uniform Resource Locator, or **URL**. The URL is the address of the Web page. It's the thing that appears in the Location or URL box near the top of your browser. It's also the thing that shows up (with most browsers) at the bottom of the screen when you move the cursor over a hyperlink. URLs are ugly, and someone should start a civil rights group to make them friendlier, but they're here and you need them.

The URL consists of two major items: the **protocol** and the **destination** (although they have all kinds of other names).

The protocol tells you what kind of Internet resource you're dealing with. The most common protocol on the Web is **http://**, which retrieves HTML documents from the Web. Others include **gopher://**, **ftp://**, and **telnet://**.

The destination can be a file name, a directory name, or a computer name. An URL such as **http://randall.uwaterloo.ca/Using_HTML.htm** tells you exactly where the HTML document is located and what its file name is. If the URL is **ftp://ftp.netscape.com/**, the URL is telling the browser to log into the FTP site on the machine named netscape.com. You get the idea.

TIP   **Happily, you don't have to type many URLs. But sometimes, when** you can't figure out how to click your way to a site, you'll want to anyway. And typing them is a great way of experimenting. If you want to see if your favorite company has a Web site, for instance, try typing **http://www.companyname.com/** in the Location box (but substitute the company's name for *companyname*).

Now you know how URLs are formed; it's time to learn what they are used for.

Putting hyperlinks to use

On the Web, you see some text that's highlighted, underlined, or in a different color—that text is probably a **hyperlink**. You'll know it is for sure if your cursor changes shape when you move it over the text. This means that the text is clickable, and if you click it you'll probably be rewarded with a new page.

How does the computer know what to send next? The answer is in the URL. You may have a link on a page that says, "Click me to get the winning lottery numbers," and as long as the URL associated with the hyperlink is correct, your browser will retrieve the document with those winning numbers. The URL tells the browser what protocol to use and where on the Net to find the file to retrieve.

Most hypertext links by themselves are part of what's known as an **anchor element**. This anchor, <A HREF></A>, surrounds the text that will describe what the link points to. The link itself must be in quotes, and it must immediately follow the definition of the anchor.

A link in HTML takes the following format:

```
<A HREF="URL">put your link text here</A>
```

So, if you want to link the text "Click here for more information" with the HTML document called moreinfo.html that resides in the infodirectory on the www.myserver.com machine, the HTML code would look like this:

```
<A HREF="http://www.myserver.com/infodirectory/
➥moreinfo.html">Click here for more information</A>
```

 CAUTION It's a good idea to make sure that your link or anchor includes a text string explaining where the link will take the reader. Otherwise, you'll have what is known as a **hidden** link. These can be fun, but they are not generally what you want. Try to make your link descriptive, too. Links that say things such as "Click here" or "Follow this link" don't give the user enough information about what he is getting into.

Q&A   ***Do I have to use text within my hyperlink? That's why they call it hypertext, right?***

Well, that is why hypertext is called hypertext. But links don't have to be textual. You can also have hyperimages. The HTML code for that would be:

```
<A HREF="URL"><IMG SRC="picturename.gif"></A>
```

As you can see, this simply replaces the "Click here..." text part with the filename of a graphic. The image appears on the screen, and the reader clicks the image, rather than a line of text.

You may be wondering about linking to Web pages that are on the same machine or about linking to other parts of the present page. These are both common occurrences. In most cases, you'll be building a series of pages that make up a "site" and you'll want to store them all on the same server. But most importantly, you'll want to link the pages to one another. If you are doing this, you don't have to include the machine name in the URL. For instance, if the file moreinfo.html was in the same directory and on the same machine as the page containing the following HTML code, the URL shown will work fine:

```
<A HREF="moreinfo.html">Get More Information</A>
```

If you want to include a link that takes the user to a different part of the page that he is already on, use a # and an anchor name. Your HTML might look like this:

```
<A HREF="#phone">Phone Number Listing</A>
```

Clicking this HTML would cause the page to scroll in the browser until the part of the page that has the target name "phone" is showing on the screen. This means that something has to be targeted, and the following HTML shows how this is done:

```
<A NAME="phone">You can contact any of our staff at the
following numbers:</A>
```

This **target anchoring** or **URL fragment identification** can be used for linking to specific places on other pages as well. If you have a link to a page that is very extensive, but your users will only be interested in a specific part of that page, you can use a target anchor so they will automatically get to that part of the page. However, if the page is someone else's, you'll have to hope that that someone will be willing to embed the target name where you need it.

Now that you've read about how URLs and hyperlinks are formed, you should try building a few yourself. You already did so in Chapter 4, but for now make a page that links to a few of your favorite Web sites. Then, once you've mastered it, keep reading, and you'll learn how to link other Internet resources into your Web page.

Hyperlinking your way to other Internet services

URLs are so flexible that you can use them to create links to practically anything on the Net. You can create links to e-mail, FTP, Gopher, News, Telnet, and the search engine WAIS. This makes it possible for Web pages to put related information together. In other words, your readers no longer have to fire up individual Internet programs to get to the information you want them to see.

Partially for this reason, in fact, the Web browser has become the single most important Internet tool. From your browser, you can do just about everything else you can do on the Net. This allows Internet users the simplicity of accessing information using just one piece of software. Figure 9.1, taken from **http://www.yahoo.com/Business_and_Economy/Companies/Computers/Software/Databases/WAIS__Inc_/**, demonstrates how browsers display URLs of several different types.

Fig. 9.1
The arrow is pointing to a link that, at the bottom of the screen, reads telnet: wais@wais.com. The link below it is to WAIS Inc.'s FTP site. But to Web users, all look identical.

An URL —

WAIS client URL —

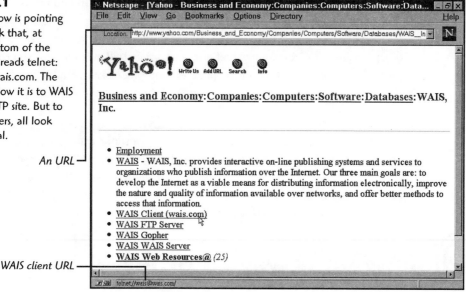

As an example of how this works with other Internet services, here's the HTML code for the bulleted list shown in figure 9.1.

```
</ul><hr>
<ul>
<LI><a href="http://www.wais.com/newhomepages/
➥jobs.html">Employment</a>
<LI><a href="http://www.wais.com/">WAIS</a> - WAIS, Inc.
provides interactive on-line publishing systems and services
to organizations who publish information over the Internet.
Our three main goals are: to develop the Internet as a viable
means for distributing information electronically, improve
the nature and quality of information available over net-
works, and offer better methods to access that information.
<LI><a href="telnet://wais@wais.com/">WAIS Client
➥(wais.com)</a>
<LI><a href="ftp://ftp.wais.com/pub">WAIS FTP Server</a>
<LI><a href="gopher://gopher.wais.com/">WAIS Gopher</a>
<LI><a href="wais://wais.com:210/">WAIS WAIS Server</a>
<LI><a href="/Computers_and_Internet/Internet/World_Wide_Web/
➥Databases_and_Searching/WAIS/"><b>WAIS Web Resources@</b></a>
➥<i>(25)</i>
</ul>
<hr>
```

Each of the items in the bulleted list (the <LI> items) begins with an anchor <A HREF>. The first item is a standard link to a Web document, as signified by the http:// protocol designation. Below that, in order, are links to Telnet, FTP, Gopher, and WAIS resources. In each case, http:// is replaced by the protocol and address for that resource. Writing these things is actually simpler than writing Web URLs; they seem to make more sense.

CAUTION **Links to other Internet tools are great things, but be careful when** using them. Your readers must have their Web browsers configured properly to make use of some of these. Many browsers need a separate Telnet program, for example. Most browsers do FTP and Gopher on their own, but only a few do newsgroups capably. Browsers can be configured to launch external programs, but don't assume your readers have done this. Make it very clear in pages that link to non-Web tools that they're doing so. Figure 9.1 is reasonably successful in this regard, but perhaps could be even clearer.

One click, and you can deluge the linkee with e-mail

E-mail is, without a doubt, the most widely used tool on the Net. E-mail lets two or more people send electronic letters to each other and talk about anything they want. When designing a Web page, many authors like to include a link to their e-mail address. This lets people who are reading your page send comments to you about it. If you have a lot of information on your page that comes from different sources, put links to them, too.

Putting an e-mail link in an HTML document is pretty easy. All you need is a valid e-mail address, which is made up of four parts: the username, the @ symbol, the machine name, and the domain name. The username is the name you typed in when you first logged in to the computer. The machine name is the name of the computer on which your account resides. The domain name indicates the company, school, or organization that gives you access to the Net. (Table 9.1 gives a short list of the most common domains available.)

Table 9.1 Some common domains

Domain	When is it used?	An example
com	Companies that are trying to make money	General Motors (gm.com)
edu	High schools, colleges, and universities	University of Southern California (usc.edu)
gov	Government or government-related entities	The White House (whitehouse.gov)
org	Special (usually non-profit) organizations	X Consortium (x.org)
net	Internet service provider	Inforamp (inforamp.net)
xx	Countries (xx can be any 2 letters)	ca (Canada) au (Australia) fr (France) etc.

Here's an example of a valid e-mail address. It happens to be my own.

```
nrandall@watarts.uwaterloo.ca
```

My username is nrandall, the machine name is watarts, and the domain name is uwaterloo.ca.

Once you have a valid e-mail address, you just put `mailto:` in front of it. An example of an e-mail link is as follows:

```
<A HREF="mailto:nrandall@inforamp.net">Send me mail!</A>.
```

Figure 9.2 shows an example of a `mailto:` link. Many authors like to "sign" their home page by putting an e-mail link at the bottom.

Fig. 9.2
When a user clicks an e-mail link on your home page, he'll be able to write messages with his browser.

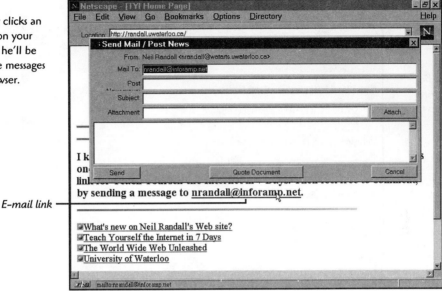

E-mail link

Creating a link to an FTP site

FTP (File Transfer Protocol) is mostly used to copy files between computers. Users of FTP have to log on to remote computers, often as guests, and get whatever files they want. Most guest accounts use the login name of "anonymous," and the password is often the guest's e-mail address.

The only thing you need to put in a link to an FTP site is the name of the site: type `ftp://site/` between the quotes for an anchor (see fig. 9.3). So if a valid FTP site was ftp.borland.com, the link would look like the following:

```
<A HREF="ftp://ftp.borland.com/">Borland's FTP Site</A>.
```

TIP   **If you're building a Web site for a company that has a lot of files** to make available, it's a good idea to put the files on an FTP server, and then just include a link to that server on your Web page. This prevents your Web page from becoming cluttered with download links.

Fig. 9.3
Here Borland has a link to the Borland tech files FTP site from the C++ page, and you can see the URL at the bottom. The mouse pointer points to the FTP link.

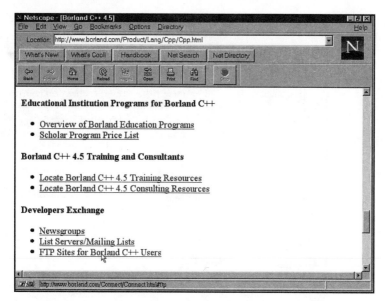

66 *Plain English, please!*

Internet users throw around the word **anonymous**, and it's hard to spend more than an hour surfing the Net without coming across it. When you log in to an anonymous FTP site, type **anonymous** as the **userid** and your e-mail address as the password.

Users can type in any old e-mail address, but many servers will only accept the valid address from which the FTP request is coming. The reason for creating anonymous login capabilities is so that people who want to download public files don't have to wait to be assigned a userid and password. It's basically the same thing as having a guest login. Figure 9.4 shows the FTP directory at Netscape Communications. 99

If you're inviting your readers to download a particular file from your site, you should specify the path for them. That is, put in the exact combination of directories to get to the file directly. This keeps users from trying to go through weird (and sometimes unknown) directories.

For example, let's say you have a program (program.exe) in your home directory (/users/myself/) that you want people to access. A link to it might look something like the following:

```
<A HREF="ftp://ftp.mycom.com/users/myself/program.exe">My
➥program</A>.
```

This will tell the Web browser to connect with FTP to the computer ftp.mycom.com, go into the directory /users/myself/, and get the file program.exe.

Fig. 9.4
FTP links provide easy access to programs and data files, not just information. If you've got a hot new program you want the world to see, use an FTP link.

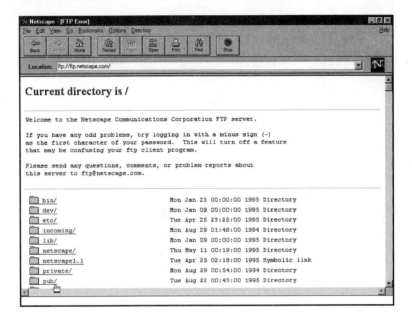

Now try a link to a Gopher server

Before the Web came into existence, one of the most popular ways of storing and accessing information was through **Gopher** sites. Gopher (see fig. 9.5) is basically a collection of text-based menus that store information in a hierarchical format. These same menus can also refer to other Gopher "holes" on other computers throughout the Net.

As you can imagine, Gopher is very similar to the Web except that it doesn't have any built-in multimedia capabilities, such as graphics or sound. You can incorporate a link to a Gopher site on your Web page by simply adding an anchor around the computer's name, and putting gopher:// in front of name. So a Gopher link would look like the following:

```
<A HREF="gopher://gopher.mycomputer.com/">My Gopher Site</A>.
```

Fig. 9.5
Browsers jazz up an
otherwise plain-text
Gopher interface and
clearly distinguish
menus from files for
Internet users.

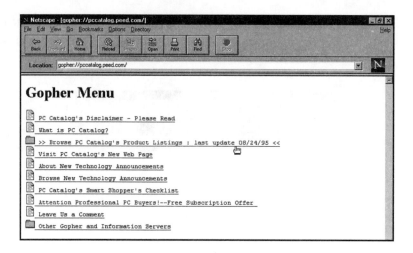

You can even link to newsgroups

A very popular activity for people who access the Net is reading and contributing to UseNet news. UseNet news is just a large collection of groups in which people talk about certain topics. You can think of UseNet as a high school or university and the newsgroups themselves as clubs that you can join.

The topics that are discussed are usually related to the name of the newsgroup, although unrelated flame wars are not uncommon. You may want to point people to a newsgroup because your home page relates specifically to what goes on in that group. Or, if you think that the user might have more questions than you can answer, you can include a link to a related newsgroup in the hope of decreasing the amount of e-mail you receive.

Whatever the case, putting in a link to a UseNet newsgroup (see fig. 9.6) is different from most other hypertext tags. To put in a link to a newsgroup, simply put in news: followed by the newsgroup name in the anchor. A typical newsgroup link would look like the following:

```
<A HREF="news:alt.tv.mad-about-you">Check out the Mad About
You newsgroup!</A>.
```

Fig. 9.6
This Ultimate TV List page shows where to find information about the show *Mad About You,* including the Mad About You newsgroup.

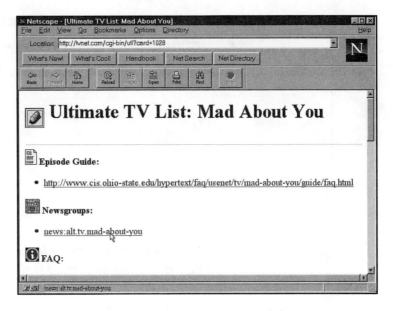

Accessing remote machines with a Telnet link

Sometimes, you'll want the user to be able to directly access other computers, which is what the **Telnet** link is for. The Telnet link actually establishes a connection with another computer and asks the user for a login name and password.

The syntax for a Telnet link is pretty straightforward: you type `telnet://` followed by the remote computer's address. A typical Telnet link would look something like the following:

```
<A HREF="telnet://mycomputer.com/">Log on to my computer!</A>.
```

Figure 9.7 shows a Telnet link.

Fig. 9.7
Telnet links are useful for businesses because they let users access their computers.

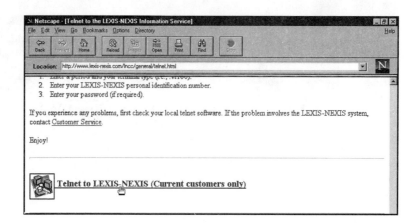

 Q&A **What's the difference between Telnet and Web links? Why don't I just use a regular http link to get the user to the other computer?**

Telnet is quite different from Web links in that it actually demotes the user's computer to a simple terminal and allows the user to make use of the resources available (including software) on the remote machine. The user is no longer really using his own system when he participates in a Telnet session. Telnet sessions are great for connecting your users to remote libraries and allowing them to browse through the libraries' online catalogs.

 TIP **You can tell users what login name to use for guest accounts.**
All you have to do is specify the login name they should use followed by the @ sign before the machine name. So if you wanted a person to access your computer with the login name of "guest," the HTML code would be:

```
<A HREF="telnet://guest@mycomputer.com/">Log on to my
system</A>
```

When the browser sees this, it notifies the user of the correct login name.

Hyperlinks are a Web designer's best friend. You'll use them constantly because they are the basis of the World Wide Web itself. Through hyperlinks, you can use the Web to access virtually the entire Internet.

10

Hands-on Step 3: Now Let's Put Part Three to Work

● **In this chapter:**

- **Mailto links**

- **Left-aligned, right-aligned, and centered graphics**

- **Images with external links**

World Wide Web construction is not all titles and pictures with links as emphasis. The real glitz and glamour come from the extra flair and personal techniques you devise to manipulate what you have learned so far . . . . ▸

Your first "hands on" experience (once you actually had a Web editor to work with, that is), gave you the basics of HTML—the things you wanted and needed to know in order to venture into the World Wide Web arena. If you've made it this far, you've successfully completed two complete World Wide Web pages with lists, links, graphics, titles, headings, and text. What more could you possibly need? Glad you asked.

This tutorial is devoted to the expansion and expert manipulation of the pages you have already created and will develop the HTML skills you have recently become acquainted with.

The programming techniques that you will discover in this tutorial represent the next step up on the HTML ladder of expertise. Your pages will soon become more interesting and will require some executive, artistic decisions. The HTML pages are now becoming your own, so why not let your audience tell you what they think?

Feedback: The straight-up truth

Criticism can be hard to take, but it is one of the only proven successful pedagogical methods around. Feedback means honesty, and it provides a new perspective that can often make or break your World Wide Web success. Although you construct your Web pages electronically, they can be highly personal and revealing representations. Having some unknown surfer thrash out at your carefully tended artwork is unnerving but healthy, so grin and bear it.

Mailto links provide the opportunity for external feedback about the style, content, and design of your World Wide Web pages and usually appear at the bottom of each page. Mailto links are simple textual links that, when clicked, display an e-mail form, usually from within the browser itself, with your address and name already inserted. Users who access this link need only fill in their address, name, and message. The message can then be sent directly from the World Wide Web site that contains it.

So who wants feedback? The band, of course. (Make sure to read chapter 4 before working through this chapter.) Let's put a mailto link in their Web site so that users all over the world can communicate with their new idols.

The easiest way to insert a mailto link in your Web pages is to use a raw text field and revert to good old HTML tags. So, in your Web editor, open the second page you created in Chapter 4 (ba2.htm) and scroll to the last line of text.

With your Web document open (Live Markup users click the Raw Text field option), type the following code:

```
<AHREF="mailto:attic@randall.uwaterloo.ca">attic@randall.
➥uwaterloo.ca</A>
```

Save your file and preview the results. When you click your e-mail address now appearing at the bottom of your Web page, you should receive the screen shown in figure 10.1.

Fig. 10.1
Mailto links keep a permanent record of your e-mail address on your pages and allow your audience to easily send forward their opinions, questions, and commentaries.

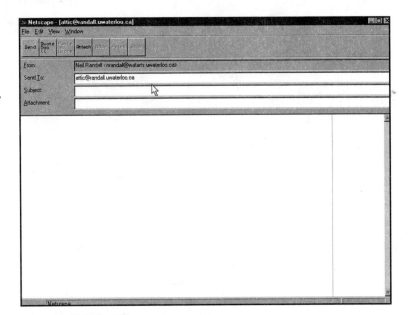

It's time for more graphics!

Because images have such a dramatic, artistic effect on the entire span of the World Wide Web, much attention must be devoted to their development and manipulation. To this point, your images have been fairly static graphical representations that appear in the same spots on all your Web documents and exist for pure visual pleasure.

Aligning graphics allows you to move them around on your screen, with text to the right, left, top, or bottom of the actual figure. As usual, these processes are much simpler using a WYSIWYG interface.

Open the graphics page you created in Chapter 4 (ba2.htm) and right-click one of the images. You should receive the screen shown in figure 10.2.

Fig. 10.2
The Live Markup menu allows you to align your text and graphics in a variety of manners. Experiment with the different styles to create variety among pages.

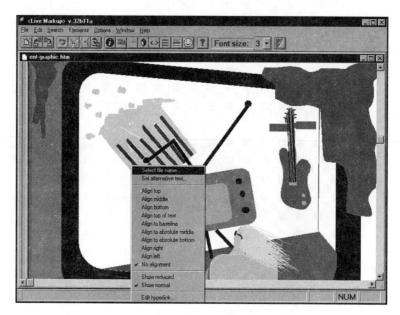

To move your graphic to the right of your screen, click the Align right option from the menu. Save your work and preview to see the results. To move your image to the left, click the Align left option, save, and preview your results. To center your image, select the Align to absolute middle option. Again, save the file and preview the results.

TIP **The fastest and easiest way to become familiar with the different** aligning options is to practice using them in your documents. Try aligning your graphics—with and without textual inserts—to see how your editor reacts. Then decide which format you prefer to use in your final document.

For code-only users

Aligning documents using a tagged Web editor requires the insertion of specific HTML within the graphic code string. The ALIGN element in most tagged Web editors accepts the values TOP, MIDDLE, or BOTTOM. The values specify that the line of text align with the top, middle, or bottom of the graphic you have inserted.

The code that places the text that follows the graphic named images/attic2.gif at the top of the graphic image is:

```
<IMG SRC="images/attic2.gif"ALIGN=top>
```

Figure 10.3 shows the result of this code in Netscape.

Fig. 10.3
The ALIGN top element moves the text that follows a graphic to the image's head—a function that is handy for screen variation.

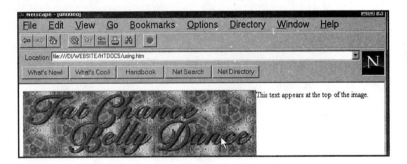

The code that places the text following the images/attic3.gif graphic in the middle of the image block looks like this:

```
<IMG SRC="images/attic3.gif"ALIGN=middle>
<IMG SRC="images/attic3.gif"ALIGN=center>
```

Both lines do exactly the same thing. The presentation of the document remains the same whether you insert either center or middle as the alignment value. Figure 10.4 shows what this document looks like in Netscape.

This line of code places the text line at the bottom of the attic1.gif graphic file:

```
<IMG SRC="images/attic1.gif"ALIGN=bottom>
```

The bottom alignment code sequence produces a document that looks something like the one shown in figure 10.5.

Fig. 10.4
Aligning a text block to the middle of an image presents the first line of characters at center position, but all further sentences appear below the graphic.

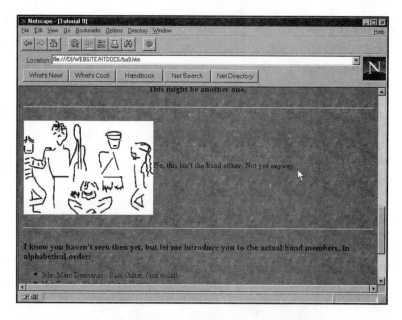

Fig. 10.5
The versatility of the ALIGN function grants users increased control of white space and document layout.

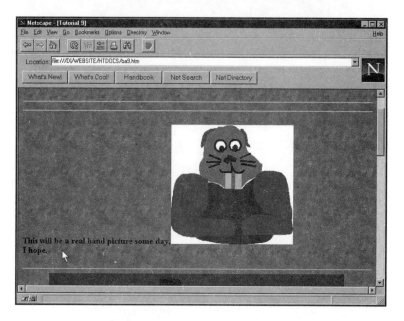

If you use right alignment, the graphic will move to the right side of the browser's on-screen display. Text typed below the image in your Web editor appears on the left side of the browser screen. Why not try it and see what it looks like?

What about a combo package?

As you have probably discovered throughout the first two tutorials and your personal surfing ventures, images and hypertext links are two of the Net's most versatile, popular, and functional elements. Unfortunately, most users class these two mega-powers as separate entities—one that covers the aesthetic side of Web production and one that really *does* something.

Why not put them together? Why not have an image that actually leads somewhere? How about a hyperimage?

Graphics that carry links (usually to a site that relates to the image itself) serve two main functions. Primarily, they color your pages, catching the reader's eye and dressing up your text blocks. But graphical links also reduce the amount of text required on a page and let the reader cut to the chase.

Creating graphic links using Live Markup or a similar WYSIWYG editor is very simple. Start the same way you would to place an image on the page: choose text block, click the image (happy face) icon, and then choose the image path or file name. Once you have your selected image, right-click once to find this menu, and choose Create Hyperlink. You'll see the screen shown in figure 10.6.

Fig. 10.6
If you right-click a graphic in Live Markup, you get a menu that enables you to align, reduce, and create a hyperlink.

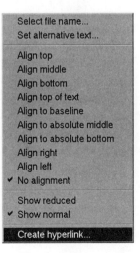

Similar to when you made a text link, you will see a hyperlink information box where you can fill in the target link. Make this link take readers back to the first tutorial page (for no particular reason). Obviously, you could send them anywhere on the Web, if you wanted to upset them.

The HTML code for this image is as follows:

```
<A HREF = "http://randall.uwaterloo.ca/ba1.htm>
➥<IMG SRC = "images/attic2.gif"></A>
```

That's it. The Bertha's Attic site is progressing nicely. In Chapter 16, you'll put in... well, I could tell you, but why spoil it now?

Imagemaps Can Be the Entire Interface

● **In this chapter:**

- **What's an imagemap?**

- **Can you use any old digital picture?**

- **Boring but necessary imagemap syntax**

- **How to write the imagemap's map files**

- **Specify clickable regions on your imagemap**

- **Available tools for creating map files**

Imagemaps are just graphics with more than one link inside, but they've become one of the most popular HTML features of all . . . . **>**

Hyperlinks reflect the way we think and act—they encourage us to be non-linear, spontaneous and intuitive. With hyperlinks, it's possible to spend hours following a diverging path of interests and whims, exploring whatever information you happen to come across. Pictures make great hyperlinks, especially when you can assign separate hyperlinks to different parts of the picture. That's precisely what imagemaps let you do.

Just what is an imagemap?

Imagemaps, in the simplest sense, are icons. When you click one, something happens; in the case of the World Wide Web, you get a new Web page sent to you. Imagemaps, however, are a little different from a simple program icon. They let you create visual navigation guides, giving users the ability to click different parts of a picture to do different things. The end result of clicking an imagemap is dependent upon which part of the map you clicked.

An imagemap is an inline picture that contains clickable regions. When you click one region, you access one Web page. When you click another, you get an entirely different Web page. This is what differentiates imagemaps from simple hyperlinked inline graphics (see Chapter 8). A hyperlinked inline graphic is a picture that has only one associated hyperlink. An imagemap is a picture with two or more associated links. Where you click determines where the hyperlink will take you.

Imagemaps work as a team effort between the user's browser and a program on the page's Web server that processes where the mouse click occurs in the image (its "pixel coordinates" for you techie-types—discussed later in the chapter). Figure 11.1 shows an example of a geographical imagemap. Each of the Canadian provinces on the map is a separate clickable region. Provincial names or abbreviations would have been a helpful addition, though, particularly for users who aren't familiar with Canadian geography.

Fire up your browser and head for **http://www.compaq.com**, **http://www.whitehouse.gov**, or **http://www.microsoft.com**. Watch the status line at the bottom of your browser, and as you move your mouse cursor across the graphic, you'll see a display of coordinates rather than a destination URL. That's how you can tell that the image is an imagemap. The coordinates have been defined by the Web author to link to specific URLs. You'll define these coordinates in this chapter.

Fig. 11.1

Clicking one of the unnamed Canadian provinces on this Web page map will give you a new page with information about business resources in that province.

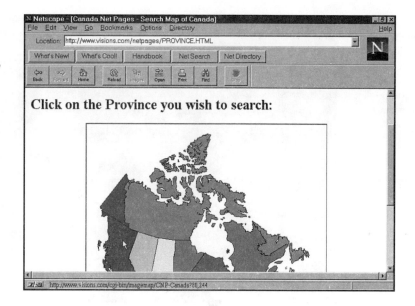

Many Web sites have navigational toolbars—clickable text and function buttons or icons—as integral parts of all the site's Web pages, so that when a user wants to go to the home page, he clicks the part of the picture that has a house on it. This is great because the imagemap is used over and over again, and the user becomes familiar with the navigational imagemap very quickly. Figure 11.2 shows a great example of an imagemap that is unambiguous and easy to use.

Imagemaps are similar to other visual graphics-based interfaces, such as Microsoft Windows. Computer games often have complex graphical interfaces that encourage you to click objects or screen areas to accomplish tasks or receive information. In each instance, the program that processes the mouse click will vary, depending on the software running on the Web server. The most popular is imagemap from NCSA, which is used with the NCSA Web server software. Another is MapServe, a package available for the Macintosh. Many new Web server packages, such as the Windows NT server from EMWAC (the European Microsoft Windows Academic Centre) have imagemap support built right in.

Fig. 11.2
Time Warner's
Pathfinder Home Page
includes a "road map,"
clickable text, and
function buttons—all
in one inline image.

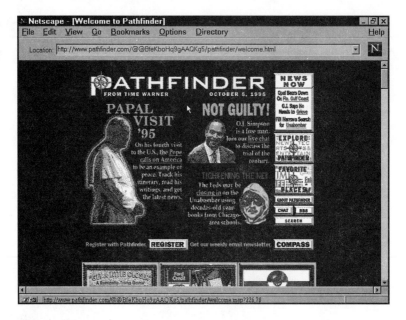

Q&A *Is it necessary to have a graphical Web browser to use imagemaps?*

Sure is. Without a browser with graphic support capabilities, someone who visits your Web page has no way to access or read your imagemaps. Even using ALT text links is tricky and clunky. If you want to cater to these users, your best strategy is to provide a "text only" page that has the same links as the imagemap and to include a text hyperlink on your imagemap page pointing to the text-only page. Your link could look something like this:

```
<A HREF = "http://www.hoodoo.com/whatsit.htm">Click
➥here for a text-only menu</A>
```

This will create the link "Click here for a text-only menu" in your Web page. Once again, however, this is entirely up to you. You don't have to cater to nongraphical browsers, but you'll alienate this particular group of users if you don't.

How do I create an imagemap?

The rest of this chapter outlines in detail how to create imagemaps. To put the process in perspective before we get into the specifics, here are the basic steps:

1 Select a graphics file you'd like to use as the basis for your imagemap.

2 Decide how you want to divide the image into regions, and decide which regions will lead to which Web pages.

3 Create the regions on the image (in effect, you're overlaying shapes on the image).

4 Assign URLs to each region.

5 Store the map file and the image file on a computer that functions as a Web server.

6 Write the HTML code in your Web page that will display the imagemap.

As you can see, imagemapping isn't an easy procedure. But practice, as they say, makes perfect, and nowhere is this more apparent in HTML design than in the creation and storage of imagemaps.

Q&A *Do I really have to put my imagemap on a Web server?*

Unfortunately, yes. You can't create an imagemap on a stand-alone computer (PC, Mac, or UNIX), not even if that computer is connected to the Internet. The machine must be set up as a Web server because imagemaps are *served*, not just viewed (as graphics files are).

Start with an appropriate image

Which graphic file should you use as the picture for an imagemap? This should be content-dependent. If you want to create a navigational toolbar that has links for a home page, e-mail, and an FTP resource, you'll probably want to create a long rectangular graphic and include icons of a house, a mailbox, and a file folder. If you want to use your company's logo, you can do that, too (as long as it can reasonably be divided into different sections), and graphically edit it to contain words that can then be linked to different pages. If your site is divided up by information pertaining to different geographical regions, you may want to use a geographical map, so that people can click the region they are interested in.

Supported graphic file formats

Imagemaps generally use a file format you've already been introduced to—the GIF format. JPEG files may also become commonplace for imagemaps, but in the meantime you should convert your digital pictures to GIFs to be certain they're fully supported.

TIP **There are many commercial, shareware, and freeware graphics** programs available today. Almost all have the ability to convert digital pictures from one file format to another. If, for example, you have a BMP file, you can usually convert it to a GIF file by opening it up in a graphics program such as Paint Shop Pro, choosing the "save as" option, and then changing the file format to GIF before you save it.

Imagemap GIFs can be in either GIF87a or GIF89a formats, and they may be interlaced. (Chapter 8 explains what these formats are and how to use them.) Images can also be transparent or regular. A transparent image has no visible background, and looks as though it is floating on the page. Take care that you do not create imagemaps that are too wide for the typical browser window, or you may find that your readers can't see or use some of the options on your imagemap. Or they may have to horizontally scroll in order to do so, and that can be extremely annoying.

Q&A *How do I know whether my image is too wide?*

There isn't really any way to tell if it might be too wide on different browsers other than by trying all of them out. However, the one thing that makes a big difference for how large an image appears is the video resolution of the machine on which the browser is running. Older machines with slower video cards often run at a lower resolution such as 800×600 or 640×480. These resolutions cause everything on the screen to be larger. If your picture works fine at 1024×768, but is too large when you switch your resolution down to 800×600, you may want to rethink your sizing. Also, you're better off having a picture that is too long vertically than too wide horizontally, because people are used to vertical scrolling on the Web.

The ISMAP attribute starts the imagemap process

Imagemaps are built around two familiar Web page components—anchor links and inline images. As the author, you have to determine which regions on your image users should click on, and then you must create a related MAP file that tells the server what links to follow for each region. The clickable regions can be round, rectangular, or polygonal (any number of sides or shapes).

TIP **Determine the shape of the clickable region by looking at the** shape of the object you want the user to click. If it's just a word within your image, make a rectangular region; if it's a globe, you can make the clickable region round. If your image is a map and you want to define a whole state as a clickable region, you'll probably need to use a polygon.

The ISMAP attribute works with the anchor element to signal to a Web browser that the current inline image is active, and that the browser should send the Web page server the coordinates of any mouse clicks on the inline image. The browser doesn't have to know if the user has clicked a clickable region or not—that's a job for the Web server's imagemap program. The syntax for using an ISMAP is:

```
<A HREF="MAP_file_URL"><IMG SRC=image_URL ISMAP></A>
```

The *MAP_file_URL* is the location of the related database of clickable regions and their actions, and *image_URL* is the inline image being used in the Web page.

For example, if your image is called **picture.gif** and is located in the **/web/ pictures/** directory on your server, and the map file is called **picturemap** and is located in **/map/mapfiles/**, your HTML tags would look like this:

```
<A HREF="http://www.company.com/web/mapfiles/"><IMG
SRC=http://www.company.com/web/pictures/picture.gif ISMAP></A>
```

Figure 11.3 shows how the imagemap is added to a Web page's code, and Figure 11.4 shows how Internet Explorer displays the new imagemap.

CAUTION **If your imagemap does nothing at all, it may be because it's not** actually on the Web. Imagemaps must be mounted on a Web server in order to work. Check with your Internet provider to see how you might develop a Web site on their server, and then add the imagemap to that site.

Fig. 11.3

The type of URL you use for the map file and the inline image—either relative or absolute—should match.

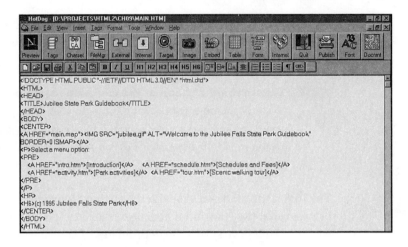

Fig. 11.4

Some browsers don't display imagemaps with colored borders like other images inside anchor links, which have borders to show they are "clickable."

Every imagemap actually consists of two files—the map file and the graphic file. The map file must be located in a directory that is at the same directory level as the graphic file, but the two files must be in separate directories. For instance the following would work: Have everything under a directory or folder called "WEB." Under WEB create two directories or folders—HTML and MAP. In HTML, store all your HTML files and graphic files. Put all your imagemap files in MAP. Then use absolute links for the image: **http://sitename/WEB/HTML/image.gif**, and absolute links for the map file: **http://sitename/WEB/MAP/image.map**. In the case of a Web server such as

O'Reilly's WebSite (see **http://website.ora.com/**), imagemaps are automatically stored in a special directory, so it's just a matter of putting your images in the correct (and supplied) directory.

TIP **A clickable region in an imagemap is a kind of hyperlink, but it** may not be encased in a definite visible border the way inline image hyperlinks are. Unless the imagemap makes it clear without explanation, it's always a good idea to tell users they should click the imagemap.

Here's what happens with the actual map files

Browsers are programmed to wait for mouse clicks. When you click, your browser sends information to the Web server where the HTML page actually resides. In the case of an imagemap, the browser sends the coordinates of the map segment that was clicked on. The imagemap program or server software responds in accordance with the map file that is included in the Anchor tag. The file is primarily a list of links that correspond to each of the clickable regions in the imagemap. If the coordinates sent do not match any in the list, the software returns the default URL value, which is usually a page saying something like, "You haven't clicked anything. Please try again."

TIP **Avoid pages that tell people they've either made a mistake or** have not accomplished anything. You're just wasting their time making their browser download another page that is irrelevant to what they want to do. One thing you can do is make the most "popular" page on the site the default URL; odds are that is where the user wanted to go anyway!

Relative and Absolute URLs

Consider a two page Web site. A relative URL link on Web page 1 is meant to get Web page 2, and doesn't contain the name of the machine or server. Thus, it is assumed that the directory and file specified for Web page 2 is located on the server of Web page 1, and is relative to the directory in which page 1 is located. If the page being linked to is not on the same server, you must use an absolute URL and specify the name of the machine or server where the file is located. You must be consistent in using relative or absolute URL links because the map file is opened and active at the same time that the image file is opened and sent.

How to create the imagemap file

Imagemap files can be created in any word processor or text editor; just be sure to save them as text files. Comments may be incorporated into map files using leading # characters to make obvious what it is you are trying to do. This is a good idea, because somebody else may come along and modify the map file you've created.

However, creating imagemaps in a word processor or text editor is far from easy. In fact, it's one of the hardest things you'll do in this book. So if you experience a little bit of trouble while working through the next few pages, you're in very good company—probably the company of everybody who's ever tried this.

The components of a standard map file entry are:

```
method URL x1,y1 x2,y2 . . . xn,yn . . .
```

Here, *method* is the type or shape of the clickable region (circle, rectangle, polygon or oval); *URL* is the URL to send back to the browser (either another Web page, an FTP connection, Gopher connection, and so on); *x1,y1* is the list of coordinates that describe the exact location of the hot spot in your inline image.

Each clickable region type uses a different number of pixel coordinates to define their shapes (see table 11.1).

Table 11.1   Defining clickable region methods

Method	Type	Required coordinates
circle	circle	2 pairs: center edgepoint
oval	oval	2 pairs: upper_left lower_right
rect	rectangle	2 pairs: upper_left lower_right
poly	polygon	"polygon" means "many-sided"; up to 100 pairs can define the vertices ("points") of the shape
point	a point	1 pair: the_point

The point method is useful as a "closest to" input (it's pretty hard to click a specific pixel in an image). If two points are defined in your map file, the one that is selected is the one that the mouse click is "closest to" (as measured by a straight line).

The map files also include a line that states the default URL for mouse clicks that are outside any of the listed clickable regions. Be careful, though, not to include a default URL in the map file for an imagemap that has a "point" hot spot—any clicks that are not in other clickable regions (like circles or rectangles) will be "closest to" the point, and the default URL will never be used.

Figure 11.5 shows the contents of a typical map file.

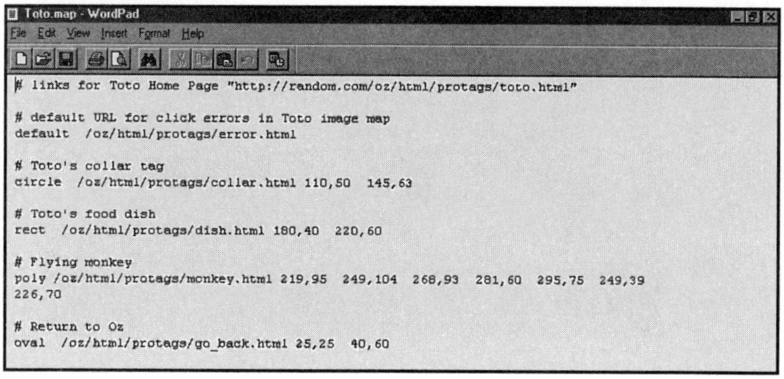

Fig. 11.5

Put one clickable region definition on each line in your map file to make it easier to read and troubleshoot in case of problems.

Fun with pixel coordinates

The most complicated part of creating imagemaps is figuring out the pixel coordinates for each of your clickable regions. It's not as if you can whip out a pixel ruler and measure them by hand. What you need is a software tool to do the job for you.

Each platform has its own tools that will do the job. If you are a professional graphics user and have PhotoShop on your computer, that will do the trick. Most people aren't that serious about creating images, and they should rely on one of the available shareware tools.

UNIX users are crazy not to use xv (available at any good UNIX shareware site), an X Windows viewer and editor that does everything you might want with your graphics—format conversions, interlacing, and transparency—as well as finding your pixel coordinates. You have to track your coordinates by hand (xv doesn't make a list for you) but as an all-purpose tool, it's one of the best.

Macintosh users should look for a tool called WebMap. This program lets you draw the clickable regions right on top of your image and then define the "action" (the URL for the hyperlink) for each region. The program then saves all the information into your map file for you. Figure 11.6 shows a typical WebMap session.

Fig. 11.6
WebMap displays each clickable region on-screen as you enter its shape, making it easy to avoid unintentional graphic overlaps.

Pixel coordinates —

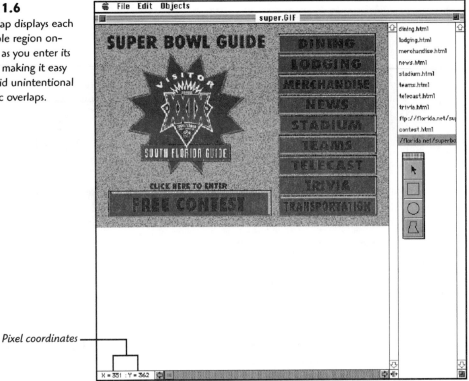

More information about WebMap is available online at the URL **http://www.city.net/cnx/software/webmap.html**.

Microsoft Windows users have two good options: Mapedit, a 16-bit Windows 3.1 utility, and Map This!, a 32-bit tool for Windows 95 users. Like the Mac's WebMap, Mapedit and Map This! let you mark out your clickable regions by drawing directly on your inline image. You can then create your map files—

complete with URLs. Mapedit will even let you change and move the clickable regions you've created. (See Chapter 26 for more information on these tools.)

TIP **On the Web, imagemaps must be created with a lot of care so** readers don't get lost or overlook available hyperlinks because they didn't recognize something as being "clickable." Ask a friend to point out all the different clickable regions on your imagemap to ensure that it's clear.

What if you don't have one of these tools, or what if the package doesn't automatically create the map file for you? In this case, you have to record the pixel coordinates by hand, and then type up your map file and insert it into your map file directory. But how do you determine the coordinates? Most graphics packages have a coordinate listing. For example, in Paint Shop Pro, you simply open up the image and point your cursor at the pixel you want as one of your coordinates; the coordinates can be read off the bottom of the screen. (This is shown in Figure 11.7.) It's kind of a pain compared to the packages that do it for you and write the map file automatically, but at least it works.

Fig. 11.7
To determine the coordinates of the smaller rectangle in this large image, you simply put the cursor over the corner of the rectangle and take note of the coordinates (456, 139) shown at the bottom.

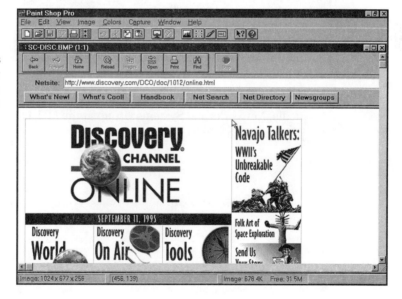

WWW Tools: MapMaker

Available at URL **http://www.tns.lcs.mit.edu/cgi-bin/mapmaker**, this Web service helps you create an imagemap for any existing inline image on a Web page already up on the WWW. It asks for the URL of your page and then maps the clickable regions you fill in (see fig. 11.8).

Fig. 11.8
After you enter your clickable regions and action URLs, click the complete imagemap button to compile the new map file and save it to your hard drive.

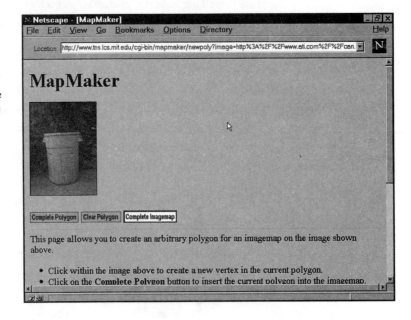

This Web service is provided by Professor David Tennehouse and the Telemedia, Networks and Systems Group at the MIT Laboratory for Computer Science.

12

Setting a Nice Table

● In this chapter:

● **The purpose and use of tables**

● **How to build a table in HTML**

● **Let's see some examples on the Web**

HTML tables are so flexible that they can be used to format your pages to look as if they've been prepared with a desktop publishing program . . . . ➤

I f the word *table* conjures up an image of a boring form of data full of statistical information found in the appendixes of long documents, do I have a surprise for you! On the World Wide Web, tables take on a new and much more interesting persona. That's because HTML allows tables to contain everything from pictures to links and even video and sound files.

Putting a table of information on the Web offers a number of interesting possibilities, but also a number of constraints. The overall effect can be quite impressive and very useful.

So, what are tables good for?

HTML tables are good for nearly anything that tables on paper are good for—sales figures, tables of contents, you name it. Because of the Web's limitations, it's true that some standard table ideas simply don't translate well. But, on the other hand, with the multimedia capabilities of the Web, information that might not be thought of as suitable for tabular format works very well in tables on the Web.

Tables that will not work well on the Web are those that are extremely large or those that contain large portions of text. This is because Internet users are confined to the viewing size of their monitors. Of course, browsers do allow users to scroll both horizontally and vertically.

CAUTION **A table that extends beyond the physical limit of the screen can** be difficult to actually use because the headings will easily fall out of view.

The opportunity provided by HTML is in the numerous types of information that can be presented in a tabular format. Think of a table that contains product and price information. It sounds pretty standard, but when you add to that information a picture that is hyperlinked to an even larger picture (and perhaps a full description of the product), the possibilities begin to become clear. A video of a product demonstration or a sound clip of music can easily become very valuable elements of a table. Figure 12.1 shows an obvious candidate for hyperlinked table elements.

Fig. 12.1
Some tables translate
really well into HTML
and onto the Web.
The Periodic Table is
a natural candidate,
allowing users to link
to information about
the different elements.

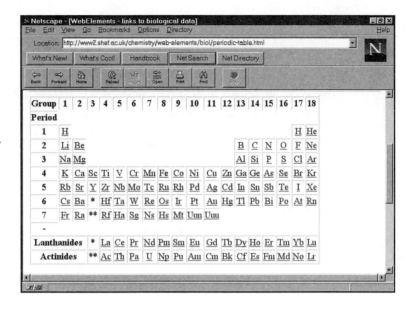

TIP **The HTML code that is used to construct tables is not overly**
complicated, but it is a bit difficult to use. Luckily, many HTML editors
available on the Internet come with built-in table features, and they're
becoming increasingly powerful.

Start small and work your way up

A table in HTML is delineated by the <TABLE> and </TABLE> tags. From
there, it is easiest to think of a table as defined by its individual cells. You
determine the maximum number of rows and columns your table will have.
(Think of the top row of a table that has only one or two headings.) Then
start defining your cells one by one. Cells are defined from left to right in
rows and then from top to bottom.

 Plain English, please!
Rows, **columns**, and **cells** are the standard terms for talking about tables.
If you've worked with spreadsheets, you already know about them. Rows go
across the screen while columns go up and down. Every place where a row
and column intersect is a cell. So a table that has 10 rows and three
columns will have 30 cells. **99**

Before you begin designing your cells, you may want to make some specifications about your whole table. For instance, you can specify whether or not it will have a border and how wide that border will be. This is done by including a `border=#` within the opening <table> tag. If the word border is left out of the tag, no border appears. If the word is in the tag but without a number, you will get a single width border.

Another specification you can make about your whole table is how wide the table is on your screen. Table width is determined by default if you don't specify it using the `width` or `colspec` attributes. The default determination of the width is based on the width of each of the columns in your table. The width of each column (unless otherwise specified) defaults to be just wide enough for your widest data element or picture. This can make your table appear cramped, but by specifying that your table is to take up 90 percent of the space between your margins, you can include a lot of nice white space. This is done by adding the `width` attribute to the opening <table> tag, as follows:

```
<table border width=90%>
```

If you want to have even more control over how your table looks, you can set the `cellspacing` and `cellpadding` attributes within the table tag. The `cellspacing` attribute specifies how much space is between cells; the default is two. The `cellpadding` attribute specifies how much space is between a cell wall and the contents of the cell. The default is one, and you probably won't want to set it to zero or your text will run into the cell and table borders. The following is an example of the usage:

```
<table border width=90% cellspacing=4 cellpadding=5>
```

Okay, now you're ready to move on and define some cells!

The data cell and the heading cell

There are two main table elements: the data cell and the heading cell. The tags that delineate a heading cell are <TH> and </TH>, but it's basically the same thing as a data cell, so we'll look at that. The tag that defines a data cell is <TD>, and it can be matched up with a complementary </TD>, but it doesn't have to be. Both the heading cell tag and the TD tag have a number of attributes: `align`, `valign`, `colspan`, and `rowspan`.

`Align` specifies the alignment of the cells contents, and it can take the value of `center`, `justify`, `decimal`, `right`, or `left`.

- If the `align` attribute is not defined, your contents default to a center alignment.

- The justify value of the `align` attribute will justify the textual contents of your cell, but only if it is practical.

- The decimal value will align everything with whatever character you specify as a decimal point.

You specify a decimal point in your <TD> or <TH> tag by writing dp=`"symbol used for alignment"`. For example, if you want everything to align to a semicolon, use the following:

```
<TD align=decimal dp=";">information to be displayed</TD>
```

This can be really useful for displaying record type information.

The `colspan` attribute determines how many columns wide that cell will be, and the default value is one. The `rowspan` attribute specifies how many rows deep your cell will be.

 Plain English, please!

Default value is the value that comes into play if you don't specify a different value. In this case, you get one column width unless you specifically tell HTML to give you more.

The `valign` attribute can appear inside a TR, TH, or TD cell, and it controls whether text inside the cell is aligned to the top of the cell, the bottom of the cell, or vertically centered within the cell. If used in the TR tag, it specifies that all the cells in the row should be vertically aligned to the same baseline.

This all may seem a bit confusing at first, but a quick example should clear things up (see fig. 12.2).

Fig. 12.2

Some cells span more than one column or row, and data within the cells can be aligned in different ways.

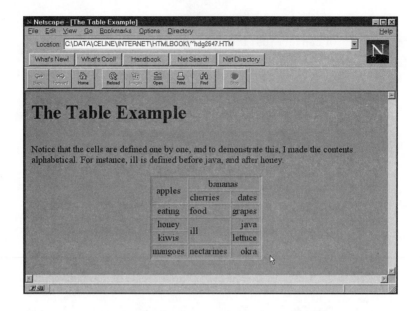

The data in figure 12.2 doesn't really mean anything, but it's a simple example that makes the HTML easy to understand. The code is in listing 12.1.

Listing 12.1— A Sample HTML Table

```
<H1>The Table Example</H1> <BR>
<P>Notice that the cells are defined one by one, and to
demonstrate this, I made the contents alphabetical. For
instance, ill is defined before java, and after honey.
<BR><BR>
<center><table border=2>
<tr><td align=center rowspan=2>apples
<td colspan=2>bananas  </tr>

<tr><td align=left> cherries
<td align=right>dates  </tr>

<tr><td align=center>eating
<td>food
<td align=right>grapes  </tr>

<tr><td align=center>honey
<td rowspan=2>ill
<td align=right>java    </tr>

<tr><td align=center>kiwis
<td align=right> lettuce  </tr>
```

```
<tr><td align=center> mangoes
<td>nectarines
<td align=right>okra </tr>
</table></center>
```

TIP It's a good idea to sketch your table out on paper ahead of time, to make sure that rowspan and colspan specifications make sense. Otherwise, you could end up with something like that shown in figure 12.3.

Fig. 12.3
The HTML for this table specified one too many columns in the colspan attribute of the first cell of the second row.

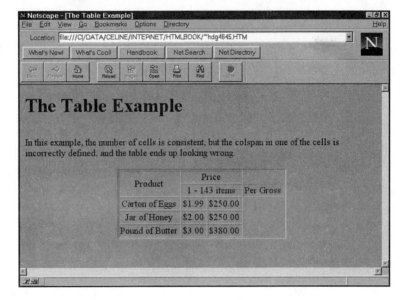

Listing 12.2 shows the first few lines of the HTML for the table in figure 12.3. You can see for yourself where the column addition went wrong.

Listing 12.2—First Lines for Figure 12.3

```
<tr><td align=center rowspan=2>Product
<td align=center colspan=2>Price </tr>

<tr><td align=center colspan=2> 1 - 143 items
<td align=right>Per Gross  </tr>

<tr><td align=center>Carton of Eggs
<td align=right>$1.99
<td align=right>$250.00  </tr>
```

Q&A *Why isn't my table appearing properly in my browser? Part of one of my cells isn't showing up.*

You probably have defined your table in a way that causes two cells to overlap. You may have a cell that is three rows deep, and in that third row, you've got a cell that is two rows wide and overlapping your deep cell. The only way to avoid errors like this is by planning ahead and double-checking. Overlapping errors are rendered differently by different browsers, so it isn't always obvious that this is a problem.

Remember to use the `width` attribute in your table tag to give your table lots of white space and to make it easy to read. Figure 12.4 shows the same table you have been working with, but made a little bit more appealing with the addition of the `width` attribute.

Fig. 12.4
The width attribute of the table tag allows you to make a table wider than its default. The default, otherwise, would make each column only as wide as its widest cell.

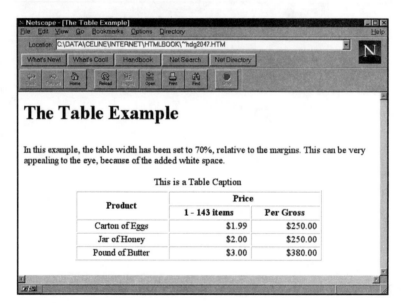

Table headings, row endings, and captions

You may be wondering about heading cells and what those <TR> tags are for. First, as mentioned previously, a table heading cell is delineated by the <TH> and </TH> tags and works exactly the same way that the table data cells work. The only difference is that the tags tell your browser that the data in the heading cells should be differentiated somehow from the information in the data cells. Most browsers will simply bold and center the information in a heading cell if it is text. For other types of content, you'll have to experiment and find out.

The <TR> and </TR> tags are the table row tags, and they tell the browser that the cells defined after the <TR> and up to the next </TR> tag are all the cells in a single row. It is the existence of this tag that makes the </TD> and </TH> tags rather useless. Table data and table heading cells are considered closed when the browser reaches the next <TD>, <TH>, or </TR> tag. Therefore, the contents of every cell will be followed by the introduction of the next data or heading cell or by the end of row tag. So you really never need to include the complementary tags </TD> and </TH>.

A table can also have a caption. This is always a good idea and can be especially useful if put at the bottom of a table. This is because a table will most often be introduced by the text preceding it. So a user scrolling down-wards will catch a glimpse of the introductory text and then see the table. Conversely, a user scrolling upwards will catch the table caption and then the table. Either way, the user gets a good idea of what the table contents are about. However, the caption will default to sit above the table unless you specify otherwise in the caption tag as follows:

```
<CAPTION ALIGN=BOTTOM>This is the caption</CAPTION>
```

Okay, so let's have a look at a table that has a number of cells specified as a heading and a caption as well. Figure 12.5 is a good example of how to use headings and captions. In this case, because the whole page is only one screen long, the caption is left at its default alignment above the table.

Fig. 12.5
The <TH> tag tells a browser that the specified cell is a heading cell and should therefore have special formatting.

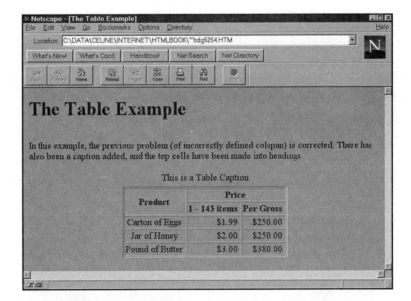

Listing 12.3 shows the HTML for the table in figure 12.5.

Listing 12.3—Code for Figure 12.5

```
<center><table border=2>
<CAPTION>This is a Table Caption</CAPTION>
<tr><th align=center rowspan=2>Product
<th colspan=2>Price </tr>

<tr><th align=left> 1 - 143 items
<th align=right>Per Gross   </tr>

<tr><td align=center>Carton of Eggs
<td align=right>$1.99
<td align=right>$250.00   </tr>
```

What can I put in a table cell?

Finally, what about including graphics in a table cell? Multimedia elements can easily be contained within a table. A cell can contain a picture, a link for a movie clip, or a link for a sound clip. Of course, if a cell can contain multimedia links, it can also contain hypertext links, which are very useful.

For tables that contain a number of brief elements and then a row or column of lengthy textual information, it is often much more appropriate to embed links to that textual information. This saves a lot of space and allows you to include as much text as you need, simply because the table size is no longer a constraint.

What about other HTML elements? Almost anything that you can put on a page can also be put into a table cell. That includes lists, forms, image maps, and even another table. You can use tables for designing impressive page layouts.

In fact, embedding a table within a table is a good example of creative page layout. This works when you have a number of different pictures, text, lists, and tables that you want to show on different areas of the screen. In this case, you define a table with all of your contents, but without a border. Make your width 100 percent. Then when you embed a table, define the nested table with borders. You'll have a great screen layout. Image maps are also really good elements for a page that has a table layout. ESPN's SportsZone (**http://espnet.sportszone.com/**) is a great example of this, as you can see in figure 12.6.

Fig. 12.6
Using an imagemap within a table can make your home page resemble the layout of a newsletter or even a magazine.

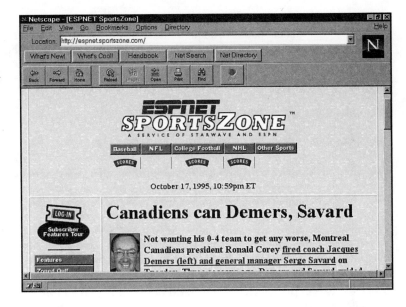

The HTML from figure 12.6 is quite extensive. Listing 12.4 shows the first bit of it to give you an idea of what's involved.

Listing 12.4—HTML Code for Figure 12.6

```
<TABLE border=1 cellpadding=8>
<tr>
<td colspan=3 align=center>
<br>
<a href="/cgi/imagemap/img/logos/front.map">
<img src="/img/logos/front.gif" border=0 alt="ESPNET
SportsZone" width="432" height="150" ISMAP></a><p>
<b><font size="-1">October 17, 1995, 10:59pm ET</font></b>
</td>
</tr>
<tr>
<td valign=top align=center width=125 rowspan=2>
<a href="/cgi/imagemap/img/login/day1.map">
<img src="/img/login/day1.gif" width="128" height="423"
 border="0" alt="Log-in"  ISMAP></a>
</td>
<td colspan=2>
<h1>Canadiens can Demers, Savard</h1><img
➥src="/editors/media/photo/1017JD.JPG"
 align=left width=65 height=90 hspace=8>
<b>Not wanting his 0-4 team to get any worse, Montreal
Canadiens president Ronald Corey <a href="/editors/nhl/
```

```
➥features/1017mtl.html">
fired coach Jacques Demers (left) and general manager
Serge Savard</a> on Tuesday. Three seasons ago, Demers and
Savard guided Montreal to the Stanley Cup;last year, the team
missed the playoffs for the first time since 1970.</b><p>
</td>
</tr>
<tr>
<td valign=top width=90%>
<img src="/img/news.gif">
<p>
<h3><a href="/gen/top/0100715001.html">Chavez testifies
 King did not pay him $350,000 fee</a></h3>
<h3><a href="/gen/top/0208812001.html">NHL's counter punch:
 Domi suspended for eight games</a></h3>
<h3><a href="/gen/top/0300777001.html">Skipper Leyland to
guide Pirates into next millennium</a></h3>
<ul><li><a href= "/gen/hln/entry.html">The Wire</a></ul></td>
```

It is important to remember that not only can a table contain many different HTML elements, but it can also be part of many HTML elements. For example, a table can be part of a list or a form or even part of a block quote. Of course, tables can't be incorporated into an image map or a graphic.

 Q&A *I have a table that has a paragraph in one of the cells, but it's not wrapping the way I want it to. Can I do anything about this?*

Yes. You can set your table data tag to contain the nowrap attribute. This means that you have to manually insert line break tags (<BR>) at the points where you want the text to wrap. This isn't usually recommended, but if you need to use it you can. The tag looks like the following:

```
<TD nowrap>text</TD>
```

Some great tables the Web has known

Although tables are somewhat new to the World Wide Web and still not all browsers can view them, there are already a number of excellent examples of table usage.

One of the most well-known pages that has a table as its whole home page and table of contents is the Zippo News Service page (**http://www.zippo.com/**). In this case, the home page is a table made to look like the front page of a newspaper with part of each column containing a story headline and maybe a few brief sentences. But of course, instead of turning to the page that contains the full article, you simply click the link. The nice part about the Zippo table is the incorporation of pictures and inline hyperlinked images. Figure 12.7 shows the Zippo page.

Fig. 12.7
The Zippo News Service page uses a table as its home page and incorporates hyperlinks and pictures into the scheme. This works great for advertising.

The HTML source for this page is pretty intense. Here's a scrap of it just to give you an idea of what can be done (see Listing 12.5).

Listing 12.5—HTML Code for Figure 12.7

```
<TR><TD  align=left Valign=top><A HREF="ftp.htm"><center><h4>
FTP Download X-Press</h4></center></a><IMG SRC="disks.gif"
ALIGN="BOTTOM"><strong>Free Web Client / Server software.
</strong> Mail, News servers and over 20,000 UNIX, NT, DOS and
Windows applications.</strong><p><hr><center><IMG
➥SRC="sz.gif">
```

```
</center><p><h5>Super Zippo / Super News. Plus Giant Ftp
➥Software Site.
 Interested in participating in Beta, contact
➥joe@zippo.com</h5></TD>
<TD align=left Valign=top><center><IMG SRC="plogo.gif"
➥ALIGN="BOTTOM"></center>
<strong>Need a great Telnet or communications
software package ?</strong> Download a full featured Trial Pak of
<a href="ftp://www.zippo.com/pub/
ftools/pipel2.exe"> Pipeline (approx. 2.6 MB) </a>
from PathLink Technology, Inc. The finest in PC to Host
 Communication Software.<hr><a HREF="comp.htm"><center>
<h4>Computer News</h4></center></a> <p><strong>Tangled in the Web?
 Got your FTP lost in your TCP ? </strong>Newsgroups covering
 virtually every computer topic and every type of computer
 system.</TD>
<TD align=Left Valign=top><center><img src="pl2.gif"></center>
<p><strong><a href="http://www.pathlink.com">Pathlink
➥Technologies, Inc.
</a></strong> Publishers of
communication software for PC based workstations. Call today at
Phone 408-720-7620 FAX 408-720-7630.<hr><a HREF="http://uttm.com">
➥<center>
<h4>CBS Up to The Minute News</h4></center><p></A> A link to the
Internet version of the CBS news show, with continual news updates
and special interest stories. Weekday updates.</TD></TR>
```

Another well-known example of table usage on the Web is found on the TV1 site (**http://tv1.com**). TV1 is a site dedicated to providing television information over the Internet. One of the most-often accessed pages on the site is "What's On Tonite!" From here, you can get a listing of what all of the major broadcast and cable stations are showing for any day. TV1 shows this information in your choice of formats, and one of the best ways to examine the information is by reading the time-station grid shown in figure 12.8.

Fig. 12.8
TV1 uses a table to let users find out what's playing on all the major television channels at any time. Notice the hyperlinks that will take a user to episode descriptions or movie details.

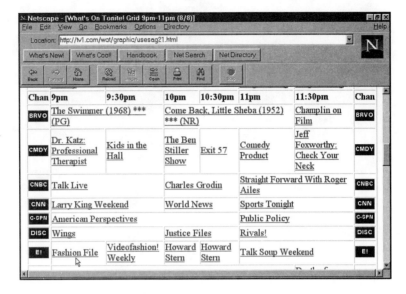

Of course, tables aren't only useful for providing information, they can also be used to get information and to place orders for products and services. This is done by incorporating a table into a form. One example of this can be seen by visiting the Ozark Ticket & Travel: Branson's 1995 Season Show Guide. This Web page contains links to information about the shows that are being advertised and, as part of the table, includes a button that users can press to order tickets. Figure 12.9 shows this page with some shows selected.

Fig. 12.9
Incorporating tables into forms is a great way to present prospective customers with a myriad of information and choices.

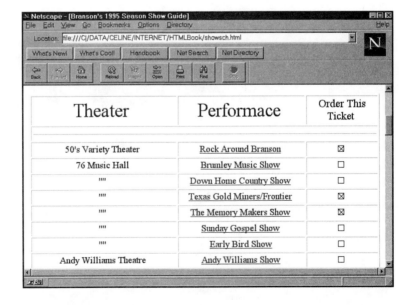

13

The World Is Run on Fill-in Forms

● **In this chapter:**

● The purpose and use of forms

● A form's relationship to a CGI script

● The form tags and what each does

While links and imagemaps allow users to move between and through Web sites, forms allow users to truly participate in your Web site. They are a great way of gathering instant feedback . . . . ❯

A form on the Web is almost exactly like a form in real life: it's made of up spaces to enter text information, lists of choices to check off, and options to select from. But while a paper form must then be turned in or mailed, a Web form is instantly submitted—and often instantly responded to. In more technical terms, forms are the **front end** to CGI scripts, and together they expand the power of the Web tremendously, making it truly interactive.

First, there's something called CGI

Before you get started on forms, there's something important to keep in mind. Forms are fun to design, and they look great. But by themselves they don't do anything. You can put a form on your Web site, and your reader can have a wonderful time filling in the blanks and clicking all the nice buttons. But when they hit the "Submit" button (or whatever you call it), something has to happen to the data they've supplied. The only way to make something happen—to direct the data to you—is to design a CGI script.

A form in HTML is the front end to Web interactivity. It's where the user enters text and makes selections, while the **back end**, the actual processing of data, is done on the Web server by CGI scripts. For more information about CGI scripting and how it relates to forms, see Chapter 15.

Okay, back to forms themselves

Forms help your site look both professional and interactive. Their power lies in the different ways they can accept and organize the user's input. Including forms in your Web site makes it something other than a simple one-way presentation. Forms are a major step toward the kind of interactivity your Web site is capable of having.

You can get a good idea of the vast number of uses for forms just by browsing around on the Web for awhile. Businesses and organizations use forms for conducting surveys, allowing online shopping and product orders, as well as for service registration. Many personal home pages have guest books that users can "sign" by simply filling in a form. To see how widespread they've become, check out the large forms on the White House site (**http://www.whitehouse.gov/**).

Here are the basic elements of a form

There are four form tags, and they're used just like any others. The first, FORM, simply defines the beginning and end of a form and how and where the information collected in it will be sent. The other three—TEXTAREA, SELECT, and INPUT—make up the part of the form the user sees and interacts with: the actual text entry areas, menu selections, and pushbuttons.

 TIP **Most of the HTML editors available on the Net support forms** creation. By all means, use them. What you're about to learn in the next few sections can almost all be at least partially automated with one of these editors.

The very first thing—the FORM tag

The <FORM> tag is used to mark the beginning of a form, while its comple-ment, </FORM>, is used to mark the end. All the other form tags are ignored outside of a <FORM>/</FORM> pairing, so you must be very clear about where your form begins and where it ends.

 TIP **Add a </FORM> immediately after you create a <FORM>, then go** back and fill in the contents. This helps eliminate accidentally leaving the end-form tag off after you've finished. Of course, HTML editors with forms creation features add the tags for you.

The <FORM> tag has two options, and they define how a particular form will behave. While the contents of the form are set by the remaining tags, these two options determine where the information entered by the user will go and how it will be sent there.

The first option is ACTION. A form's ACTION defines what URL the information entered into a form will be sent to. It appears inside the FORM tag in the format, as follows:

```
<FORM ACTION="URL">
...
</FORM>
```

URL may be any URL, though for the data entered into the form to be pro-cessed correctly, URL should point to a CGI script that was designed to handle that particular form. If an ACTION is omitted, the URL of the page containing the form is used by default.

The FORM tag's second option is its METHOD. A form's METHOD defines how the information collected by that form will be sent to the ACTION URL, and may be one of two choices: "GET" or "POST". The "GET" method is the simpler of the two, while "POST" allows far more data to be transmitted. Which METHOD you choose depends entirely on how the CGI program that will process the form data is written, but a well-written CGI program will handle both. METHOD has no effect on the form itself, only how the gathered information is sent.

 TIP **It's pretty well always a good idea, when writing CGI scripts, to** use a library that parses form data automatically no matter which METHOD you use. These libraries are covered in Chapter 15.

The METHOD option is used inside the FORM tag like this:

```
<FORM METHOD="POST">
...
</FORM>
```

 CAUTION **Though it's possible to leave off a form's METHOD and have it work** perfectly well, it's not generally a good idea. You should be as explicit as you can with your HTML, both to remind you what you intended to do in a specific case and to avoid relying on defaults that may change in the future or be different for different browsers.

So, which of the two methods should you use for your form? While the "GET" METHOD is simpler for CGI scripts to handle, it limits the amount of data that can be sent, usually to slightly less than one kilobyte. If there is any chance that your form will generate more data than that, you should use the "POST" METHOD.

Of course, ACTION and METHOD may both be set for a form. This is, in fact, the most common usage, as seen in the following example:

```
<FORM ACTION="http://my.server.com/cgi-bin/form.sh" METHOD="GET">
...
</FORM>
```

Once your form has defined how it will be used with the FORM tag, you must fill it with controls that the user can see and interact with.

Let 'em write: Allowing users to input free-flow text

The TEXTAREA tag allows users to enter free-form text information in an open-ended edit field. TEXTAREAs are defined with a beginning <TEXTAREA> and a closing </TEXTAREA> with the default contents held between them, as follows:

```
<FORM ACTION="/cgi-bin/form.sh" METHOD="POST">
    Type your comment here:<BR>
    <TEXTAREA>
Everything was wonderful!
    </TEXTAREA>
</FORM>
```

This code sample produces figure 13.1.

Fig. 13.1
A TEXTAREA can be created with hopeful defaults: "Everything was wonderful!" However, users can very easily type over this text with less enthusiastic comments.

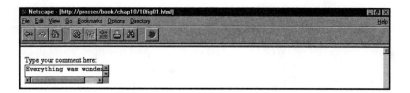

CAUTION No HTML tags used inside a **TEXTAREA** pair will be interpreted. In many ways, TEXTAREA acts like an editable PRE section with a fixed-width font being used and all line breaks being preserved.

Like FORM, TEXTAREA also has options that may be set inside the initial tag.

The first tag is NAME, and it is not actually optional. The name of the TEXTAREA is what will be paired with the contents of the area when the user submits the form. You must always give a NAME, as this is how the control is identified and its value retrieved.

The other two options are ROWS and COLS, each defining how big the TEXTAREA is to be in character heights and widths. If left off, ROWS is set to one and COLS is set to 20, allowing for only a very small typing area, as in the following example.

```
<TEXTAREA NAME="comment" ROWS=4 COLS=60>
I love your product!
I wish I had found it sooner.
</TEXTAREA>
```

This snippet of HTML will result in figure 13.2.

Fig. 13.2
This TEXTAREA is named "comment," and is 60 columns wide and four rows tall.

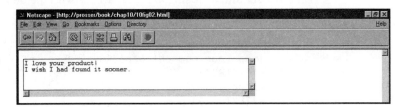

Q&A

What if I have no idea how much text the user will want to type?

A TEXTAREA allows users to type in as much as they like. The specifications for row and column only determine how big the TEXTAREA appears in the Web browser. If users type past the right "margin," a horizontal scroll bar will appear, and if users type in more lines than there are rows, a vertical scroll bar will appear. Note that TEXTAREA does not include a word-wrap feature, and so users must hit the return key if they want to wrap their sentences to the next line.

Giving users choices

While TEXTAREAs allow users to enter free-form text information, it is often a better idea to allow them to make limited choices from a predefined list—just what the SELECT tag was designed to do.

The SELECT tag itself is simple, just a <SELECT>/</SELECT> pair with three options:

- NAME, like TEXTAREA, defines a name that will be paired with whatever value the user selects.

- SIZE defines the height of the list of selections to show the user. If it's left off or if it's set to one, the user is shown his choices as a pop-up menu, as shown in figure 13.3.

- MULTIPLE takes no value and simply defines if this SELECT group allows multiple selections at one time. If omitted, the user will only be able to make one choice from the list; if included, the user will be able to make any number of choices, including zero. Also, as a side effect of specifying MULTIPLE, the list will be shown as a scrollable list even if SIZE is set to one.

Fig. 13.3
Only the current selection is shown if SIZE is set to 1.

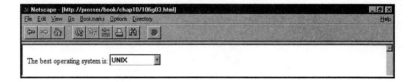

Once the SELECT tag is defined, OPTION must be defined within it. The OPTION tag defines each individual choice that the user will see and is only recognized inside a <SELECT>/</SELECT> pair. Like the LI tag, an OPTION's text does not need to be closed with </OPTION>, though it doesn't hurt, as seen in the following example:

```
<FORM METHOD="GET">
    Select your favorite food:
    <SELECT NAME="food">
        <OPTION>Cold pizza
        <OPTION>Cold Chinese
        <OPTION>Cold fried chicken
    </SELECT>
</FORM>
```

The OPTION tag itself has two variants:

- VALUE is what will be associated with the NAME if that option is chosen by the user. This is used by the CGI script to identify the option, but does not need to correspond to the text the user sees. Creative use of this can make selections easier to deal with from the CGI side of a form. If VALUE is omitted, it is defaulted to the text that follows the OPTION.

- SELECTED defines which OPTIONs are selected by default when the choices are first displayed. If SELECTED is not set on any options, none of them will be chosen; if more than one is marked as SELECTED, those will all be marked. Usually, the single most common selection should be set as the default.

For instance, if you wanted to allow customers to rate your service people, you might use something like the following:

```
<FORM ACTION="/cgi-bin/service_logger.sh" METHOD="GET">
    Please rate the service you received:
    <SELECT NAME="service">
        <OPTION VALUE="100">Excellent
        <OPTION VALUE="75" SELECTED>Good
        <OPTION VALUE="60">Fair
        <OPTION VALUE="50">Poor
    </SELECT>
</FORM>
```

Note that the VALUEs of the OPTIONs relate to your scoring system rather than the actual text of the OPTION. This example results in figure 13.4.

Fig. 13.4
Web sites can generate information for you as well as provide information to the people who visit the site.

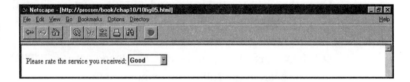

The multi-talented INPUT tag

The final tag, INPUT, is far and away the most flexible and the most complex. While TEXTAREA produces editable fields and SELECT produces lists of choices, INPUT can be used to create six different input methods: TEXT, PASSWORD, CHECKBOX, RADIO, RESET, and SUBMIT.

Each kind of input is specified by an option to INPUT called TYPE. All the other options to INPUT are based on what TYPE is set to.

One-line TEXT input fields

The TEXT option produces a single line text entry field, like a single row TEXTAREA.

If the TYPE of an INPUT is TEXT, a NAME must be specified along with three other variants: SIZE, MAXLENGTH, and VALUE.

The SIZE of a TEXT INPUT is how many characters wide the text entry field will be; MAXLENGTH specifies the maximum number of characters a user may enter into the field. If MAXLENGTH is bigger than SIZE, the text field will scroll to allow the user to enter more data. If SIZE is excluded, the default is 20 characters; if MAXLENGTH is excluded, there is no limit on the amount of text that may be entered.

The VALUE option may be set to the default contents of the field or left off entirely if there are none, as shown in the following example:

```
Please enter your name, first then last:
<INPUT TYPE="TEXT" NAME="first" SIZE="15" MAXLENGTH="13" VALUE="John">
<INPUT TYPE="TEXT" NAME="last" SIZE="30" MAXLENGTH="28" VALUE="Smith">
```

This results in figure 13.5.

Fig. 13.5
Default values can be used to show the format of the re-quested data even when no realistic defaults are possible.

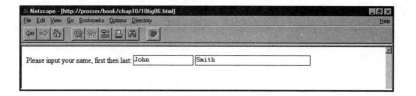

Hidden inputs for PASSWORD-type content

The PASSWORD tag is a lot like TEXT—they share all the same options—except that any characters typed into a PASSWORD TYPE are hidden. This, of course, allows passwords and other secret data to be entered:

```
Password: <INPUT TYPE="PASSWORD" NAME="pass" SIZE="8" MAXLENGTH="8">
```

If the user types into this code snippet, it will appear like figure 13.6.

Fig. 13.6
No matter what characters are typed in, a PASSWORD field will hide them from prying eyes.

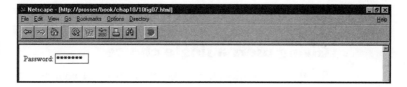

Q&A ***Does using a password field ensure that the information entered is secure?***

Even though a PASSWORD field prevents your secret data from being read on the screen, it is still passed over the network as plain, unencrypted text. It can even appear in the URL that way. So the answer is no—don't let PASSWORD lull you into a false sense of security.

Why not give your readers a checklist?

The CHECKBOX tag is simply a toggle; it can be either on or off. CHECKBOX is great for the simple, yes or no choices on your form. CHECKBOX has three options: NAME, VALUE, and CHECKED.

NAME is the name that will be delivered to the Web server, paired with the VALUE, if the checkbox is selected when the form is submitted. If VALUE is left off, it is automatically set to on. If the final option, CHECKED, is included, the default state of the box is on instead of off.

```
Select the condiments you would like:
<INPUT TYPE="CHECKBOX" NAME="mayo" CHECKED> Mayonaise
<INPUT TYPE="CHECKBOX" NAME="mustard" CHECKED> Mustard
<INPUT TYPE="CHECKBOX" NAME="relish"> Sweet Relish
```

This HTML code produces figure 13.7.

Fig. 13.7
The CHECKBOX tag allows for yes or no choices that are independent of one another.

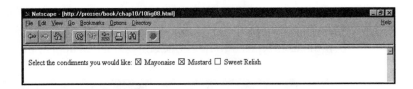

Giving users a single choice

RADIO is a lot like checkbox, but only one toggle in a group may be selected at a time. All RADIOs in a single form that share a NAME are considered members of a single group, and if one is chosen by the user, any already selected button is cleared. Otherwise, RADIO functions exactly like CHECKBOX even down to the options it uses.

You may notice that this functionality sounds a lot like a non-MULTIPLE SELECT, and they end up accomplishing almost exactly the same thing. Which you choose depends largely on the look and feel you want your page to have.

This code demonstrates the RADIO TYPE:

```
Select the type of bread:
<INPUT TYPE="RADIO" NAME="bread" VALUE="white" CHECKED> White
<INPUT TYPE="RADIO" NAME="bread" VLAUE="wheat"> Wheat
<INPUT TYPE="RADIO" NAME="bread" VALUE="roll"> French Roll
<INPUT TYPE="RADIO" NAME="bread" VALUE="rye"> Rye
```

The result is figure 13.8.

Fig. 13.8
RADIOs are designed for allowing the user a single choice among many.

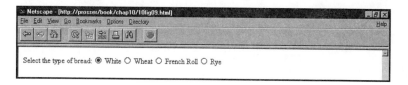

CAUTION

As with SELECTs that are missing a SELECTED entry, it is possible for no member of a RADIO group to end up CHECKED if you don't specify a default value. Always be sure to mark the most common choice as the default with CHECKED.

Letting users start over—the RESET button

RESET TYPE creates a button on the screen that clears the form and returns all the settings to their original default values. Its only option, VALUE, may be set to the text that you want the button to have. VALUE may also be left off, resulting in the text "Reset." See the following example:

```
<INPUT TYPE="RESET" VALUE="Press here to reset form to defaults">
```

You should always include a RESET button because it's very easy to input incorrect information, especially if your form is several screens long.

When they're finished—the SUBMIT button

The final TYPE, SUBMIT, works a lot like RESET but achieves an entirely different result—exactly the opposite. While RESET will clear a form of user-entered values, SUBMIT will gather them up and send them to the URL specified way back in the ACTION tag. A SUBMIT button is the "Go" switch that every form must have to let the user click when he or she is done entering information.

The only option to SUBMIT is VALUE, which sets the text of the pushbutton. If excluded, the default is "Submit Query," as in the following example:

```
<INPUT TYPE="SUBMIT" VALUE="Press here to submit your input">
```

 CAUTION **If the text of a button is very short, "OK" for example, the button** will usually end up looking ugly. You can avoid this by padding the VALUE of the button with an equal number of spaces on both sides to widen it.

Cheating 101: Looking at other people's HTML

One great way to figure out how to build forms is to look at how other people build forms. You can often even scam their code, although you'll usually have to do some customizing to suit your particular needs.

If you spend a fair amount of time surfing the Web, you're likely to come across some very well-designed forms or some forms that are different than the usual. You can easily find out how the Web authors created their forms by looking at the HTML source. Most browsers have a "view source" button, which you can use to get the HTML coded version of the page.

Even if your browser doesn't have that option, you can save the page to your hard disk, and then open it up in a text editor or an HTML editor. This is a great shortcut for run-of-the-mill forms as well, especially if you need to get the form up and running in a hurry. You'll still have to write your own CGI script to accept the data, but that's inevitable. You just have to make sure that you change the ACTION URL so that the form gets sent to the right place when the SUBMIT button is clicked.

Note that this method of cheating can be used for other HTML coding aspects as well, but it works especially well with forms because you don't have any special graphics or media files to contend with.

Design Your Forms for Maximum Usability

● In this chapter:

- **General guidelines for effective forms design**

- **How to control the horizontal layout of forms**

- **Controlling the vertical layout of forms**

- **Outlines and organized lists**

Forms can range from single, one-item toggles to complex, multi-screen pages, but the truly important thing is to come up with a solid design . . . . ●>

The design of a form affects not only how it looks, but how well it works. An attractive layout encourages people to peruse your forms and to fill them in with the information you need to know. A well-designed form is also a usable form, and it's the usability that makes the difference between something that's glanced at and something that's pored over.

66 *Plain English, please!*

Usability means "degree of ease of use." Software companies such as Novell, Apple, and Microsoft make extensive use of usability labs, where typical users try out design features to see if they can be understood and... well, used. *Usability* is a good word to keep in mind, even if it's becoming a bit overdone these days. 99

Some general issues of form design

There are a few things you should keep in mind when you design forms. These are simple rules that can make simple forms exciting and complex forms easy to use.

Figure 14.1 is a form in need of some help.

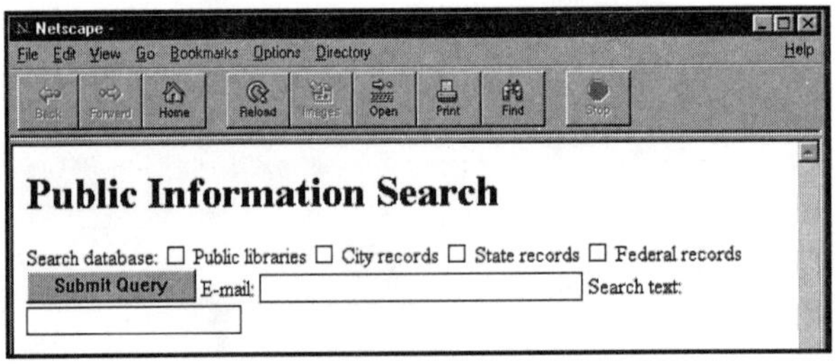

Fig. 14.1
This form requests all the data the Webmaster wants, but doesn't make it easy for the user to enter it.

There are general design rules you can follow to correct these problems:

- **Explain yourself**. A small bit of explanatory text next to your inputs can really help a user who otherwise might just give up.

- **Make sure your form has a flow**. Request input from the user in a logical order, preferably starting with something familiar.

- **Group related items together.** Collect all the information about a single subject in the same place.

- **Make each field the right size for the data you're requesting.** Too little room is discouraging, while too much wastes space.

- **Use the space *between* fields as well.** White space—the blank areas between actual content—can be as important as what data the page contains.

The redesigned form is shown in Figure 14.2.

Fig. 14.2
General design rules, along with a few tricks, can make your pages welcoming instead of forbidding.

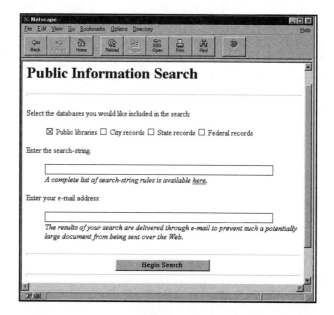

Using multiple forms in a page

Though there is no technical reason not to, you should avoid using multiple forms on one page. From a designer's point of view, a page with a form should fill a *single* purpose. Crowding forms onto one page will only confuse your visitors and make your site harder to use.

That said, there are a few instances in which multiple forms on one page will make things *easier* to use. For example, it's okay when the forms you are using have only one or two fields. This works well when you want to give users a choice of search queries.

Q&A *I have multiple forms on my page, but they're all coming out as one big one. What's going on?*

You probably forgot a </FORM> tag along the way. Because forms cannot be nested, a second <FORM> encountered before a </FORM> will be ignored.

Working with horizontal controls

The elements of a form, like almost every HTML tag, do not have their line-breaks preserved as they are laid-out in the code. While this can be very useful for long blocks of text, it makes forms appear disjointed and ugly. The <BR> tag and the <P> tag can help.

The line-break (<BR>) tag

If you have two fields you want the user to fill, their first and last name, the HTML code could look like this:

```
<FORM>
    First name: <INPUT TYPE="TEXT" NAME="first" SIZE="15">
    Last name: <INPUT TYPE="TEXT" NAME="last" SIZE="15">
</FORM>
```

But when this code is viewed through a browser, it looks like figure 14.3, which is probably not what you intended.

Fig. 14.3
The default layout of forms can be hard to look at—even ugly.

By adding a line-break tag (<BR>) after the first field, the second INPUT will appear on the next line and against the left margin, regardless of how wide the user sizes his browser.

```
<FORM>
    First name: <INPUT TYPE="TEXT" NAME="first" SIZE="15"><BR>
    Last name: <INPUT TYPE="TEXT" NAME="last" SIZE="15">
</FORM>
```

This piece of HTML, with the <BR> tag after the first INPUT field, looks like figure 14.4.

Fig. 14.4
The <BR> tag allows you, instead of the browser, to decide where a line ends.

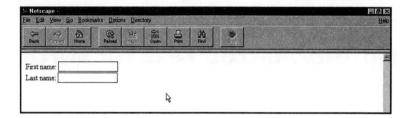

The <BR> tag is also useful for putting any prompting text above a large field, instead of to its left. This is especially important for wide fields.

```
<FORM>
    Please enter your comments:<BR>
    <TEXTAREA ROWS="4" COLS="60"></TEXTAREA>
</FORM>
```

Using the paragraph (<P>) tag

The <P> tag works a lot like the <BR> tag, but its use in forms can lend a subtle distinction that distinguishes a slapped-together form from a crafted one.

While the <BR> tag simply breaks the line, the <P> tag inserts extra space between the current and previous line. This can be used to separate fields without making the separation so obvious as to break the flow of the form.

This code demonstrates the use of <P> in forms:

```
<FORM>
    Name: <INPUT TYPE="TEXT" NAME="name" > <I>Optional</I><P>
    Please enter your comment:<BR>
    <TEXTAREA ROWS="4" COLS="60"></TEXTAREA>
</FORM>
```

The result is figure 14.5.

Fig. 14.5
The <P> tag allows you to set off sections from each other while keeping them in a single visual scope.

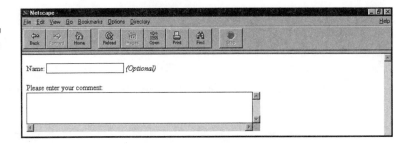

Using preformatted text for vertical alignment

Once you have each of your entry fields divided onto separate lines, you'll notice that there's another problem. While all the fields start at the left-hand margin, the actual entry area starts immediately after the prompt text, completely unevenly. This can make your forms look haphazard and unprofessional.

This HTML code demonstrates the problem:

```
<FORM>
     Name:                <INPUT TYPE="TEXT" NAME="name"><BR>
     Street Address: <INPUT TYPE="TEXT" NAME="addr"><BR>
     Sex:                 <INPUT TYPE="RADIO" NAME="sex" CHECKED> Male
                          <INPUT TYPE="RADIO" NAME="sex"> Female
</FORM>
```

Though this looks nice laid-out in the source code, it appears in browsers like figure 14.6.

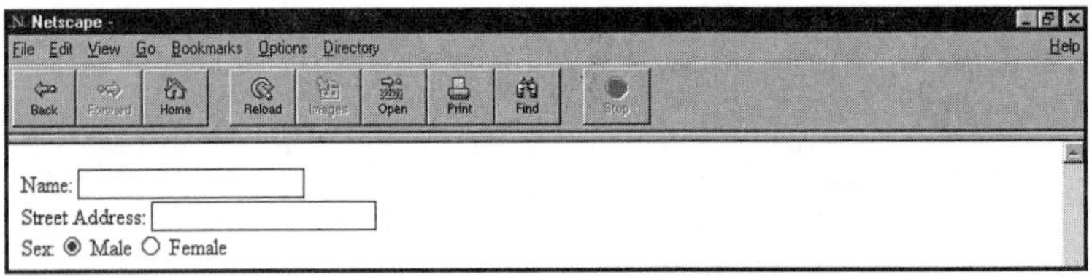

Fig. 14.6
Though the fields are well laid-out horizon-tally, they need vertical alignment.

The trick to get around this problem is to use the <PRE> tag. <PRE> stands for preformatted, and it forces the browser to use a fixed-width font and the layout you specify. So, you can control exactly how much space is used between the left margin and the prompt text, and between the prompt text and the entry area. The above code would be rewritten like this:

```
<FORM>
     <PRE>
     Name: <INPUT TYPE="TEXT" NAME="name"><BR>
Street Address: <INPUT TYPE="TEXT" NAME="addr"><BR>
        Sex: <INPUT TYPE="RADIO" NAME="sex" CHECKED> Male
                <INPUT TYPE="RADIO" NAME="sex"> Female
     </PRE>
</FORM>
```

And it would appear like figure 14.7.

Fig. 14.7
The <PRE> tag allows you to control the vertical.

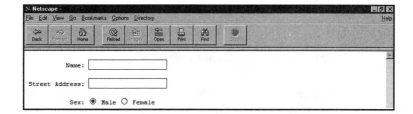

Because the <PRE> tag preserves all spacing, and because text entry fields use exactly the same font as words inside <PRE> tags, it seems logical that you could create an even right-hand margin by carefully counting spaces. But you can't unless you limit yourself to the same number of fields per line and start counting out character and blank spaces. This is because the border and internal padding of each text entry field widens the line, depending on how many fields you have.

Using lists

Though the <BR>, <P>, and <PRE> tags give you incredible flexibility when laying out forms, there is a much simpler way to do certain types of design, especially outlines and numbered choices: the list tags.

Definition, ordered, and unordered lists work inside forms just like they work on plain text. This makes creating form-based outlines incredibly easy:

```
<FORM>
     Where would you rather live?
     <UL><P>
          California
          <UL>
               <INPUT TYPE="RADIO" NAME="home" VALUE="la" CHECKED> Los Angeles<BR>
               <INPUT TYPE="RADIO" NAME="home" VALUE="sf"> San Francisco
          </UL><P>
          New York
          <UL>
               <INPUT TYPE="RADIO" NAME="home" VALUE="ny"> New York City
          </UL><P>
          Illinois
          <UL>
               <INPUT TYPE="RADIO" NAME="home" VALUE="chi"> Chicago
          </UL>
     </UL>
</FORM>
```

This sample appears in figure 14.8.

Fig. 14.8
A well-designed outline becomes painless with list tags.

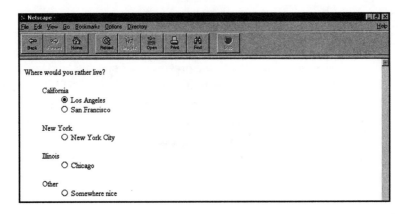

This method for creating outlines and lists can be used with any type of form element and any of the list tags. They can even be nested!

15

Introduction to CGI

● **In this chapter:**

- **CGI and what it does**

- **The languages for programming CGI scripts**

- **How can you use CGI to give your pages extra features?**

- **The information you need to keep in mind while programming CGI scripts**

- **Here's what other CGI artists have done**

The Common Gateway Interface (CGI) is the doorway between your Web server and the computer it runs on. Understanding CGI, both what it is and how it works, can help you expand the capabilities of your site tremendously . . . . ⊘

Themes problem with creating fill-in forms for your Web pages is that they don't actually do anything. Your readers can fill them in to their hearts' content, but when they click the Submit button, the data won't go anywhere. That's where Common Gateway Interface (CGI) comes in. By developing CGI scripts, you can make your forms—and other features on your Web pages—truly interactive. CGI scripts bring your static Web pages to life—returning requested data, responding to user input, and logging accesses. Interactivity is a large part of the allure of the Web, and CGI programming is the **back end** that makes it possible.

What is CGI?

Think of CGI as the way in which a Web browser can run programs directly. In this way, it's much the same as the way Netscape or Mosaic use **helper applications** to display picture formats that they don't know about internally. The big difference is that CGI programs run in the browser itself; you don't need an external program to make things happen.

To a user, a link to a CGI program looks like a link to any other URL. It can be clicked like any other link and will result in new information being displayed, just like any other link.

But, under the hood, a CGI program is much more than a normal Web page. When a normal URL is selected, a file is read, interpreted, and displayed by the browser. When a URL to a CGI program is selected, it causes a program to be run on the server system, and that program can do just about anything you want it to: scan databases, sort names, or send mail. CGI scripts allow for complex back-end processing.

CGI changes the definition of what a Web page is. While normal pages are static and unchanging, CGI programs allow a page to be anything you want it to be.

One small note: The terms **CGI programs** and **CGI scripts** are used interchangeably in this chapter just as they are on the Web itself.

A CGI success story

Imagine Pete's Trucking. Pete and his shipping department need to keep their customers informed about the location of various shipments. Currently, a customer phones in a request and a service rep faxes a response. The system works, but only during office hours. It also seems clumsy, requiring a verbal request for a fax that may then have to be scanned back into a computer. Errors and delays crop up often.

By using CGI, Pete can extend the functionality of his Web site. A customer service page might request a customer's name and password. Based on that information, it scans the manifest database and returns a response—in seconds, at any time, without interrupting the service rep. And instead of a fax, the customer now has a digital copy of the data he wanted and can print it, e-mail it, or save it to a disk. By writing a small CGI program, Pete has solved a nagging problem—invisibly, conveniently, and elegantly—and his customers are happy. The result is shown in figure 15.1.

Fig. 15.1
Pete's biggest customer finds out that his driver is very lost.

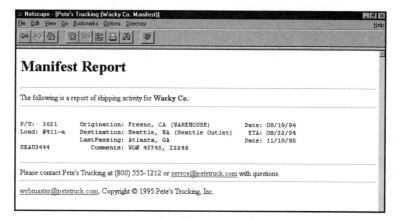

Why reinvent the wheel?

CGI programming can be extremely frustrating in the beginning. There are many rules to follow, most of which can be obscure or complex. Even getting a simple script up and running can be a chore.

One of the best ways to get over these first few hurdles and start CGI programming is to look at existing code. By reviewing (or simply using) existing CGI scripts, you can not only save yourself a lot of time, but teach yourself new techniques.

Existing code almost always makes a good base to expand from. Instead of implementing a new script from scratch, an older program can often be modified to suit your needs. Collections of CGI programs can be found on the Web, and a good starting point is **http://hoohoo.ncsa.uiuc.edu/cgi/**.

Most experienced CGI programmers will almost always be happy to share their code and talents with you. They've probably already solved any problem you might have and can save you hours of frustration with a word or a clue. Just ask. And be sure to return the favor when you become an expert. That's part of the fun of being on the Web.

Pick a language, almost any language

You do not write CGI scripts in HTML like you write the Web pages themselves. CGI scripts are written in other computer languages, such as UNIX shell scripts, Perl, C, or Visual Basic, and to write them you'll need knowledge of at least one of these languages. Although a discussion of even one of them is beyond the scope of this chapter, there are strengths and weaknesses to each, and many excellent references exist.

UNIX shell scripts (or Windows NT or 95 batch files) are a good choice for small or temporary CGI programs. They are easy to write and you can see results immediately. But you're not limited to simple scripts. Your CGI programs can be as complex as you want to make them.

Perl is a good choice for medium-complexity programs, and most platforms support it. It's fast, easy to program, and it's interpreted, meaning that it doesn't need to be compiled like C. Perl allows you all the advantages of a full computer language and a shell script combined. Also, a Perl library exists that will automatically translate any data sent to your CGI program into a usable form. You can get this library from **ftp://ftp.ncsa.uiuc.edu/Web/httpd/Unix/ncsa_httpd/cgi/cgi-lib.pl.Z**. Note that it is available only for UNIX users.

Information on Perl itself is available all over the Web, including at **http://www.yahoo.com/Computers_and_Internet/Languages/Perl**, **http://www.yahoo.com/Computers_and_Internet/Internet/World_Wide_Web/Programming/Perl_Scripts**, and **news:comp.lang.perl**.

For very complex data manipulation, it's best to use a full-fledged computer language, such as C. It will give you the fastest response and let you work with your information in the most flexible way. A C library also exists for decoding submitted data, and is available at **ftp://ftp.ncsa.uiuc.edu/Web/ httpd/Unix/ncsa_httpd/cgi/ncsa-default.Z**.

Here are a few CGI examples

The best way to learn what CGI scripts can do and how they do it is by example. The four examples below progress from using CGI programs to display simple static data, to more complex dynamic data, to using server-provided information, and to the ultimate end of CGI: reacting to user input.

First, a simple example

Although CGI programs can become extremely complex, they can also be quite simple. One of the simplest is the UNIX shell script in listing 15.1 (and shown in fig. 15.2)

Listing 15.1   A Simple CGI Script

```
#!/bin/sh
echo "Content-type: text/html"
echo ""
echo "<HTML><HEAD><TITLE>Sample</TITLE></HEAD>"
echo "<BODY>This is a <EM>simple</EM> CGI script.</BODY></HTML>"
```

Fig. 15.2
The output of CGI scripts can look exactly like HTML.

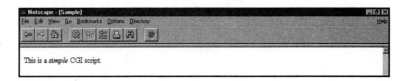

The first line of this script (#!/bin/sh) tells UNIX what shell this program is written for; if the program were a Windows NT batch file, the line could be excluded.

The second line (echo "Content-type: text/html") tells the Web server what type of information is to follow in MIME (Multipurpose Internet Mail Extension) format. **MIME** is a method of delivering complex binary data using only ASCII text characters. There are hundreds of standard MIME formats now registered, but the two most common for CGI applications are "text/html" (for HTML output) and "text/plain" (for plain ASCII output).

The third line (`echo ""`) is simply an empty space to tell the server that what follows is the data described by the `"Content-type."`

CAUTION   **Be sure to use the correct** `"Content-type:"` **for the type of** output you are generating. If your CGI program outputs HTML but your `Content-type` is listed as `"text/plain,"` none of the HTML tags will be interpreted, leaving your page looking like an HTML source code listing.

Finally, the fourth and fifth lines are the actual HTML data. These are sent through the server to the browser and interpreted just as the same instructions would be if they'd been read from an HTML file.

Installing and referencing a CGI script

While conventions among servers differ, most require that CGI programs be installed in a special CGI directory. This subdirectory is usually off of where the server software itself is installed, and is usually called cgi-bin. If you don't have the permissions needed to install your program in that directory, talk to your system administrator. The system administrator will also tell you how to install the script itself, which is usually a matter of copying it from your own computer to the appropriate directory of the main Web server.

Once your CGI script is in place, you can reference it from a browser like any other URL. For example, if you installed a program called simple.sh in the cgi-bin directory, its URL would be as follows:

http://my.server.com/cgi-bin/simple.sh

If complex.pl (a more complex Perl program) is installed in cgi-bin/sales/order (a typical directory dedicated to sales orders taken over the Web), its URL would be as follows:

http://my.server.com/cgi-bin/sales/order/complex.pl

These URLs can be used like any others, including as HREFs from other Web pages.

Q&A ***I keep getting errors when I try to run my CGI program. What do they mean, and what's the best way to debug my script?***

The most common error is "500 Server Error." It means that you either forgot to send the "Content-type:" line before your data, or your CGI program failed somehow part way through. Both cases mean that you have some debugging to do.

If you get "403 Forbidden," you need to set certain permissions on your CGI script. Talk to your system administrator to correct this problem.

Now for a dynamic example

Of course, the simple CGI program in Listing 15.1 only outputs static data, and your reader wouldn't be able to tell it from a normal Web page. The real power of CGI scripts can be seen when they go beyond this and start generating dynamic data— something that's impossible for a normal page to do.

The CGI script in listing 15.2 (displayed in fig. 15.3) displays a new wise saying each time you jump to it.

Listing 15.2   A Dynamic CGI Script

```
#!/bin/sh
echo "Content-type: text/html"
echo ""
echo "<HTML><HEAD><TITLE>Fortune</TITLE></HEAD>"
echo "<BODY>Words of wisdom:<HR><PRE>"
FORTUNE='/usr/games/fortune'
if [ "$FORTUNE" = "" ]; then
    echo "A wise system administrator installs 'fortune'
    ➥for his users."
    echo "        — Anon"
else
    echo $FORTUNE
fi
echo "</PRE></BODY></HTML>"
```

Fig. 15.3
Web users are given new words of advice from the UNIX fortune command each time they jump to this script.

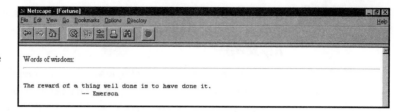

Instead of just displaying a predefined message, this script—through the UNIX fortune command—shows dynamic information each time it is run. If a user were to select the link that ran this script twice in a row, it would produce totally different results. This works because fortune has been installed in the games directory of the UNIX computer in advance. If it's not there (check with your system administrator), the script won't do anything at all.

Just about any UNIX utility, or combination of utilities, can be used in place of the fortune command in the above example. The real power of CGI scripts is to allow the entire capability of the computer to go into generating the Web page, and this example only hints at the possibilities.

Making use of input provided by the server

Dynamic Web pages can be even more powerful if they use some of the information that the server automatically provides to every CGI program.

When a CGI script is run by the server, several **environment variables** are set, each containing information about the server software, the browser the request came from, and the script itself. These variables can then be read by the CGI program and used in various ways.

For example, the program in listing 15.3 logs (keeps track of) each machine that connects to it and responds with a greeting (see fig. 15.4). Instead of being written as a UNIX shell script, this CGI program is written in Perl, which allows for greater control over how the log information is displayed.

Listing 15.3 A CGI Program That Uses Server Information

```
#!/usr/local/bin/perl
print "Content-type: text/html\n\n";
# Find out where they're from
$remote_host = $ENV{'REMOTE_HOST'};
if (length($remote_host) == 0) {
    $remote_host = $ENV{'REMOTE_ADDR'};
}
# Log this access
($sec,$min,$hour,$mday,$mon,$year,$wday,$yday,$isdst) = gmtime;
open(FILE,">>access.log");
if ($mon < 9)   { print FILE "0"; }; print FILE ++($mon),"/";
if ($mday < 10) { print FILE "0"; }; print FILE "$mday/$year     ";
if ($hour < 10) { print FILE "0"; }; print FILE "$hour:";
if ($min < 10)  { print FILE "0"; }; print FILE "$min:";
if ($sec < 10)  { print FILE "0"; }; print FILE "$sec GMT
➡$remote_host\n";
close FILE;
# And output the HTML

print "<BODY>Hello\!  You are connecting from $remote_host.
➡</BODY></HTML>\n";
```

Fig. 15.4
This CGI program not only tells users that you know where they live, but it keeps a log of that information too.

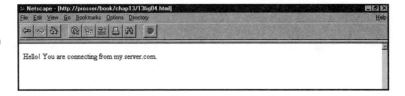

This program uses two environment variables set by the server to find out the name of the machine running the browser: REMOTE_HOST and REMOTE_ADDR. REMOTE_HOST will normally contain the Internet host name of the browser's machine, for example, my.server.com. But if, for some reason, this variable is empty, REMOTE_ADDR will always contain the Internet address of the browser: 123.45.67.123, for example.

That's what the fourth through seventh lines of the program are doing: getting this information. The rest just gets the time and date, writes them to a file, and returns a message to the user.

There are many variables like these. The most common ones are shown in table 15.1.

Table 15.1   CGI environment variables

Variable	Contents
REMOTE_HOST	The Internet name of the machine the browser is running on; may be empty if the information is not known
REMOTE_ADDR	The Internet address of the machine the browser is running on
SCRIPT_NAME	The program currently running
SERVER_NAME	The Internet name or address of the server itself
HTTP_USER_AGENT	The browser software that the user is running

A complete list of CGI environment variables is available at **http://hoohoo.ncsa.uiuc.edu/docs/cgi/env.html**.

By using these environment variables creatively, you can do all sorts of neat things. Combining SERVER_NAME and SCRIPT_NAME can produce a URL to the currently running script, allowing it to reference itself. HTTP_USER_AGENT can be used to check what browser the user is running and send the appropriate page to the user (i.e., Netscape users get one page, Lynx users get a different one, and so on).

Making use of input supplied by your readers

By far the most popular, most powerful use of CGI programs is to transmit information users type into fill-in forms. CGI scripts can take the input that a user provides in a form and process it in any way you choose. This allows your Web site to become truly interactive.

For example, the program in listing 15.4 is a "Guestbook," an electronic version of the familiar visitor log used by hotels and museums. It first displays a list of signers, then uses a form to ask the current user to add his signature. It is written in Perl and uses a form-input **parsing** (i.e., analyzing) library called cgi-bin.pl. The guestbook appears in figure 15.5.

Listing 15.4   A CGI Program That Uses User Input

```
#!/usr/local/bin/perl
print "Content-type: text/html\n\n";
# Load the library
do "cgi-bin.pl" || die "Fatal Error: Could not load cgi-bin.pl";
&ReadParse;
# Set the location of the guestbook
$guestbk = "guestbk.gbk";
# Get the sign-ins name
$name = $in{'name'};
# Only add to the log if they entered something
if (length($name) > 0) {
    open(FILE,">>$guestbk");
    print FILE "$name\n";
    close FILE;
}
# Show the current sign-ins
print "<HTML>\n<HEAD><TITLE>Guestbook</TITLE></HEAD>\n";
print "<BODY>\n<H1>Guestbook</H1>\n<H2>Current signees:
➥</H2>\n<HR>\n<UL>\n";
open(FILE,"<$guestbk") || print "You'll be the first\!\n";
while (<FILE>) {
    print "<LI>$_";
}
close FILE;
print "</UL>\n";
# Request new sign-ins
print "<HR>\n<FORM METHOD=\"GET\"ACTION=\"$ENV{'SCRIPT_NAME'}\">";
print "Your name: <INPUT TYPE=\"text\" NAME=\"name\SIZE=\"20\">";
print "<INPUT TYPE=\"submit\" VALUE=\"Sign in\!\"></FORM>\n</BODY>
➥\n</HTML>\n";
```

Fig. 15.5
Guestbook is a nice
way to make your site
more personal.

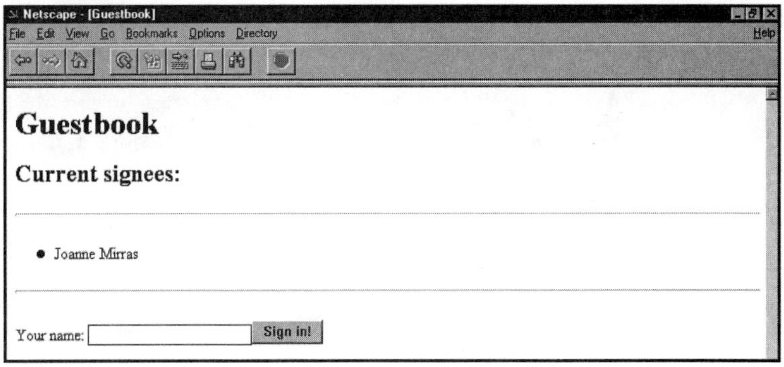

By using the cgi-bin.pl library, the information entered into a form by the user is extracted from the request and stored in a Perl table called "in." You can get the VALUEs of each form INPUT by asking in for it by referencing its NAME. For instance, if a form INPUT has the NAME "address," the following line of Perl code would return the value the user entered:

```
$addr_variable = $in{'address'};
```

Before you can use in, you must have loaded cgi-bin.pl and called the library routine that sets up the table. Both these procedures are handled in lines four and five in listing 15.4.

CGI and Security

When creating forms and CGI scripts, you should be aware that, normally, none of the data passed between the browser and the server is encrypted. This means that any private data (credit card numbers, love letters, etc.) can be stolen by machines between the sender and receiver. Thankfully, more and more browsers (such as Netscape) have the ability to automatically encrypt data and make secure data transfer possible.

Another point about security: there are people out on the Web who would love nothing more than to cause you trouble. Purely out of a sense of vindictiveness, they will try to make your life as hard as it can be. Your CGI scripts need to take this into account.

For example, cleverly written queries can be used to gain privileges on your server that you never intended to grant. One common trick involves sending a shell command appended to some piece of requested data, so that when the CGI program uses that piece of data in an external command, the **piggy-back** command is executed as well.

Imagine a user entering savola@usc.edu;rm -rf/ into a form (rm in UNIX means delete). A badly written CGI script might simply add the UNIX command *finger* to the front of the request and execute it as a shell command, causing both commands to be run and deleting a lot of files. One good reason to borrow CGI scripts from elsewhere is because other authors have already thought of these things.

CGI in the real Web world

The power of CGI is being used every day on the Web, from individuals who run small personal sites spiced up with a simple form to multinational corporations that are using the Web as a new frontier for sales and customer interaction.

Commercial sites

There's a lot to see out there. For instance, it's already possible to place orders over the Web for flowers, pizza, or software. You can buy glasses, stuffed animals, and clothing without having to get up out of your seat.

Check out the virtual malls listed on Yahoo (**http://www.yahoo.com/ Business_and_Economy/Companies/Shopping_Centers**). All these shopping sites use CGI scripts to answer requests, process orders, and complete transactions. And while the scope of these commercial sites is probably beyond what you will want to do yourself, there are dozens of professional designers who, for a fee, will set up a site for you that will rival anything else on the Web.

The public domain

Don't assume, however, that you need a professionally designed page for professional results. With a little help, almost anybody can put together a great looking, interactive, CGI-based Web site—especially if he takes advantage of public domain programs that already exist.

Often rivaling the capabilities of custom scripts, many public domain CGI programs exist free for the taking, and more are being created every day. Even if these scripts are too general for your needs, they can be mined for techniques and methods that you can then use in your own programs.

You can find many public domain CGI scripts at **http://www.yahoo.com/ Computers_and_Internet/Internet/World_Wide_Web/Programming/ CGI**, **http://ftp.ncsa.uiuc.edu/Web/httpd/Unix/cgi**, and **news:comp.infosystems.www.authoring.cgi**.

The cutting edge

Check out some of the following sites, which make good use of CGI scripts and interactivity:

- **http://www.sci.kun.nl/thalia/funpage/startrek**

- **http://www.hotwired.com**

- **http://kuhttp.cc.ukans.edu/cwis/organizations/kucia/uroulette/uroulette.html**

- **http://bf.cstar.ac.com/bf**

- **http://www.inference.com/~hansen/talk.html**

- **http://www.usc.edu/dept/garden** (see fig. 15.6)

Fig. 15.6
The gardening department at the University of Southern California lets you exercise your green thumb from thousands of miles away.

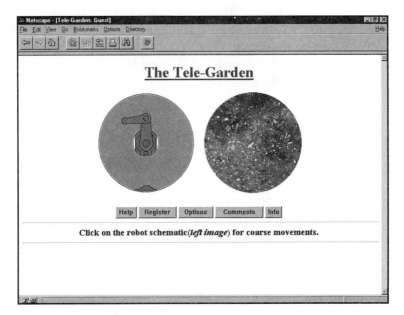

CGI isn't easy, and increasingly it's handled by specialists. But you can do a great deal on your own, and the results can be both impressive and immensely helpful. In many ways, CGI puts the final touches on your Web site, because it allows you to collect data rather than just present information.

16

Hands-on Step 4: Getting the Most Out of Part Four

● **In this chapter:**

- **Create an imagemap**

- **Put together an HTML table**

- **Design your first HTML form**

This part of the hands-on tutorial takes you through the stages of creating imagemaps, tables, and forms—three of the most popular items on the Web. . . . . **>**

The colorful interface—your first imagemap

In Chapter 11, you discovered how to create imagemaps, those wonderful graphical files with multiple links inside. Here, you'll design an imagemap to act as an interface to three important pages on the Bertha's Attic site.

For this hands-on step, I used MapEdit for Microsoft Windows, which is readily available on software sites around the Net (such as **http://www.tucows.com/**). You may use any imagemap creation program you want, of course, or you can simply type the code into your favorite text editor. The appropriate code is shown at each step of the tutorial.

First, you need a graphic file to work with. You'll find one on the Web at **http://randall.uwaterloo.ca/mapgraphic.htm**. Go there in your browser, then right-click the graphic image to download it to your computer. Save it in the directory where you've saved the other graphics files for your Web pages. Call it atticmap.gif.

Create the map file itself

Next, load MapEdit. To make things easier, maximize the screen. Choose File, Open/Create to bring up the Open Create Map dialog box. Click the Browse button, and go to the directory where you've stored all your HTML documents so far (*not* where your graphics files are stored). Call this imagemap attic.map (make sure it has the .MAP extension). Click OK to return to the Open Create Map dialog box.

Now you need to select the graphics file that will form the basis of your imagemap. Click Browse, and find the atticmap.gif file, which you downloaded a minute ago. Select it and click OK, and you'll be back at the filled-in Open Create Map dialog box.

Finally, you'll be asked to choose the Type of imagemap you're creating. Unless you have reason to change from the default NCSA selection, leave it at NCSA, the default. This dialog box will now look like figure 16.1.

Now, click OK and then confirm that you want MapEdit to create the MAP file.

Fig. 16.1
Be sure to select a graphic file, and remember to save your .MAP file with your other HTML documents.

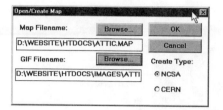

Dividing the graphic into separate clickable regions

At this point, MapEdit will still be open, but now you see the graphic displayed. Here's where imagemap creation gets fun. The trick is to divide the picture into different regions and to assign each region a separate URL (Web address). Assigning these separate URLs is what makes imagemaps work.

There are three items on the graphic: a lyric sheet, a musical icon, and an icon for an order form. When your readers click the lyric sheet, they'll be taken to a separate HTML document with lyrics to Bertha's Attic songs. Clicking the musical icon will take them to a page where they can download samples from Bertha's Attic recordings. If they click the order form, they'll retrieve a form for ordering the full cassette.

For this hands-on step, you'll create the sound samples page and the order form. In Chapter 21, you'll add the lyric sheet.

First, choose one of the tools in MapEdit's Tools menu—the rectangle is a good one—and surround the lyric sheet icon on the picture. MapEdit is a bit confusing here. You make your selection by using the left button, and as soon as you're finished, you must right-click to actually do anything.

Right-clicking yields the Object URL dialog box where you fill in the destination URL for the lyric sheet. In the box labeled "URL for clicks on this object," type **http://randall.uwaterloo.ca/lyrics.htm** (see fig. 16.2).

Fig. 16.2

If you want, you can fill in the comments box, but it's for your use only and won't actually appear on your Web page.

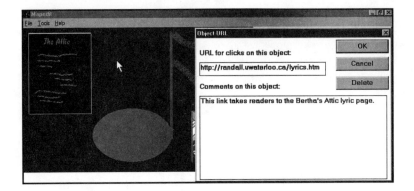

Click OK. You'll see that the selected area (the lyric sheet icon) is now highlighted. If you want to change the destination URL or the comment, double-click this area.

Now that you know how to do this, the rest is easy. You have two more areas to assign: the musical icon and the order form icon. Draw a rectangle or a polygon around each, and assign the following URLs to the regions:

- Assign **http://randall.uwaterloo.ca/sounds.htm** to the musical icon.

- Assign **http://randall.uwaterloo.ca/orders.htm** to the order form icon.

Finally, you should assign an URL to the regions of the image that aren't covered by the shapes you've created. In other words, if readers click outside the rectangles or polygons, they should at least go somewhere. For now, just have them come back to the imagemap.

Choose File, Edit Default URL. Type **http://randall.uwaterloo.ca/ atticmap.htm** in the box. Click OK.

You're done. Now it's a matter of putting the imagemap into an actual HTML document.

Now tell your HTML documents to put the imagemap to use

As I was writing this, there wasn't an HTML editor out there that seemed to handle imagemaps completely. So I won't bother having you reload Live

Markup at this point. Instead, load your favorite text editor to create a brand new HTML document. Call the document atticmap.htm—which, of course, is the destination for the default URL in the imagemap.

In your text editor, type the following code:

```
<HTML>
<HEAD>
<TITLE>Bertha's Attic Imagemap</TITLE>
</HEAD>
<BODY>
<A HREF = "/~imagemap/attic"><IMG SRC = "images/atticmap.gif"
➥ISMAP></A>
</BODY>
</HTML>
```

Note that you might have to modify this code to suit your own directory structure. You might have your MAP file in a different directory from mine, and your atticmap.gif file in a different directory as well. The important point is that you specify the correct directory and you include the ISMAP element in your HTML code.

In a better world, your HTML editor would take care of all the tiny bits. And HTML editors are getting better at this all the time. For now, though, you might have to do it by hand, and it never hurts to know exactly what goes on.

Save the text file as **atticmap.htm** in the correct directory.

Test your imagemap

Now for the fun part. Fire up your browser and load atticmap.htm. There it is: your brilliant creation.

Only one problem. The map won't work the way you expect it to. To make an imagemap actually do anything, it has to be stored on a computer that's set up as a Web server. If you ever get around to making your machine a Web server, the server software will contain instructions on where to put your imagemaps and graphics files.

Many Internet providers offer imagemap services to their subscribers. Check to see if yours is one of them.

Until then, point your browser to **http://randall.uwaterloo.ca/ atticmap.htm**, and see what the finished product does.

It's time for a simple table

Here, you'll produce a table that will form the basis of an HTML document named sounds.htm. Above, you linked the musical icon of your imagemap to this page, and now it's time to create the document itself.

By now, most HTML editors contain a feature for creating tables. If yours does, by all means go ahead and create the table that way. For now, and partly because my version of Live Markup didn't do tables at the time of this writing, let's just create it the old-fashioned way by using text. It's ugly, but it works.

Starting it up

Use your favorite HTML editor to get started. Open a new page, and give it the title Bertha's Attic Sounds. Now give it an <H1> level heading of Sounds from the Attic, and then center this heading. You already know how to do all this, of course, from previous hands-on steps.

Add a table to this page that will allow readers to download samples of Bertha's Attic songs. You want the table to lead them to the lyric sheets for those songs. Here's what the table will look like after it's created:

Song Title	Click Here	Lyrics
The Attic	Download	"In the attic she finds herself..."
The Hermit	Download	"I'll be looking for peace to sit and just remember..."
In the Mix	Download	"We can talk of magic spells..."

This is easy to do in a spreadsheet or a word processor, but in an HTML table the cells of the table can act as links. That's the fascination of tables—they can be very orderly and attractive mini-HTML documents.

Create the actual table

Again, if your HTML editor supports tables, use it. If not, load your text editor and type the HTML code in listing 16.1. If you don't feel like typing it, go to **http://randall.uwaterloo.ca/sounds.htm** and use the Save or View Source command to copy the file. Then load the HTM file into your editor.

Listing 16.1   The Sounds from the Attic table

```
<CENTER><TABLE COLSPEC="L20 L20 L20" BORDER=10
CELLPADDING=5 CELLSPACING=5><CAPTION ALIGN=top>
BERTHA'S ATTIC SOUND FILES</CAPTION><TR><TH>SONG TITLE</TH>
<TH>CLICK HERE</TH>
<TH>LYRICS</TH></TR><TR><TD><EM>The Attic</EM></TD>
<TD><A HREF="http://randall.uwaterloo.ca/sounds/attic.wav">
Download!</A></TD>
<TD><A HREF="http://randall.uwaterloo.ca/lyrics/lyric01.htm">

"First line of song"</A></TD></TR><TR><TD><EM>Song # 2</EM></TD>
<TD><A HREF="http://randall.uwaterloo.ca/sounds/song2.wav">
Download!</A></TD>
<TD>"<A HREF="http://randall.uwaterloo.ca/lyrics/
lyric02.htm">
First line of song"</A></TD></TR><TR><TD><EM>Song #3</EM></TD>
<TD><A HREF="http://randall.uwaterloo.ca/sounds/song3.wav">
Download!</A></TD>
<TD><A HREF="http://randall.uwaterloo.ca/lyrics/lyric03.htm">
"First line of song"</A></TD></TR></TABLE></CENTER>
```

Save the file (sounds.htm), and load it into your browser. It should look like figure 16.3.

Fig. 16.3
The table is centered, and the sound files and lyrics can be accessed by clicking the appropriate links.

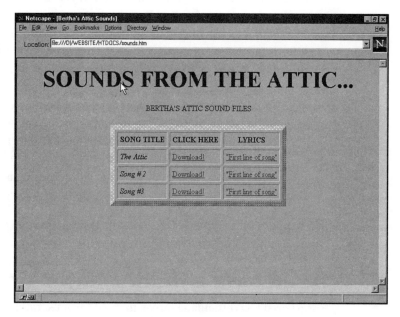

Notice that the hyperlinks inside the cells for the sound files and the lyrics pages point to separate HTML files. To get the sound files themselves, go to **http://randall.uwaterloo.ca/sounds.htm**, then right-click the hyperlink and download the file to your hard drive. You can then reference the sound file directly from there if you wish. The lyric sheets can be found at **http://randall.uwaterloo.ca/lyrics.htm**. You can download these to your hard drive as well.

Congratulations! You now have an imagemap that leads to a table. This is sophisticated stuff!

Wanna buy an attic?

You read about forms in Chapters 13–15, and now it's time to design one for yourself. This form will let your readers order the Bertha's Attic cassette or CD. They'll fill in their names, addresses, and e-mail addresses; select either the cassette or CD version; and then offer comments if they feel like it.

Here are two issues to keep in mind. First, this order form isn't designed to let your readers order directly. You need a secure Web server to do that safely, and unless you intend to set up a Web form for users to transmit sensitive information, you aren't likely to have a secure server. Also, you're probably not registered to sell products through Visa or American Express, something you have to do before you can accept credit card numbers. In fact, there's a good deal more to do than just register, and you're advised to consult a financial advisor from your local bank to determine what's involved in selling products through credit card acceptance. The form you'll produce here is simply designed to e-mail information to the Web site, at which point the reader will receive an e-mail message with ordering instructions.

Second, just as with the imagemap, the form you design won't actually work unless your computer is set up as a Web server. You can see the form in action by going to **http://randall.uwaterloo.ca/orders.htm**.

If you have a forms creator

Forms aren't as difficult as tables to create from scratch, but they're not much fun. Increasingly, HTML editors are including forms creators, and sometimes these are even easy. HotDog Professional does the job quite well, as do others. WebForms, for Microsoft Windows users, is designed expressly to create HTML forms. As always, these are available on the Net itself from the software sites, including the TUCOWS site at **http://www.tucows.com/**.

As of this writing, Live Markup (the program I use most often) doesn't do forms. As a result, I present the code in text format only as I did with tables. This is a bit of a pain, but one nice thing is that the code is easy to change. Nonetheless, if you have a forms creator, by all means use it.

Doing the job with a text editor

You'll need a new HTML document for your form. At the beginning of this chapter, remember, you provided a link from the Order Form icon in the imagemap to an URL named **http://randall.uwaterloo.ca/orders.htm**. As a result, your HTML file will be called orders.htm.

Title your HTML document "Bertha's Attic Order Form." Next, give it a centered level-1 heading of "Play the Attic in Your Car!". Then, type a normal paragraph as follows:

```
Now that you know how good Bertha's Attic is, why not pick up
    their full-length cassette or CD? Fill in this form, then hit
    the "Send me info!" button. In a day or so, you'll get an
    e-mail message telling you how to place your order.
```

Now that you've instructed your readers what the form is all about and what will happen when they submit it, it's time to create the form. Refer to Chapter 12 for help if you wish, but the entire code for the form is in Listing 16.2.

Listing 16.2 HTML Code for the Feedback Form

```
<FORM ACTION="http://randall.uwaterloo.ca/cgi/order" METHOD="POST">

    <p><PRE>First Name:        <INPUT TYPE="text" NAME="First Name"
                               ➡SIZE=20></PRE>
    <p><PRE>Last Name:         <INPUT TYPE="text" NAME="Lastname"
                               ➡SIZE=20><PRE>
    <p><PRE>E-mail:            <INPUT TYPE="text" NAME="E-mail"
                               ➡SIZE=20></PRE>
    <p><PRE>Address1:          <INPUT TYPE="text" NAME="Address1"
                               ➡SIZE=30></PRE>
    <p><PRE>Address2:          <INPUT TYPE="text" NAME="Address2"
                               ➡SIZE=30></PRE>
    <p><PRE>City:              <INPUT TYPE="text" NAME="City"
                               ➡SIZE=30></PRE>
```

```
    <p><PRE>State/Province:        <INPUT TYPE="text" NAME="State/
                                  ➥Province"SIZE=20></PRE>
    <p><PRE>Country:               <INPUT TYPE="text" NAME="Country"
                                  ➥SIZE=20></PRE>
    <p><PRE>PostalCode:            <INPUT TYPE="text" NAME="PostalCode"
                                  ➥SIZE=15></PRE>
    <p>How do you listen to your music?<br>
    <p><menu>
        <INPUT TYPE="radio" NAME="medium" VALUE="Cassette" CHECKED>
        ➥Cassette<br>
        <INPUT TYPE="radio" NAME="medium" VALUE="CD" >CD<br>
    </menu>
    <p>Would you like to comment on our Web site?<br><TEXTAREA
    ➥name="Comments?" rows=8 cols=50></TEXTAREA><p>
<p>

    <p><INPUT TYPE="hidden" NAME="WebFormID" VALUE="1">
    <p><INPUT TYPE="submit" VALUE="Send me info!">
    ➥<INPUT TYPE="reset" VALUE="I screwed up - start over">
</FORM>
```

If you don't feel like typing all of this, set your browser to **http://randall. uwaterloo.ca/orders.htm** and copy and paste the code from there.

The most noteworthy element here is the <PRE></PRE> containers surrounding each line. The purpose is to force your reader's browser to display a monospaced font (such as Courier). While this isn't necessary, it allows you to align the form boxes so they look nice. As an experiment, get rid of a few of the <PRE></PRE> tags, save the file, and see what happens.

This form isn't extensive. It gives differently sized boxes to the reader to fill in with name and address, and then it offers a radio button selection ("medium") of cassette or CD. Next it provides a comments box asking, "Would you like to comment on our Web site?". Finally, it provides two buttons: one to submit the form and one to reset it. Your form should look like figures 16.4 and 16.5.

Fig. 16.4
The top half of the form shows the lead-in and the first few fill-in boxes.

Fig. 16.5
The form's bottom half displays the radio button, the comments box, and the submit and reset buttons.

Congratulations! Your Web site is coming along nicely. In Chapter 21, you'll put together a lyric sheet, and that'll finish the site for now.

17

So Much for Technique—Now It's on to Content

● **In this chapter:**

- **The page design process is crucial to your success**

- **Great content doesn't just happen**

- **Keeping your content fresh and alive**

- **How do I develop good HTML habits?**

Unless your pages are breathtaking in their beauty, they'll be judged in the long run by what's inside them. Here's what you need to keep building great content . . . . ▶

You know the hype that's happening over the 500-channel universe? Head straight along the information highway, the pundits tell us, and eventually we'll have cable systems with 500 channels or maybe more with all kinds of specialized content at our disposal. Maybe you find that exciting, or maybe you feel like Bruce Springsteen with his "57 Channels and Nothing On." Whatever the case, the fact is that you can get a taste of this watch-whatever-you-want universe by touring around the World Wide Web today.

From one standpoint, the World Wide Web can be compared to the ultimate cable television system: thousands upon thousands of channels are available for you to browse. Entertainment channels, educational channels, financial channels, cult channels—you name it, it's out there. Unfortunately, like a lot of cable TV these days, most of it consists of bad programming, worse execution, and blatant self-promotion.

And reruns. How can you have reruns on the Web? Just look at Web pages whose chief function is to link you to people's favorite Web pages. Having hundreds or thousands of links to Wired Magazine's HotWired site **(http://www.hotwired.com/)** is like having hundreds of TV channels all showing *I Love Lucy* episodes.

So how can you avoid becoming just another voice in the crowd or worse: ending up with a reruns-only Web page? Start, very simply, by telling yourself that you have something worth offering the world in the first place. That way, you'll stop yourself from providing links to every other Web site on the planet with no real content of your own. This chapter is about how to start making that happen.

Start with a process

If you join a production team these days, you're certain to find yourself wrapped up in a process. People make careers out of designing and implementing processes, and keeping processes on track is a major requirement of middle management in any number of industries. Walk into a meeting, and you'll hear talk about goals, milestones, subprocesses, and all kinds of other elements of process.

Why? Because the goal might be a product, but a product can only result from a process. That holds true whether you're manufacturing cars or designing an operating system. On a much smaller level, it also holds true when creating your Web site. What you want is a complete and full site, rich with worthwhile content and equally rich with visual appeal. The problem is getting there.

The following points outline a process worth following when designing your Web site. (Astute readers will note that this is a numbered list, not a bulleted list, because the steps are to be completed in a specific order. See how well we listen to our own press?)

1 Define your goals for the Web site. What's your point? What information do you want your audience to take away with them? Who's your audience anyway? Will the tone of the site be serious or humorous?

2 Think about the final product: what you want your Web site to look like in its entirety. Think about the opening pages and the closing pages, then go back and think about how the user will navigate through them. Sit down in front of a large piece of paper or, better still, a chalkboard, and draw a quick mock-up of each screen and the links between that screen and the others. Be sure to understand exactly how you will keep the reader aware that your site is a unified site, not a collection of poorly linked pages.

3 Carefully consider your links. In fact, this might be the most crucial decision you make. Kazillions of Web sites open by offering links to other sites. Given the tendency of Web users to click the first hyperlink they see, this is the equivalent of watching the opening credits for *ER* or *Friends* and seeing an invitation to flick to another channel. Even further into your site, be careful about where you place links and where they lead. Keep in mind that once your users are gone, they aren't likely to come back.

4 Create your information. This includes writing all of the text for the pages, getting your photographs scanned and saved in a standard file format, finding (or creating your own) buttons and icons that people will use to navigate your documents.

5 Start designing your actual pages using your favorite HTML editor. Link the pages together until the site actually works, making sure to include a selection of opening pages, interior pages, and closing pages.

6 Now that you have something to look at, step back and rethink your initial site design. Don't be afraid to scrap everything you have and start over. But keep your existing pages stored because you might very well discover that they'll fit anyway.

7 Design your tables using a spreadsheet or word processor. If you're using tables for formatting your pages rather than for storing information, use your word processor to get the design the way you want it. Once that's done, use your HTML editor to put your tables in the appropriate pages. Fire up your browser and make sure they work.

8 Work on your fill-in forms. Figure out what information you want users to send you, then put together a form to make this happen. Be careful not to include forms that are too lengthy because people won't want to fill them in at all. Concentrate on which questions you'll ask, and exactly how you'll ask them. Now, place the forms in your Web pages, and get to work on the CGI scripts you'll need to go with them.

9 When the site is done, test it. Then test it again. Then change the resolution of your computer and test it again. Now test it with a slower modem. Then grab a different kind of computer and test it. You've no doubt detected a pattern here. Don't let your readers find the errors. And there *will* be errors; it's inevitable, no matter how careful you are.

Naturally, you don't have to work through all these steps. You may feel comfortable skipping a step here or there after writing a few Web pages. That's fine as long as you keep in sync with the overall process. If you're managing other people who are putting together, or helping with, the Web site, this process will help keep everybody on track.

A few practical tips for great content

Having something to say on the Web is one thing, making yourself heard is another. Many Web designers seem to think that big, flashy graphics, streaming digital audio, and list after list of hyperlinks are all that is required to get their site recognized as a good one. That's just not the case. These things can help, but they can also hinder.

A site as simple as Federal Express's **(http://www.fedex.com/)** has only one reason for visiting: you can track your shipments. But it's one of the most popular sites on the Web, especially for business users. Even if you're not on the scale of FedEx, you can make great statements with a minimalist kind of design.

 Plain English, please!

> **Streaming digital audio** is a sound file that is played with a program called the RealAudio Player or another called Internet Wave. As the file is received by your computer, the player immediately plays the sound instead of waiting for the entire file to be transferred (as in standard digital audio).

Are my Web pages easy to use?

That's the first issue: usability. The Web is a dream information environment, combining text and graphics in an intuitive, point-and-click interface. Many authors get so caught up in the interactive nature of the Web that they forget the first rule to a good Web page: it *must* be easy to use.

Design your Web site so readers spend very little time figuring out how the pages work, and nearly all of their time accessing the information you're providing. Text should be brief, well-written, and efficient. Waste your readers' time, and they'll be sure to stay away.

Multimedia content—images, sound bites, video clips—should be clearly marked and informative. If you want people to retrieve them, let them know what they're in for by including information about file sizes, formats, and the quality of the multimedia information. Better yet, tell them how long it will take to retrieve this file at various modem speeds, and tell them where they can get this information if they don't want to download large files. Figure 17.1 shows an example of this kind of author consideration.

Fig. 17.1
These media links show
the individual file sizes,
so readers know how
long downloading the
files might take.

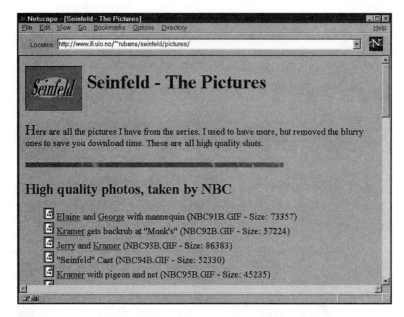

 Q&A *Doesn't good usability depend on testing and labs and all that?*

Sure, if you're Microsoft, Apple, Lotus, or Novell. Or, for that matter, if you're creating any software product designed to be used by nontechnical business people or home users. You can set up a lab with one-way mirrors and run an entire sample of typical users through a lengthy series of trials.

On the other hand, if you're just trying to get a Web site as usable as you can, given the fact that you don't have a huge amount of surplus cash lying around for sophisticated testing, you can test for usability yourself. Start by getting rid of the feeling of self-congratulations you've naturally and justifiably built up over the course of constructing the Web site. Put yourself in a Web surfer's shoes, and enter the Web site with an "I'm from Missouri; why don't you show me" attitude.

Ask yourself these basic questions: Does the page take too long to load? Are the graphics worth looking at? Do I know what the site's about? Do I find the writing insulting? Do I have an overwhelming desire to click the first link and leave? Do I have any interest at all in going deeper into the site? Could I find my way to the next logical page even if I wanted to? Is there enough information for me to continue?

Be critical, and be prepared to change anything that has to be changed. Nobody out there cares how many hours you spent designing the site; they just want it to work for them. If you think about usability at all times—and this means thinking as a user rather than as a designer—you shouldn't have too many problems.

TIP **A good measuring stick for transfer times is the 14,400 bps (bits** per second) connection rate—a midpoint between 9,600 and 28,800 bps transfer rates.

The point is this: *Make your Web site one you'd visit yourself.* If you don't find it easy to use, it's not likely anyone else will either.

Help them navigate

If readers can't find their way around your site, they'll leave and probably never come back. There are simply too many sites and too little time to bother with a poorly designed site.

The great disappearing act

The Web used to be a textual medium. Now it's a graphical medium. That's not consistently true of course; many "serious" sites—mostly academic or issues-oriented sites—still offer large doses of text. But the Web sites most of us keep going back to are controlled by graphics with text provided only where necessary.

Why? The temptation is to attribute it to the much ballyhooed loss of reading skills. Maybe. But book sales are still pretty good (hey, you bought this one, didn't you?), so that's an unlikely explanation. The more probable reason is that the Web has increasingly emulated the advertising industry.

Look at the big newspapers from the early part of this century, and you'll see ads that were primarily text (sometimes wholly so) with graphics added only as a bit of spice. Look at ads today, and you'll see graphics with only a smattering of text. Ads are done this way because we respond to them. We don't generally respond to blocks of text any more, especially if it's an item we don't expect will take us much time to get through.

The Web is an information medium. But it's a unique information medium. People don't read Web sites as if they're books—rarely even as if they're magazine articles. Web pages are a fascinating cross between ad and article, and soon—as browsers become more capable—they will combine the characteristics of ads, articles, programs, and even games. How we communicate all those things in our Web designs remains to be seen.

Navigation tools are essential for user-friendly Web pages. It's as if you are creating the interface for an online software program: you want all of the features and functions to be available at people's fingertips. This means including text links to other pages (including your main Web page and other reference-types of pages) and to the `mailto:` feature so they can send you feedback on your content (which helps you fine-tune your information and make it more accessible in your pages). It also means well-designed imagemaps, graphical navigation clues, and other helpful items.

Make your message clear

More and more often these days, Web sites are being designed for viewing, not reading. Text is disappearing on the WWW, just as it's becoming less prominent in almost every other form of mass communication.

Communicating by text is not the same as talking to your readers. You lose all sorts of subtext and non-verbal hints found normally in discussions: there's no body language, facial expressions, or proximity distances to help you figure out what the message is. There's also no voice inflection to clue you in to attempted sarcasm or humor—two very big challenges for communicating over the Internet.

 CAUTION   **Before trying to be funny, make sure you know how to do it.** Humor is probably the hardest thing in the world to write. (Do you ever wonder why there aren't very many humorous songs?) Most people just can't do it—not even those who are knock-down hilarious to listen to. Some designers suggest that, if you are kidding or trying to be funny, be sure to indicate it by using those fancy **smileys** (a.k.a. **emoticons**) you've encountered elsewhere on the Net. However, because the author of the book you're now holding hates smileys with an undiminishing passion (good writing *never* needs smileys), he will not, under any circumstances, agree with this point. So there!

Some Web pages are themselves an in-joke. Figure 17.2 is one of them, and it's not clear what you're getting into. As it turns out, it's quite fun, but not everyone is on the Web to have fun.

Fig. 17.2
Web pages like
The Spot, which are
tongue-in-cheek plays
on common cultural or
social icons or events,
should provide a clear
disclaimer for readers
who may not get the
joke.

Watch your language!

The Communications Decency Act notwithstanding, this section isn't a call for wholesomeness on the Internet. Instead, it's a warning about using nonstandard English (or German, or French, or whichever language your content will be in). Your information should avoid colloquialisms or slang that your intended audience just might not "get." If your Web pages are aimed exclusively at a particular group (motocross fans, for instance), then take advantage of the common jargon. Otherwise, try to use direct and clear English (or German, or French, and so on). Remember that the Web is *international*, and some of your readers won't know English well at all.

 Plain English, please!

> **Jargon** is vocabulary that isn't part of general experience. The act of buying a book with HTML on the cover means you're already a jargon user (go ask your grandparents what they think about HTML if you don't believe it). Jargon isn't bad at all unless it's used out of context. Remember: jargon is jargon only if you don't understand it. **99**

CAUTION **Don't translate your pages into other languages unless you're** certain that you know what you're doing. If you feel you have to translate, hire a translator. Otherwise, you're almost certain to wind up with unintentionally funny or even insulting information.

Don't people want huge amounts of information?

Keep your pages lean and mean. If your readers wanted vast gobs of information, they'd go to the library.

Your pages must get to the readers' desktops as fast as possible. Megabytes of travel photos, music, home videos, and unedited musings only serve to strain your audience's patience, not to mention the Internet's resources. Don't give them shovelware, give them worthwhile content. And give them the option of retrieving the content themselves: If you put huge inline images into your Web pages without warning, chances are they won't stick around to get the whole page, and they won't be back to visit your Web site in the future.

 Plain English, please!

Shovelware is a term that comes from the CD-ROM industry and refers to CD-ROM products that are obviously only older software "shoveled" onto a CD and sold as a new version of the product. Forcing older content into new distribution packages without adapting to the new medium detracts from the advantages of the medium and weakens the market for new cutting-edge products.

Provide users with "text-only" Web pages that don't include inline images. You can even provide transcripts of audio and video clips that people can retrieve first to see if they want to retrieve the media files. Give your readers a way to avoid being turned off.

TIP **Even links to partial transcripts on your graphical Web pages will** provide readers with an idea of what the linked data file is about. The smaller and faster your Web pages are, the easier they are to use and enjoy.

What if I want to present myself on the Web?

There are thousands of Web pages on the Internet, and yours will just be a small drop in a big ocean. To keep people's attention and interest, you need to find fresh and creative ways to give them what might be considered "run of the mill" information.

As you're creating your Web pages, you'll develop a strange kind of affection for them. They're yours, all yours, and they matter to you. The point, though, is whether or not they'll matter to your readers. One thing you learn very quickly while navigating the WWW is that people's lives (at least the people who have Net access) are, for the most part, very similar worldwide: we all have loved ones (boyfriends, girlfriends, spouses, pets), we have jobs we either like or dislike, we have individual musical tastes and preferred physical and mental hobbies. We all also have our favorite Web links.

At a certain point, the spontaneity of these sites grows thin. You begin to dread the next mile-long hotlist on your neighbor's Web page. What you need—what we all need on the WWW—is a way to share our information in fresh and engaging ways. Consider the following methods.

Breaking the mold

Find new ways to introduce yourself to the Web audience: poetry, fiction, photo collages. Explore your own passions, give your opinions, engage in debate. Use the Web as a tool for creating a global discourse (or for exchanging chocolate chip cookie recipes). Talk about your favorite foods, films, or authors. Or give people something weird, something unexpected. Figure 17.3 (**http://www.vv.com/~gilmore/head/heads.html**), for example, is just strange enough to draw people back for more.

Fig. 17.3
This Web page does
something, doesn't it?

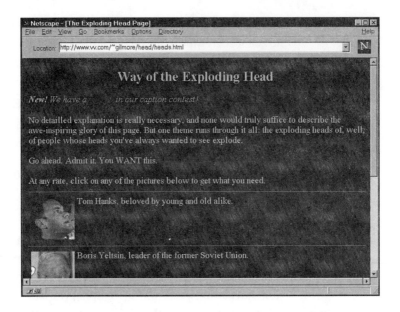

Keep it fresh!

This is, unquestionably, *the most important rule of Web site design*. If you don't change the content, don't expect people to return. Why would they?

Change your Web content as often as you can. The WWW is a dynamic environment. Take advantage of it! Expand your information, and explore your content. Post feedback from readers who've taken the time to respond to your efforts. If you start a controversy, run with it! And be sure to update your links to keep users from heading for nonexistent pages.

 CAUTION If nothing else will get you to update your Web site at least every couple of weeks, try this: People are now keeping track of non–updated sites, and you can expect to see lists of them appearing in Web pages shortly. They're called, appropriately, **cobweb sites**.

You should also keep your directory listings up to date.

Design, don't just present

Develop your own artistic muscles by changing the design of your Web pages. So maybe you aren't all that artistic, or you have two right brains when it comes to artistic skills. You do know what you like, right? You've seen Web pages that just jump out of the browser and catch your attention (and maybe your breath). Don't be afraid to borrow from the masters. Use your browser's View Source feature to see how they've used HTML to create the on-screen effects that you like. Adapt their techniques to match your own information. A page like figure 17.4, for example, might offer clues for your own designs.

Fig. 17.4
This page's dynamic use of text and graphics may be just the kind of design you'd like to emulate.

CAUTION It's very simple: don't plagiarize. The WWW is an open community of people who are more than happy to share their energies, resources, and ideas. If you blatantly borrow and fail to give credit where it's due, the Web community's wrath is also very swift. This is a virtual honor system, and you are expected to be an honor scout. It matters.

Asking yourself the right HTML questions

Writing *good* HTML is not only a smart practice, it'll save you time and effort down the road when new standards come along that will enforce some of the HTML concepts more stringently. Design your Web pages with the following tips in mind.

Do I know who my audience is?

It's not enough to create dazzling content. You have to anticipate your audience and how it will be using the World Wide Web and browsers. Anything you can do to make the experience more enjoyable for your whole audience will help make your Web pages stand out.

Some users love to cruise the Web by text only. They may be limited to text because they are using Lynx or some other text-based browser, or they may be using text only to zip around the Web at top speed. You can anticipate the needs of this crowd by providing a **front door** that they can use to go directly to a text-based version of the home page. Figure 17.5 shows an example of a commercial Web site that provides this service for Web users.

Fig. 17.5
Always remember to duplicate graphics–based hyperlinks with text versions if your Web page may have a mixed audience of readers.

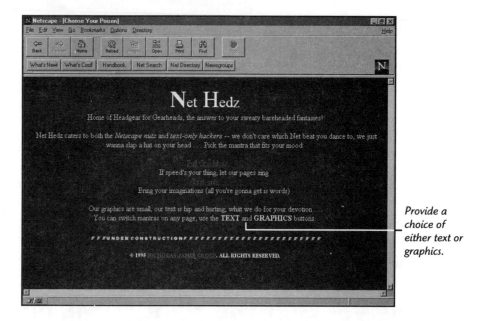

Provide a choice of either text or graphics.

Other users are on powerful systems with fast Internet connections, and they want as much color and flash as they can get. These users can be offered a **high graphics** version of the Web site if you've got lots of graphical content for them to browse.

Date stamping

Users should know how old your information is. There's just no point in making them search your Web pages looking for something new if it isn't there. If a page has a statement such as "Last revised 12/25/95," then users will know that you were diligently putting up new content on Christmas Day (which means you got a new modem for Christmas, you have no life, or your particular faith doesn't celebrate Christmas).

Some pages absolutely must have date stamps, such as those related to investment advice or other **real time** activities. Figure 17.6 shows one such page.

Fig. 17.6

Some day, editors may automate dates on your page like word processors do by using a variable that records the current date when you publish your pages in HTML format.

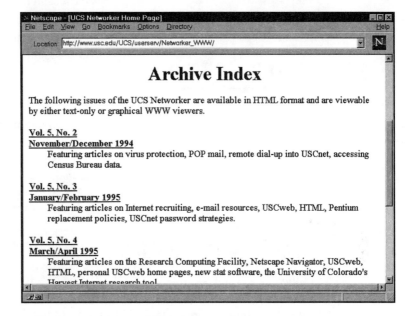

What's in a name?

Tell 'em who you are! Include your e-mail address somewhere on the page, and invite your users to contact you via e-mail. A signature can be as simple as an e-mail address (as in fig. 17.7) or as complex as a description of your job duties. As the author, signing your work is akin to signing a painting—it lets readers know who is responsible for the impressive work.

Signatures can be written into your head section with the <LINK> element. More commonly, authors provide a text hyperlink on-screen via a `mailto:` hyperlink that opens a mail form when clicked. Readers can send you feedback (congratulatory or not), and the message is sent directly to your mail box. Figure 17.7 shows both forms of signatures as they are written in HTML.

Fig. 17.7
<LINK> is rarely used by authors today, but may become more prominent in the future as other Internet services begin to access Web documents.

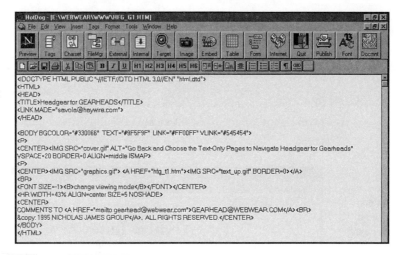

You might also consider including a link to your personal home page if the current Web page has a different type of content. If your Web page is providing information that might require some sort of verification of your authority on the subject, this is a handy way to present your background and qualifications. Many readers also just like to learn more about Web authors as a way to personalize their experience.

HTML's text entities

I've talked about the characters that HTML reserves for its own use, such as the *greater than* and *less than* symbols (also called the right angle bracket and left angle bracket characters). If you want to impress your non-English speaking audience and use characters like the accented *e*, take advantage of HTML's text entities. These are strings of characters (a string is just a short group of letters or words) that browsers interpret and display as special characters. You can use these characters either as their HTML entity definitions or by their standard **ISO Latin-1** character codes.

 Plain English, please!

> **ISO Latin-1** is an international definition that describes each character in the alphabet plus international characters as a 7-bit data value. Each character has a number that corresponds to its definition. For example, ISO Latin-1 value 169 is reserved for the copyright symbol (©). 🙶

CAUTION **Do not cut and paste special characters into your HTML editor** from other applications. Newer operating systems (such as Windows 95 and Macintosh System 7) use 8 bits of information to define each character. The Internet software that is the foundation for the World Wide Web (the HTTP protocol) is based on 7 bits and can't transmit 8-bit characters. HTTP and your computer use a little **bit shuffling** to convert the incoming and outgoing characters to the appropriate sizes.

Using HTML entities is easy. The standard format is

&*name*;

where *name* is the entity label or the ISO Latin-1 character number. Entities can be inserted into any normal line of text, as in figure 17.8.

Fig. 17.8
These entities can be used inside text style containers (like <PRE>) and enlarged with Netscape's <FONT SIZE> element.

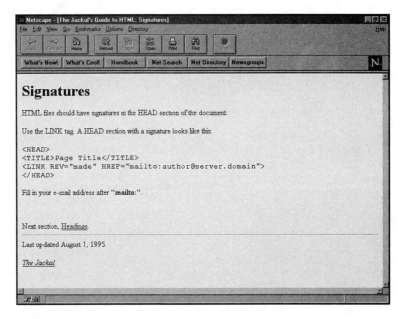

Character entities are especially useful for displaying non-keyboard and foreign language characters. Table 17.1 provides a complete list of HTML entities you can use.

 CAUTION **Text entities must be written in lowercase, or many browsers will** not be able to translate them properly.

Table 17.1 HTML Entities

Reserved HTML characters

&lt;	for < character
&gt;	for > character
&amp;	for & character " for " character
&reg;	Netscape 1.0 extension, for registered trademark symbol
&copy;	Netscape 1.0 extension, for copyright symbol

Accented characters

&AElig;	for capital AE diphthong (ligature)	&Icirc;	for capital I, circumflex accent
&Aacute;	for capital A, acute accent	&Igrave;	for capital I, grave accent
&Acirc;	for capital A, circumflex accent	&Iuml;	for capital I, dieresis or umlaut mark
&Agrave;	for capital A, grave accent	&Ntilde;	for capital N, tilde
&Aring;	for capital A, ring	&Oacute;	for capital O, acute accent
&Atilde;	for capital A, tilde	&Ocirc;	for capital O, circumflex accent
&Auml;	for capital A, dieresis or umlaut mark	&Ograve;	for capital O, grave accent
&Ccedil;	for capital C, cedilla	&Oslash;	for capital O, slash
&ETH;	for capital Eth, Icelandic	&Otilde;	for capital O, tilde
&Eacute;	for capital E, acute accent	&Ouml;	for capital O, dieresis or umlaut mark
&Ecirc;	for capital E, circumflex accent	&THORN;	for capital THORN, Icelandic
&Egrave;	for capital E, grave accent	&Uacute;	for capital U, acute accent
&Euml;	for capital E, dieresis or umlaut mark	&Ucirc;	for capital U, circumflex accent
&Iacute;	for capital I, acute accent	&Ugrave;	for capital U, grave accent

Accented characters

&Uuml;	for capital U, dieresis or umlaut mark	&igrave;	for small i, grave accent
&Yacute;	for capital Y, acute accent	&iuml;	for small i, dieresis or umlaut mark
&aacute;	for small a, acute accent	&ntilde;	for small n, tilde
&acirc;	for small a, circumflex accent	&oacute;	for small o, acute accent
&aelig;	for small ae diphthong (ligature)	&ocirc;	for small o, circumflex accent
&agrave;	for small a, grave accent	&ograve;	for small o, grave accent
&aring;	for small a, ring	&oslash;	for small o, slash
&atilde;	for small a, tilde	&otilde;	for small o, tilde
&auml;	for small a, dieresis or umlaut mark	&ouml;	for small o, dieresis or umlaut mark
&ccedil;	for small c, cedilla	&szlig;	for small sharp s, German (sz ligature)
&eacute;	for small e, acute accent	&thorn;	for small thorn, Icelandic
&ecirc;	for small e, circumflex accent	&uacute;	for small u, acute accent
&egrave;	for small e, grave accent	&ucirc;	for small u, circumflex accent
&eth;	for small eth, Icelandic	&ugrave;	for small u, grave accent
&euml;	for small e, dieresis or umlaut mark	&uuml;	for small u, dieresis or umlaut mark
&iacute;	for small i, acute accent	&yacute;	for small y, acute accent
&icirc;	for small i, circumflex accent	&yuml;	for small y, dieresis or umlaut mark

Netscape provides two additional non-standard character entities: the registered trademark symbol, ® (defined as ®), and the copyright symbol, © (defined as ©). These entities are supported by a number of browsers, even those that are not strictly considered Netscape-compatible. HTML can also show these symbols using their ISO Latin-1 characters: ™ for the registered trademark symbol and © for the copyright symbol.

Text Doesn't Have to Be Boring

● **In this chapter:**

- **Create dynamic page titles**

- **Using lists for all kinds of information**

- **How should horizontal rules be used?**

- **Linking internally**

- **How to create navigational text links**

- **How can I control on-screen font sizes?**

Graphics dominate the World Wide Web, and sound and video are appearing on more sites every day. But good old text still gets the point across, and with creative HTML work, it need not look dull . . . . ▶

Your first fifteen minutes on the Internet will make you realize that the Web relies primarily on text to communicate the majority of its information. But no one will read a poorly designed Web page when there are millions of others to choose from. The number one goal of all successful HTML authors is to entice viewers—to lure an audience into their tangled archives of information. The tips and tricks in this chapter will help you construct seductive Web pages.

 TIP Some of the WWW's most appealing documents stretch the programming rules outlined up to this point in order to create personal, artistic pages. The Web doesn't have to be your canvas for masterful self-expression and explosive prose, but—with a few hints here and there—you will find that it's easy to apply a personal flair to the web you build.

Even titles can be dynamic

One of the more conservative "rules" of the Web mandates short, descriptive page titles. What this rule fails to tell you is that most WWW browsers will recognize multiple <TITLE> values in a head section. After displaying the first value (or character) in the document window, browsers repeatedly insert the next available value until the last available setting is found and displayed.

The result? Animated titles of course! By choosing your title values carefully, you can create many different textual effects, such as scrolling headings (see listing 18.1).

Listing 18.1   Creating Animated Titles

```
<TITLE>!</TITLE>
<TITLE>o!</TITLE>
<TITLE>lo!</TITLE>
<TITLE>llo!</TITLE>
<TITLE>ello!</TITLE>
<TITLE>Hello!</TITLE>
```

The result of this somewhat tedious manipulation of the <TITLE> element is that the word "Hello!" scrolls in from the left of the browser's window title bar. To construct a title that scrolls onto the screen from the right, complete the alterations to the pattern shown in listing 18.2.

Listing 18.2   Animated Title That Scrolls from the Right

```
<TITLE>     H</TITLE>
<TITLE>    He</TITLE>
<TITLE>   Hel</TITLE>
<TITLE>  Hell</TITLE>
<TITLE> Hello</TITLE>
<TITLE>Hello!</TITLE>
```

The first line has five blanks before the H, the second line four blanks, the third three, the fourth two, the fifth one, and the sixth none. Your document's title will now scroll into an area that is six spaces wide.

Do you remember the Nike television commercial in which promoters flashed a series of individual words on the screen to create associations and visual imagery for the viewers? You can do something similar with your Web page title (see listing 18.3).

Listing 18.3   Flashing Words in the Title

```
<TITLE>THIS</TITLE>
<TITLE>IS</TITLE>
<TITLE>MY</TITLE>
<TITLE>HOME</TITLE>
<TITLE>PAGE</TITLE>
<TITLE>!!!!!</TITLE>
<TITLE> </TITLE>
<TITLE>s W</TITLE>
<TITLE>'s Wo</TITLE>
<TITLE>m's Wor</TITLE>
<TITLE>om's Worl</TITLE>
<TITLE>Tom's World</TITLE>
```

The commands in listing 18.3 instruct browsers to flash the words "THIS IS MY HOME PAGE !!!!!!" one at a time on-screen. Then, like a curtain opening, the text "Tom's World" is revealed from the center, extending out to both sides of the title bar.

 Q&A *Can HTML editors format titles to appear on the screen as if a word processor was entering the text directly onto the title bar?*

To accomplish this scrolling effect, insert the same commands as those in listing 18.2, but place the blanks spaces after the characters instead of before them. Better yet, leave the spaces out entirely. This process displays the title's text as if you were typing it directly into the browser's window box.

TIP **If you want to experiment with multiple lines of text in your title,** try this. Insert <TITLE> values in the middle of your body section so that, as the Web page is being retrieved, alternating values replace the title as they are read. This is a fun way to play with your readers who are loading pages with lots of graphics or text content.

Using lists for greatest effect

As a Web author, think of lists as a sure thing. Practically every browser, either graphical or text-based, uses the same on-screen formatting for these elements.

Lists allow users to combine and manipulate a variety of screen styles for eye-catching effects. Numbered lists are somewhat more limited in the roles they play for viewers (after all, numbered items inherently possess fairly solid hierarchical connotations). Bulleted and defining lists are more useful for presenting information and content in new and interesting ways.

Figure 18.1 shows how to use definition lists for on-screen formatting, and figure 18.2 shows how a browser, such as Netscape, displays them.

Fig. 18.1
It can be effective in HTML to put other HTML elements (like text styles or lists) inside definition lists.

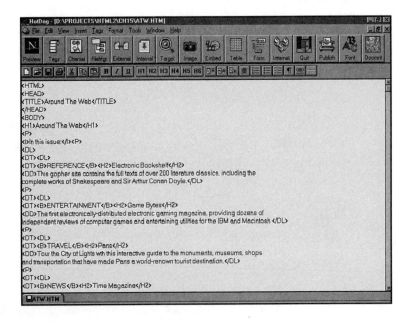

Fig. 18.2
Make sure that you close each definition list with the **</DL>** tag to avoid letting your on-screen formatting run amok.

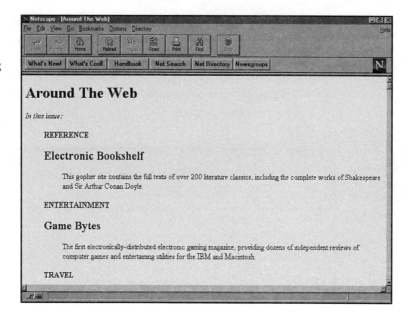

Here's what horizontal rules are really about

World Wide Web artists use horizontal rules (straight lines across the page) to separate anything and everything that appears in their documents. Rules provide white space, disjoin text and graphics, and separate ideas in a concrete fashion. More and more browsers are able to display rules of different widths and heights, and, consequently, more and more Web pages are surfacing with monstrous stylistic problems.

It's time to step back and take a look at horizontal rules from a creative and functional perspective. You should have a specific purpose in mind when you insert a rule in your Web pages. Consider not only what horizontal rules represent, but also what effect they have in your Web pages.

What horizontal rules represent

A horizontal rule represents a separation, a change of direction or of subject, a new beginning, a shifting of gears. Rules can represent (in a fictional context) the passage of time or a change of location, but whatever the association, one thing is clear: horizontal rules tell the reader to consider the content that follows as something new and different.

CAUTION **As an author, you can use the horizontal rule element to create** Web pages with well-divided content, but be careful—an overuse of rules can have a negative effect (as in fig. 18.3). An overabundance of dividing lines masks the document's content and makes the separating force meaningless. To avoid catastrophe, remember that everything on your page must be there for a purpose.

Fig. 18.3
This online catalog uses horizontal rules too much; they just don't have a clear function.

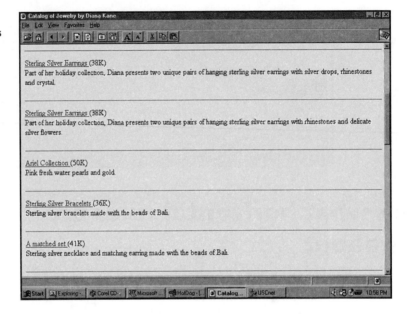

How do you make sure your readers pay attention to your horizontal rules? By establishing a clear logic to their use. Plan how they will function in your pages and stick to your guns—don't randomly break your own rules about rules.

After establishing some regulatory guidelines, survey your work with a critical aesthetic eye. Ask questions like the following:

* Does it make sense to use three rules for every section break?

* Are double underlined headings appropriate or necessary?

* Have you switched gears, changed ideas, or begun a new point?

* Is the structural layout of your page in relation to your use of horizontal rules aesthetically pleasing?

Your own taste and sense of what works should steer you away from the kinds of errors that are far too common on the Web.

Some of the effects of good horizontal rules

Horizontal rules may be used to show that an area on the page is not part of the flow of information. They're similar to the sidebars (shaded boxes) you have seen in this book. An online sidebar might look like the one in figure 18.4.

Fig. 18.4
You can combine line breaks with horizontal rules to help create the illusion of a text sidebar.

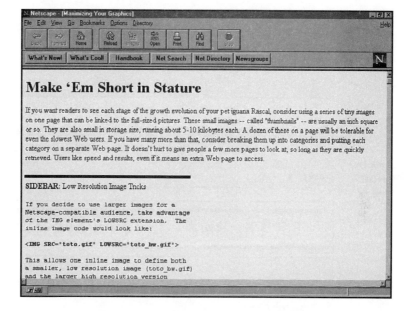

Another interesting opportunity to use rules surfaces when you are creating navigation buttons at the bottom of a page with text and graphic links (as in fig. 18.5).

Two or more horizontal rules can also be used together to create a graphic banner across the browser window. Using Netscape's extensions, banners may be displayed with one or two rules, as in figure 18.6.

Fig. 18.5
Text navigation links
can be made to look
buttonlike, or they can
have a style all their
own.

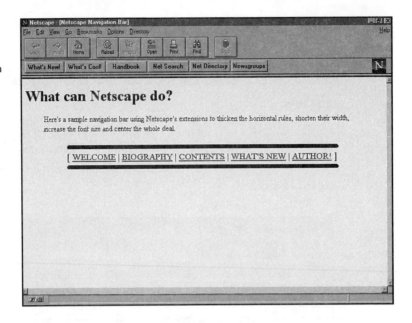

Fig. 18.6
Netscape's extensions
give the user control
over how horizontal
rules look and feel.

Power to the hyperlink!

A well-designed hyperlink (which you explored in Chapter 9) jumps right out at you and clearly identifies its destination. But in your efforts to spin the perfect Web, don't overdo your use of links: too many and you'll create a lot of noise that drowns out your readers' enthusiasm for your content. Worse, it practically begs your readers to leave your site for greener pastures (the page you haven't clicked on always seems better than the one you're reading).

 TIP **The key to any effective link is to balance the possible detours for** a reader's attention with the material in your Web page. Try to place links at the end of thoughts, not smack dab in the middle, so that the progression from your idea to the link reference and back is natural.

Let your readers navigate link by link

Web pages don't have built-in navigation capabilities. Instead, browsers provide buttons and keyboard shortcuts that move users forward and backward along the pages they've already visited. As a WWW author, it's up to you to create navigation links inside your own pages to simplify how people read and find your information.

Navigational links should provide a means of doing the following:

- Moving back to the page that comes before the current page
- Going forward to the next page
- Returning to the main page
- Acquiring help or other information about the Web page or you (the author)
- Sending an e-mail message to you
- Reaching other Web pages with similar information

Figure 18.7 shows a few of the ways that simple horizontal lists of text links can be written to resemble button-like interfaces.

Fig. 18.7
Navigation links should
be grouped together
in a browser window.
Consider using hori-
zontal rules to separate
them from the rest of
the information on the
page.

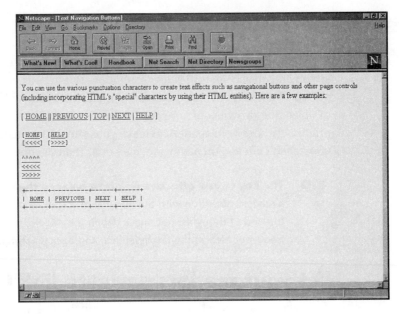

TIP When creating text links, avoid specific references to the linking
action. For instance, stay away from using the phrase "click here" to indicate
a link. Users can see that there is a link, so focus on its destination instead.

Do I have any control over font sizes?

Netscape extensions give you control over how large or small text looks on-
screen. The *value* is either an actual text size (one through seven) or relative
to the normal size of the body text (from +4 down to −4).

    <FONT SIZE=value>

To change the entire document's basic font size, use the Netscape extension
<BASEFONT SIZE=*value*>. Again, the *value* can range from one through
seven (the standard browser text size is three).

Text control enhances pages for users with Netscape-compatible browsers.
Use the <FONT SIZE> to do the following:

- To use small capital letters in your text, just capitalize all of the body
  text and raise the first letter of each capitalized word by +1.

- To use large initial capital letters, set the value of the first letter to five or six, depending on how large you want the first letter to be.

- Create the effect of approaching text by beginning with a font size of one and increasing each letter by one until all of the remaining text is in size seven.

- Create a receding text effect by setting all of the text to size seven, then reducing the size of the end letters by one until the last letter is size one.

Figure 18.8 shows a document using different text effects. Remember, these are only visible for readers using Netscape-compatible browsers.

Fig. 18.8

Don't get too elaborate with your text. A single effect at the appropriate time will have much more impact than a Web page loaded with all sorts of text effects (which only shows that you lack a critical eye).

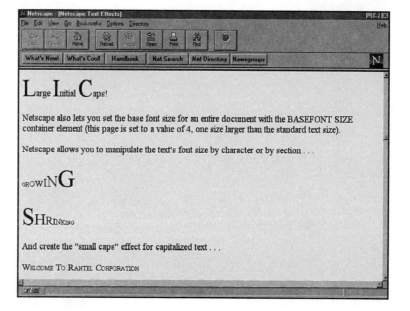

19

Maximize Your Graphics

● **In this chapter:**

- ● **Keep your pictures clear**

- ● **The size of the graphics matters**

- ● **Making interlaced and transparent GIFs**

- ● **You can even use pictures of text**

- ● **Create graphics that help with navigation**

Communicating graphically is both fun and challenging. Graphics can help eliminate the problems of global communication, but they can do much more as well . . . . ❯

When the World Wide Web appeared on the Internet a few years ago, users applauded the medium's potential for worldwide communication. Soon thereafter, users began to realize that *mis*communication could result as well. Part of the problem was that Web pages had text, and because they logged in from all over the world, not all Web users knew the same language. Then, as graphics became more commonplace, users started to see the value of visual representation (signs) as accurate and persuasive communicative devices.

You can insert images and icons in your WWW document in much the same way that you manipulate hypertext links. Both imagery and linking act as physical representations that condense text by replacing it with a smaller visual clue or keyword. But be careful: dependence on a visual medium to communicate messages and intentions is tricky and can cause serious comprehension problems for your audience.

Figures 19.1 and 19.2 display some of the hazards that surface with the use of graphical communication: users can become lost and bored, and may eventually tune out a confusing Web site entirely.

Fig. 19.1
RezN8's home page is aesthetically pleasing and professional, but confusing for the first time reader. What do the icons do?

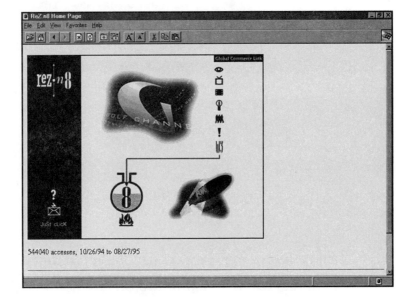

Fig. 19.2
This tour of the book store is artistically competent, including the beautiful 3-D navigation tool, but clicking the various visual perspectives does nothing. So what's the point?

Choose your images for clarity

Any graphics contained within your personal Web space must reflect a common set of functions whose meanings are clear on a more or less universal basis—a challenge for novice and expert alike. Thankfully, WWW authors have access to international organizations that define the meanings commonly assigned to regional and global symbols, such as the question mark.

TIP　Most users will understand that clicking a graphical button containing a question mark will transport them to a Help page.

Only the most effective visual codes can successfully send the same message to each individual reader. For this reason, many images and image maps provide complimentary text labels that provide readers with written instructions. Figures 19.3 and 19.4 display World Wide Web pages that combine images with text to ensure clarity.

Fig. 19.3

The home page of Magnet Interactive Studios uses text and related graphics to ensure the clarity of their functions.

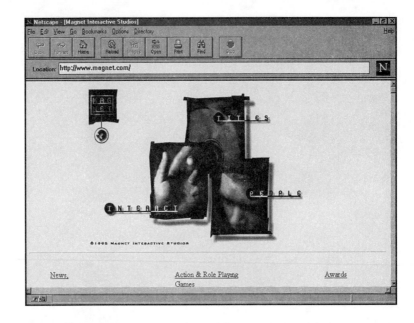

Fig. 19.4

The Microsoft Network's home page represents another successful combination of text and images.

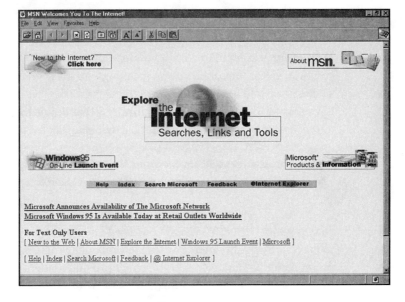

Clarity makes or breaks your WWW success. Confusing pages are tossed aside as quickly as they appear in favor of other, more effective sites. As you create your Web pages and the images that will be used on-screen, focus on how well components act together to make your ideas and intentions clear. If you have any doubts about the functions or harmony of your icons, add descriptive prose to the image for clarity.

What about the size of the graphics of my pages?

Among other things, the World Wide Web is a mass distributor of images. Art portfolios, photo journals, and concert shots clog the Web and often trap users while anxiously downloading half a megabyte of graphics. Graphic archives do serve a functional purpose on the Web, but the organization and distribution of these typically large sites often leave something to be desired.

How then can you distribute large graphic files without losing your somewhat impatient audience? How can an online art gallery post its latest show on the Web? How can a real estate broker give you a proof sheet for each home listing? The answer is simple: use smaller images. There are two measurements of size on the WWW: the amount of the screen that an image consumes, and the storage space it claims.

Make the picture smaller

All that any WWW user can hope for is speed and results, and if possible, speedy results. To facilitate this dominating need for rapid efficiency, consider inserting small **thumbnail** images on a page that link to other WWW documents that contain the full-sized graphics.

 Plain English, please!

Thumbnails are tiny graphical representations that link to a full screen reproduction of the initial image. Thumbnails are usually 2–3 cm square and run about 5–10 kilobytes each in storage size. Even the slowest Web user can tolerate 10–12 thumbnails on a single Web page, but if you have many more than 12, consider breaking them up into categories with a separate Web page devoted to each. Figure 19.5 shows how the "Travels with Samantha" Web site uses thumbnails as links to the corresponding full-sized images.

Fig. 19.5

This travel site presents over 220 full-sized JPEG images as inline thumbnails, allowing readers to retrieve only the full-sized images they want to see.

Make 'em a lower resolution

If you decide to use larger images for a Netscape-compatible audience, take advantage of the IMG element's LOWSRC extension. The inline image code would look like the following:

```
<IMG SRC="toto.gif" LOWSRC="toto_bw.gif">
```

This coding allows one inline image to define both a smaller, low resolution image (`toto_bw.gif`) and the larger, high resolution version (`toto.gif`) of the same image.

On the first pass through, Netscape-compatible browsers load the image defined by the LOWSRC attribute. After all the low resolution images and body text have been loaded, browsers return to the IMG element and load all images defined by the SRC statement. This dual process allows users to see the better looking image after first getting an idea of the page's content.

The low resolution extension also allows users to select a link without waiting for all of the page's images to be loaded. Browsers that do not support LOWSRC will ignore the Netscape extension.

Trick #1: Use black and white LOWSRC images and color SRC images to make the low resolution images load lightning fast.

Trick #2: Define the LOWSRC image as the first step in a two-image sequence. For instance, if the LOWSRC image was a genie lamp, the SRC image could be the genie lamp with smoke pouring out of it. When the Web page loads, first the lamp loads, then the browser retrieves the lamp with smoke right on top of the first image, adding a dynamic element to your Web page.

Trick #3: Define the LOWSRC image as a background image, like a blurred picture. Create the SRC image smaller than the LOWSRC graphic. When the SRC image loads, the LOWSRC file will act as a background border underneath the SRC image. (Alternatively, create the SRC with a drop shadow and a transparent background to make it look three-dimensional in the browser window.)

Put 'em in smaller files

As you must realize by now, smaller images mean faster retrieval. An Internet surfer of even the most minimal experience quickly comes to appreciate compact and concise graphics for the speed and efficiency they bring to the Web. To minimize the size of your graphics, consider using JPEG formatting. JPEG coding compresses images to one-third or one-fifth of the total size of GIF styles.

 CAUTION **Before converting all of your larger GIF files to JPEG format,** remember that during compression, JPEG removes the information it perceives as the least important to the image's final quality. The higher the compression, the greater the loss, which creates the potential for patterns to appear in solid or gradient colors.

To further reduce the size of your images, highlight your graphics with only a limited number of colors. Every image you create has a **palette** of colors that may be added for animation and aesthetic appeal. GIF files support palettes of up to 256 colors, while JPEG files have access to over 16 million different shades.

By removing the palette entries for colors that do not appear in your graphic image, you can reduce the amount of file space reserved for the palette information. Limiting your images to fewer colors (64 or 100 for GIFs and 1–2000 for JPEGs) dramatically reduces the size of your images. Programs like Photoshop, Paint Shop Pro, and xv give you control over the palette information of your graphic files.

Creating interlaced and transparent GIF graphics

Because HTML offers only limited manipulation and handling of graphics, more advanced image applications must occur before the file hits the Web server. The creation of both interlaced GIFs and transparent GIFs require such special handling from external sources.

With interlacing, a browser displays the graphical image in stages, presenting the file information to the reader as soon as it is read. The image revealed to the user displays a "horizontal blinds" effect, with pieces of the picture folding over one another as if slatted blinds were being closed.

Users might also see interlaced images as low-resolution, chunky graphics that refine themselves with each successive pass. This is somewhat like watching a blurry slide come into focus with an automatic slide projector. Figure 19.6 shows the horizontal blind effect.

Fig. 19.6
The larger the file size, the longer the browser takes to retrieve the file and show it "in focus."

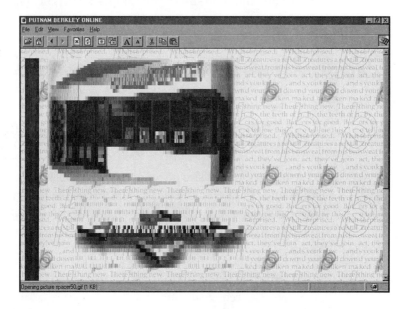

Transparency is available with GIF89a formatting but remains nonfunctional with the original GIF87a standard. To construct transparent images, assign one of the palette colors to the background of your GIF89a file as a transparent channel. When a GIF89a compatible browser loads the file, the transparent portions of the image will be replaced by the information behind them (often the color of the background or the background bitmap). Transparency constructs graphics that float on top of the background and are not defined by a standard square picture frame (fig. 19.7).

❝ *Plain English, please!*

GIF89a is one of many graphics formats. Most graphics programs let you create graphics in GIF89a format or convert other types to GIF89a. GIF89a offers special features, including transparency. **❞**

Fig. 19.7
Every instance of the transparent palette entry will show through to the background, so do not choose a color that is found in the graphic itself.

Graphics can be saved as GIF89a files using a graphic tool, such as Lview Pro or xv. Separate utilities, like the Mac's Transparency and GIF converter programs, function solely to create transparent images.

Consider transforming your text into graphics

Although you, as a Web artist, have little control over how browsers will display your font applications, **pictures of text** add a stimulating effect to the visual display of information. "Pictures of text" are really just graphics files—you create fancy text in a graphics program and save it as a graphics file. Figure 19.8 displays text that has been inserted in the Web document as a graphical image.

Fig. 19.8
The text effect simply adds the "Q" highlight and a larger text font to make the form question easy to recognize and read.

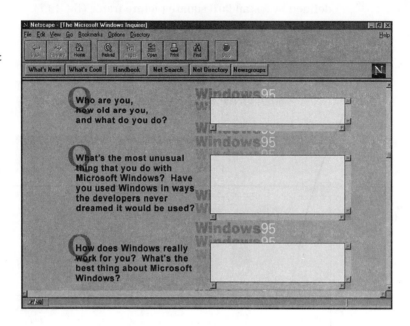

CAUTION **Inserting pictures of text raises some vital considerations** concerning display capacity and image size.

First, text-only browsers will display only the ALT text string—and that's *if* and *only if* it is supplied by the Web author. Remember that using pictures of text may diminish a large portion of your potential audience.

Second, the extended retrieval time required by pictures of text can be unappealing (to say the least). To solve this problem, keep the number of colors in your text and enhancements to five or so, and use transparency to let the background shine through around your text graphic. Be careful to keep the width of your images small enough for all browsers to display— usually no wider than 400 pixels.

Give your readers some buttons to navigate by

Most Web authors allow their readers to move smoothly from page to page within their personal archives by inserting the necessary navigational tools. However, Web authors rarely provide navigational tools that direct readers to new Web locations—somewhere they've not yet visited. To add to your readers World Wide Web enjoyment, use graphic and textual representations to link to your main page, to subdirectory pages, and even to e-mail or special interest pages.

TIP **Navigation graphics provide authors with the freedom to pick** and choose which controls will appear on which pages while ordering and aligning them in any number of ways. Figure 19.9 displays a WWW page with separate navigation graphics.

Fig. 19.9
These navigation graphics may be aligned horizontally or vertically (using line or paragraph breaks).

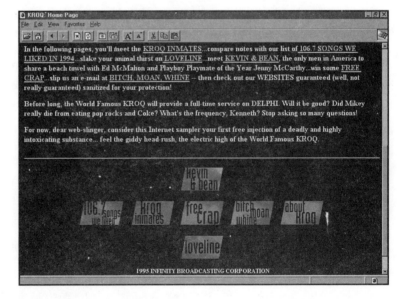

There are an abundance of navigation-style icons and buttons available for public use on the World Wide Web. Refer to Appendix B for a list of graphic resources on the Web. Figure 19.10 shows a Web page that provides a navigation image map.

Fig. 19.10

Using image maps as navigational tools allows users to stray from the typical "square button syndrome" to a more whimsical style that incorporates text and composite graphics within the Web page.

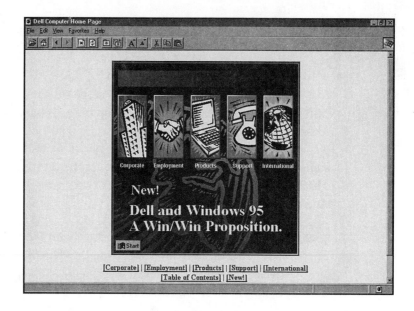

The visual world proposes a graphical means of communication that is as vast and explicative as any human language. Thus, just as we maximize our World Wide Web textual language, we must also maximize the language of our images in order to create a clearly functional site. After all, with a few basic instructions, anyone can create a standard World Wide Web page, but it's the added flair and the special touches that form exceptional documents.

20

Make Your Pages Move!

● **In this chapter:**

● **How pictures "move" on the Web**

● **Types of animation supported by Web browsers**

● **Using a Perl CGI program for server-push animation**

● **How to incorporate other animation or video files**

Pictures are nice, but pictures that move are even better. While you're not about to re-create Snow White, your Web pages can have a degree of animation and in doing so can capture your reader's attention . . . . ▶

Over the past twenty years, television and film have become society's most applauded forms of entertainment, virtually replacing the written and spoken word (books and story telling, respectively). So when the World Wide Web arrived on the Internet scene a few years ago, its promise of a multimedia experience appealed to users who were anxious for a dynamic, graphic-based version of the Net.

There's only one problem: the WWW doesn't do motion pictures very well.

How do animated images work?

The technology behind motion pictures is based on a natural phenomenon called **persistence of vision:** a series of still images shown one after another (as rapidly as possible) imprints a kind of continuity between the objects in the pictures. The result is a perceived sense of movement between images. Creating persistence of vision requires technology that can zip through a lengthy series of pictures at a steady pace.

Unfortunately, the World Wide Web cannot perform anywhere near the acceptable speed standards for persistence of vision. Even a 1K image requires almost half a second of transfer time using the fastest connections available. So what can the WWW do to provide dynamic, moving content? The Web supports two kinds of animation—**pull animation** and **server-push animation**—while linking to other animated media (such as digital video files).

 CAUTION Only a few browsers can show Web-based animated sequences—those that are Netscape-compatible, such as Netscape Navigator, OS/2 Warp's Web Explorer, and Microsoft's Internet Explorer. Fortunately for animators, these three browsers command most of the browser market.

Using pull animation

Creating pull animation is the easiest form of moving pictures on the Web. All it takes is a little artistic ability and some new HTML commands in your Web pages.

Remember when you were a kid and you could get little booklets with multiple drawings, each slightly different, of the same figure? You'd flip the pages quickly, and the figure would appear to move. Basically, that's what pull animation does, although at a much slower rate.

Pull animation relies on the reader's browser to retrieve each animation page one after another via commands to the software. Instead of the seamless, smooth movement we have come to expect from television and motion picture animation (TV operates at 30 frames per second; movies are slightly slower), images are displayed a few seconds apart. The result is slow animation that does not place a constant drain on the Web server that delivers its pages.

Creating pull animation pages

The first thing you need to create pull animation pages is a set of figures that represent an animation sequence, such as a moving sports car (see fig. 20.1). These images should be in JPEG or GIF format.

Fig. 20.1
The car is a 3-D object that moves along a path in a 3-D program. Taking a screen capture at each position produces the entire sequence as GIF files. Combining this series of images in the proper sequence will create the illusion of the car driving towards you.

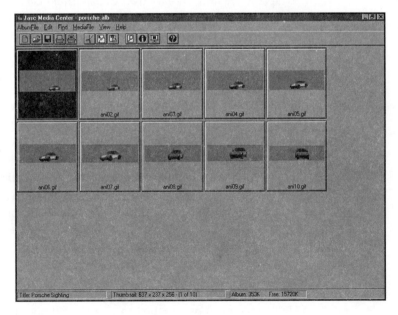

Plain English, please!

A **screen capture** is a picture of the text and images that appear on your browser screen at any given time. Utility programs (such as Nikon) and commercial software alike (Paint Shop Pro), allow you to choose the image's file format and color palette and save the screen's contents as a file on your hard drive. More advanced programs can even keep track of a screen capture sequence—assigning such names as car1.gif, car2.gif, car3.gif, and so on—as you *shoot* and *reshoot* the on-screen images.

Next, create a separate Web page for each image. Make sure that you place each image's HTML reference in exactly the same place on each HTML page. If you want the animation to travel across or down the screen, control the image's progression across the page with <P> paragraph tags or invisible **spacer GIFs**.

 Plain English, please!

A **spacer GIF** is a very small GIF file that doesn't actually show anything. Spacers are invisible—save them as transparent GIF89a images so that the page's background shows through. You can create a spacer with any graphic program that supports the GIF89a format, such as Lview Pro.

Using the META element

Finally, add a META statement to the HEAD section of each Web page (for more META information, refer to Chapter 5). The META statement instructs the browser to finish downloading the current Web page, wait a specific length of time, and retrieve the next Web page in the animated sequence. The last page in the sequence doesn't require a META statement, although you may include one to tell the browser to download an alternative site.

```
<HEAD>
<TITLE>My Animation</TITLE>
<META HTTP-EQUIV=REFRESH CONTENT="1;
 URL=http://hostname/directory/filename">
</HEAD>
```

This META statement orders the browser to wait one second after loading the current page and before retrieving the next (**http://hostname/directory/filename**). Users can control how long the browser waits by replacing the one with a larger number—for smooth animation, set the value to zero.

Try to keep your animation files small enough to prevent impatient readers from pulling the switch on your site. Anticipate that someone might stop the animation (by accident of course), and include a link to the main Web page on each animation document.

Using server-push animation

Server-push animation instructs Web servers to send a continuous stream of animation data to the browser. This **live feed** of graphics creates smooth animation, but mandates an **open** data connection between server and browser. Such demand places considerable stress on the Internet pipeline (the wires that carry information between the browser and the Web server) and the server itself, so it's best not to overuse it.

When many users connect to the same Web server, clogging the connection's pipeline route, your animation may start to break up or **stutter**. As authors, you cannot prevent this, but you can limit it by keeping the animated series as short as possible and reducing the size of each animated picture.

 Plain English, please!

The **Internet pipeline** includes all of the wiring and data transmission that make up the physical Internet network. These consist of long-distance phone lines, fiber-optic data cables, satellite relay transmissions, even your twin-pair phone cable that attaches to your computer's modem. This pipeline carries all the information that extends across the Internet. If users move too much information simultaneously on the same wires, the system bogs down and everyone has to wait longer to get data. **"**

Using CGI to animate your graphics

With server-push animation, CGI (Common Gateway Interface) applications control the animation GIF files. Using CGI scripting languages to create WWW forms is discussed in detail throughout Chapter 15, but sending continuous animation files also falls on CGI turf. See Chapter 15 for an in-depth discussion of CGI.

Perl, C, and Visual Basic are the most common programming languages for CGI scripting. Perl scripting for server-push animation is written and distributed freely, and can be accessed from the Server-Push with Perl archive at **http://www.romantasy.com/test/server_push.html**. Feel free to use this scripting for your own animation.

The two main files that control server-push animation are called cycleimages.pl and ci_config.pl. The file cycleimages.pl distributes a series of GIF images in a continuous stream to the reader's Web browser, creating the animated sequence. The ci config.pl file lists this GIF file s equence. When specifying your graphic sequence, use your own GIF file names so that the cycleimages script will know which graphics to access.

Installing the Perl files

The first step for Perl installation is to ensure that your provider's server computer supports Perl scripting (Version 5 is the most common) and that its HTTP configuration allows animation to run. The only way to know these things is to check with your systems administrator or your Internet service provider or to read the documentation (which is usually on the Web itself) for your Web server program.

 TIP **If you receive access or data type errors when attempting to view** your server-push animation pages, contact your provider's customer support (or your system administrator if you are on a company network). The server administrator will alter either the server's configuration or the configuration of your personal Web account, creating full animation support.

The next step in Perl installation is to cut and paste the lines of animation code, found at the server-push animation WWW site, into two text files. (When saving these files, make sure that you select the ASCII or Text Only option from the file format list.)

Place the text-only script files in your Web account's public directory (often called public_html), and make them group-executable (using the chmod command in UNIX, for example). Ask your systems people for help with this. Depending on the nature of your WWW account, your server provider's support staff may have to make the files group-executable for you—contact them if you are not familiar with this process.

Now edit the ci_config.pl file (see Listing 20.2) to point to the directory on your Web account where you have uploaded your animation GIF files; make sure the correct GIF file names are listed on the line that begins @IMAGES.

Listing 20.1 is the cycleimages.pl file.

Listing 20.1   The cycleimages.pl Code

```perl
#!/usr/local/bin/perl
#cycleimages.pl
# " 1995 Brian Valente, all rights reserved
# You may freely copy this script, so long as this copyright
# statement is intact
# a simple little server push script in Perl

require ("ci_config.pl");

#Misc Constants
$TRUE=1;
$FALSE=0;

#Server push constants

$HEADER="Content-type: multipart/x-mixed-replace;
boundary=ThisRandomString\n";
$RANDOMSTRING="\n--ThisRandomString\n";
$ENDSTRING="\n--ThisRandomString--\n";
$CTSTRING="Content-type: image/gif\n\n";

$Continue=$TRUE;

$Counter=0;

$MaxImages=@IMAGES;

####################################
print(STDOUT $HEADER);
print (STDOUT $RANDOMSTRING);
while ($Continue){
     sleep($SLEEP_TIME);
     print (STDOUT $CTSTRING);
     if (open(FHandle,
"$IMAGE_PATH$DELIM$IMAGES[$Counter]")){
          while (<FHandle>){
               print;
          }
          print (STDOUT $RANDOMSTRING);
          close(FHandle);
```

continues

Listing 20.1   Continued

```
                # reset counter to 1 if at max # images,
           otherwise increment counter
                if (($Counter+1) < $MaxImages){
                    $Counter=$Counter+1;
                } else {
                    $Counter=0; # reset counter
                }
                # $Counter = (1) ? ($Counter >= ($MaxImages-1)) :
         $Counter++;
            } else {
            $Continue=$FALSE;
            }
        }
```

The ci_config.pl file is shown in listing 20.2

Listing 20.2   The ci_config.pl Code

```perl
#!/usr/local/bin/perl
#ci_config.pl
# These are the only variables you will need to edit
# to make cycleimages.pl work!

# path to image files (assumes all images are in the same
# directory)
# (notice there's no end slash - keep it that way!)

$IMAGE_PATH="/home/ftp/pub/<your_login_name>/public_html";

# how many seconds delay between displaying images
# (1 sec. is usually good)

$SLEEP_TIME=1;

# path delimiter for portability
("/" for UNIX, "\" for DOS, Windows, and ":" for Mac)

$DELIM="/";

# list all images in array
# using the format "filname1.gif", "filename2.gif", and so on.
# your image files MUST be gif format!!
# you images must also be in the same directory (see above)

@IMAGES=("logotest1.gif","logotest2.gif","logotest3.gif",
 "logotest4.gif", "logotest5.gif");
1; #indicates successful finish
```

Now that your scripts and GIF files are finally in place, it's time to add animation to the page. Figures 20.2 and 20.3 show what happens when the Perl script is used to animate a graphic.

TIP **When running a Perl script from a Web page, pretend that you are** loading an image in HTML using the <IMG SRC=> tag. For example, if the script is located in the directory **www.haywire.com/website/logo/**, the HTML reference would be **<IMG SRC="http://www.haywire.com/ website/logo/cycleimages.pl">** (see fig. 20.2).

Fig. 20.2
Perl-based animation uses the inline image element to display the animated images in your Web pages.

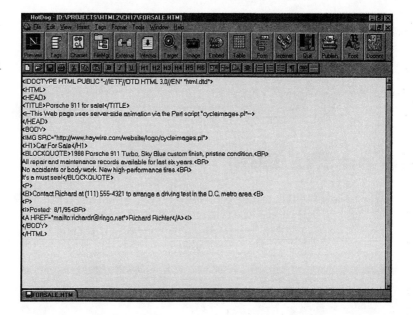

For a live example of service-push animation using cycleimages.pl, see the Web site at **http://www.romantasy.com/test/server_push.html**.

Fig. 20.3
Initial access to this site prompts the Porsche to drive towards the viewer, where it then remains in this static position.

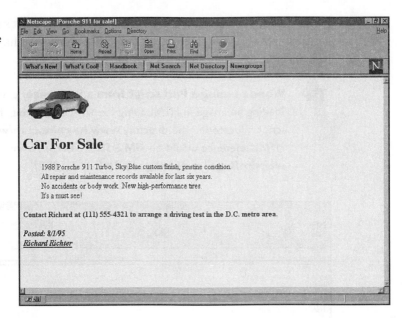

Video on the Web

Although video applications on the World Wide Web remain limited, digital video clips provide users with a similar but small-scale experience. Hyperlinks to digital video files in Web pages allow readers to download

What about other animation formats?

Many multimedia programs on the market today support the creation of animation files. Some of the more common include Autodesk Animator (which creates FLI animation files), Macromedia Director (which makes MMM director application files), and Asymetrix ToolBook or Multimedia ToolBook (which create TBK ToolBook application files).

You can easily run these programs on your personal computer using basic software applications. But how can these file formats be used on the World Wide Web? The answer is simple: just like any nonstandard file formats with helper applications.

When a reader selects a hyperlink to FLI, MMM, TBK, or any other multimedia application file from your Web page, their browsers will prompt them for directions to the program that will handle the data file. Users may also customize their browsers' helper application settings to always access specific viewer programs with these data files.

these files to their hard drives and view them using helper programs, such as QuickTime's Player software or Windows 95's Media Player utility.

Making digital video has become a fairly simple and affordable task. Start by obtaining a **video capture card:** a computer component that saves the video sent to it by your VCR or camcorder as regular data files on your hard drive.

After capturing the video sequences onto your hard drive, use a program like Adobe Premiere to edit your clip. Premiere enables you to cut and paste video frames; add transitions, such as fades and dissolves; and even edit more than one video clip together.

With your video clip ready, you need to build a link to it in your HTML file. This is no different from building a link to a graphics file (see Chapter 8). Your readers will need programs that play video files, and you'll want to tell them about that on the page itself.

Two important exceptions exist to this rule of the need for external programs: Netscape Navigator 2.0 offers built-in support for Macromedia Director files and Apple QuickTime video files. In addition, other companies will be constructing Netscape add-ins to make the program display their files directly as well. Microsoft Internet Explorer 2.0 comes complete with the capability to display Windows video files (AVI files) directly in the browser window. Go to **http://home.netscape.com** and **http://www.microsoft.com** for more information about these new techniques.

Observe the following guidelines for creating and distributing digital video over the World Wide Web:

1 Keep your video clips short. The shorter the video, the smaller the file, the less time people will need to invest in downloading the file so they can view it.

2 Make sure your video content corresponds to the Web page that contains it. A Web page on the Industrial Revolution linking to a video clip that displays your nephew's recent soccer game will lose credibility and diminish your audience. Keep track of your videos by logging their content as you edit them.

3 Don't use video just for the sake of using video. Sure, it's a neat technology, but it carries high costs for both your readers and the World Wide Web.

4 Tell people what to expect. When you link a video file to your Web page, inform your audience of its content and size. You may also want to indicate the quality of the clip in case it doesn't meet their expectations (for example, if there is no sound or if the compression technique breaks up the image).

Adding dynamic elements, such as server-push animation and digital video clips, will make your Web pages stand out from the crowd. Keep in mind that, as with any *cutting edge* feature, animation and video is most effective when used in small doses. Limiting your Web animation will ease the burden placed on your provider's Web server and on the Internet pipeline. Fast service will bring "Internauts" back to your pages again and again!

Hands-on Step 5: Give Your Web Site Its Finishing Touches

● **In this chapter:**

- **Work with text enhancements to create a lyric sheet**

- **Test your Web site to ensure that everything works**

- **Double-check your web to ensure accuracy of links**

- **Adding missing elements for user navigation**

In this final hands–on step, you'll create a new page that uses some advanced HTML elements to create an attractive, professional-looking lyric sheet for the band. . . . . ❯

So far, you've worked your way through the basics of headings, lists, hyperlinks, and graphics. You've also worked with backgrounds, imagemaps, tables, and forms. In other words, you've learned all the really important features of HTML.

What's left? A great deal, actually. But most of it's up to you. Go out onto the Web, retrieve the pages you like, and then use their HTML code to make your pages look as you want. That's the fundamental rule of HTML coding.

One more time back to the attic

In this hands-on step, you'll basically soup up your Web site. The only thing you don't really have is a lyric sheet for a Bertha's Attic song, and the goal here is to create a nice one. Then you'll test the entire site to make sure everything works.

Create a lyric sheet

There's nothing special about the basic lyric sheet you're going to create. It's just a simple HTML file with a background that makes it look somewhat like an old piece of paper—the kind you'd find in an attic, that is.

Using your HTML editor, create an HTML file with the title "The Hermit Lyric Sheet." This will become a page showing the lyrics to the Bertha's Attic song "The Hermit." Your code should look like the following:

```
<HTML><HEAD><TITLE>The Hermit Lyric Sheet
</TITLE></HEAD>
```

Next, how about a good background graphic? Go onto the Web and look for one in the usual places or fire up **http://randall.uwaterloo.ca/graphics.htm** and select the one called tan_paper.gif. Download it to your hard drive, and put it in the directory with your other graphics files.

Add it to the Web page either with your editor or by typing the following code:

```
<BODY BACKGROUND = "images/tan_paper.gif">
```

Note that the actual directory and file name might be different from that shown here.

At this point, it's time to add the lyrics to the song. Give the song title an <H1> heading, The Hermit, and <CENTER> it. Now type the words of the song (see listing 21.1).

Listing 21.1   Lyrics of "The Hermit"

```
There's a part of me that wants to be a hermit
When my journey's done my life will be my permit
Won't complain that my life was full
But I found what I'm looking for, as a hermit

I'll face life forever, refuse to run from problems
I'll remember you all your pictures in my albums
Sometimes I need to get away, to be alone
To be afraid to find the strength

You will be there, a pain in my heart a memory
You will be there, in the shine of lonely weather
I'll never let things go

Oh - I wanna be a hermit
Oh - I wanna be a hermit!

I'll be looking for peace to sit and just remember
And life will fall away like old leaves in November
Inside me there's a scream
A little boy who needs to find a reason

You will be there, a pain in my heart a memory
You will be there, in the shine of lonely weather
I'll never let things go
Oh - I wanna be a hermit
Oh - I wanna be a hermit!

Saw my life in pictures
Never thought it'd be this way
Burning sun on my head
And the colours quickly fade

Oh - I wanna be a hermit
Oh - I wanna be a hermit!
```

If you don't feel like typing all this, go to **http://randall.uwaterloo.ca/ lyric.htm** and copy and paste.

Now, fancy it up a bit. First, center the entire text by placing <CENTER> </CENTER> containers before the first line and after the last. Next, add a horizontal rule between the title of the song and the first line. To make it subtle, use the NOSHADE option. Your code will look like the following:

```
<HR NOSHADE>
```

Now you're going to spice the page up even further by making use of a new Netscape extension: font colors. If you're not using Netscape 2.0 or higher, you won't see these (although other browsers will quickly catch up).

The way to specify font colors is to place the <FONT COLOR = "#xxxxxx"></ FONT> container around the text you wish to color. #xxxxxx is the color code for the specific color. You can find a color code chart at **http:// web.idirect.com/~gmc/color.html**.

Create a sequence of greens and browns to fit with the theme of the old manuscript in the attic. Start by giving the song title (the <H1> heading) a rich green color. Your updated code for the <H1> line will be as follows:

```
<H1><FONT COLOR = "#009900">The Hermit</FONT></H1>
```

Now add a slightly lighter shade to the first verse, as follows:

```
<CENTER>
<P><FONT COLOR = "#009933">
There's a part of me that wants to be a hermit<BR>
When my journey's done my life will be my permit<BR>
Won't complain that my life was full<BR>
But I found what I'm looking for, as a hermit</FONT></P>
</CENTER>
```

Next, apply other shades to the remaining verses and choruses. Here they are (listing 21.2) with just the first line of each verse. Don't forget the closing </FONT> tag at the end of the verse (as above).

Listing 21.2 Applying Font Colors

```
<CENTER><P><FONT COLOR = "#007700">
I'll face life forever, refuse to run from problems<BR>
<CENTER><H4><FONT COLOR = "#005500">
You will be there, a pain in my heart a memory<BR>
<CENTER><H3><FONT COLOR = "#009900">
Oh - I wanna be a hermit<BR>
<CENTER><P><FONT COLOR = "#004400">
```

```
I'll be looking for peace to sit and just remember<BR>
<CENTER><H4><FONT COLOR = "#333300">
You will be there, a pain in my heart a memory<BR>

<CENTER><H3><FONT COLOR = "#009900">
Oh - I wanna be a hermit<BR>
<CENTER><H5><I><FONT COLOR = "#663300">
Saw my life in pictures<BR>
<CENTER><H3><FONT COLOR = "#009900">
Oh - I wanna be a hermit<BR>
```

Okay. You're done. Now load the page in your browser and see what it looks like. If you can increase the resolution of your system to high color (16-bit) or full color (24-bit), you'll see even more of a difference.

I'd show you what the screen looks like here, but because the book is in black and white, it won't be impressive. To compare your version with the one I had in mind, go to **http://randall.uwaterloo.ca/lhermit.htm**.

Making sure your Web site works

The last thing your readers want to do is find your Web site, start clicking around, and realize that part of it doesn't connect to other parts. One thing you *must* do when you've finished constructing your pages is fire up your site and make sure that all the links function properly. The only way to do this is to click every single link and see what happens.

In the hands-on steps in this book, you've constructed the following:

- The Bertha's Attic front page
- The Bertha's Attic graphics page
- An imagemap linking to lyrics, sounds, and an order form
- The sound files table
- The order form
- The lyrics sheet for one song

The first two pages remain unlinked to anything. Add a link now from the Bertha's Attic front page to the graphics page. Put it on the front page so that readers will see it but won't be tempted to move to it instantly. A simple **next link** message would be fine.

On the graphics page, add a link to the imagemap. Call it Enter the Attic. From here, ensure that the imagemap links to the sounds table and the order form properly. Those links were established in Chapter 16. Also, make sure that the sounds table links properly to the first lyric sheet. You'll want to rename the songs and change the text of the first line in the link to The Hermit.

Finally, create a table similar to the sounds table, and call it Bertha's Attic's Lyrics. Link to here from the imagemap, and provide links from the table to the lyric sheet for The Hermit. You can add whatever other links you want from here.

Now go back and try it all again. Should you offer other links? Probably. And there's much, much more to add as well. To see what I've done, go to **http://randall.uwaterloo.ca/Bertha's_Attic.htm** and take a look. It will be different from yours, but you'll recognize many of the parts.

Good luck! You're well on your way.

Bertha's Attic thanks you.

22

Everything's Done, and Now I Want to Show the World!

● In this chapter:

- How do I get my work online?

- Announcing your Web pages on the WWW

- Talking up your site on UseNet

- Are there virtual "storefronts" on the Web?

- Maintaining your Web pages

Now that you've created your very own Web site, it's time to take the plunge: publish your work on the World Wide Web and see what people think! . . . . ▶

This is what it all comes down to—actually showing the world the fruits of your labor. Ready? Then let's go. But what do you actually need to do to get online and onto the World Wide Web? That's what this chapter lets you know.

Why can't my friends see my Web pages?

The greatest Web site in the world is no good to anybody if it's not being **served** to the Web. Served? Yep, served. For a Web site to be accessible by any computer other than the one it's actually stored on, it has to be placed on a computer that has been set up as a World Wide Web **server**. This computer will **host** your site.

So where do you find a Web server? The following are the options:

- Use your existing Internet account. If your Internet provider or the place where you work already has a Web server, find out from them if they will host your Web site.

- Rent Web space from an Internet presence provider. Several firms have set themselves up as **presence providers** and host Web sites for a monthly or yearly fee. You can find many of these in the Yahoo listings (**http://www.yahoo.com/Business_and_Economy/Companies/ Internet_Presence_Providers/**).

- Put your site on a commercial online service. The major commercial online services (PRODIGY, America Online, and CompuServe) either offer or will soon offer Web hosting services for their members. Log in to your account and check out the membership information.

- Turn your own computer into a Web server. If you're connected to the Internet through an Ethernet connection or a SLIP or PPP connection, you can often establish your own computer to serve your web. Your machine will need its own unique IP (Internet Protocol) number, and you should have a 24-hour connection. If you're ambitious, you can do all this through a modem, but it means having a separate phone line and a 24-hour account. The most common direct way to serve a Web site this way is to have your computer networked to an organization that in turn has a high-speed Internet connection.

Finding a Web provider

The first step for new Web authors is to find a provider who can maintain your files on his Internet host computer. Chances are you aren't going to set up your own host on the Internet—this requires a substantial amount of hardware and money (including monthly fees based on the speed of your rented connection). Instead, it makes sense to rent space on an existing server.

When you're considering signing up with an Internet provider, ask them the following questions:

- Can I serve my Web site from your computers?

- If so, does it cost extra?

- How many megabytes of file storage is included?

- Will I be charged for heavy traffic?

- Do you offer Web creation services?

- Does your server handle imagemaps and forms?

- Can someone help me write CGI scripts?

If you get a "yes" answer to everything, and if the cost is reasonable (about $10 per month for standard Web storage, up to $75 for advanced storage and assistance), consider it a good deal.

Using your basic Internet account

The cheapest and easiest option for publishing your Web pages is to add the service to your existing Internet account. Many providers use low cost WWW home pages as an incentive for enrollment, while others charge a marginal fee for their users to have a noncommercial Web presence. Unless you are interested in running a business online or advertising a commercial product, this option may be the best bet for you.

If your provider does not allow you to have a Web page, there are many Internet hosts that are giving people free pages for noncommercial use. You don't even have to buy your basic service from them! One well-known and popular service is Turnpike Metropolis (**http://turnpike.net/turnpike/metro.html**). Others can be found through the Internet Presence Providers and Internet Service Providers listings in Yahoo (**http://www.yahoo.com/**).

Announcing your arrival

Once you know how, publishing information on the Web is easy. It only takes your own time and energy (and money if your provider isn't free). Great content is work, but it's work you can do without anyone else's cooperation. Having people look at your work, on the other hand, can't be done alone. Although you can give people the opportunity to see your Web work, it's up to them to choose to do so.

The WWW is all about opportunities, and it's up to you to take advantage of them. One way you can do this is to let people (preferably those who might be interested to read your information) know where it is. This takes more work, but it's well worth the trouble.

Use the newsgroups

UseNet newsgroups cover thousands of special interest discussions. One of these is for new Web page announcements. Called **comp. infosystems.www.announce**, it's a forum where people post notices of new pages and of new content to existing pages.

The www.announce group follows a specific format for posting new messages. At the bottom of every posting is an e-mail address where you can get guidelines and other information about the group. The moderator also posts the group's guidelines regularly—it is highly recommended that you read these before sending in a posting for the first time.

 TIP **The comp.infosystems.www.announce newsgroup is very busy,** often posting over a hundred new messages a day. The moderator may need up to a week to process new posts, so make sure you give him plenty of time to handle your request when you decide to announce your new Web pages.

You may find that your Web pages center around specific topics of interests, such as Japanese literature or beach volleyball. UseNet has a separate discussion group for nearly every topic and issue conceivable. Use your Network News reader (or a browser like Netscape Navigator, which includes support for newsgroups) to search the list of current groups.

It's a big list—as many as eight thousand, depending on how your News server is configured—so be prepared to wait while your software retrieves the master list. Once you have it, use the program's text search capabilities (if available) to search for your keywords.

Subscribe to the groups you find and read some of the **threads** or discussions that have been posted recently. Make sure that this group is talking about the same things you want to share via your Web pages—many groups are created to ridicule their subjects, so don't wander into a target range by accident. Barney the Dinosaur lovers should stay out of the **alt.barney.die.die.die** discussion group or risk being skewered alongside the big purple lizard!

Once you are comfortable that you've found the right group, consider participating in the discussions as well as posting a general message about your new Web resources. It's a great way to establish yourself in the online community, which will attract more readers to your site.

Web page directories

One of the most difficult aspects of the World Wide Web is that it lacks organization—it reflects the open and unstructured qualities of the Internet. How do you find what resources are available, and how do you make sure others can find yours? Probably the most popular service on the Web today is directories. These are listings of Web pages that you can search through and link directly to them from the directory entries. Web directories are becoming a big business—the most well-known directory, Yahoo, went commercial after being started up by two students at Stanford University. It now sports a redesigned interface and corporate sponsorship.

Other similar directories have experienced the same type of interest and growth. Their success is a direct result of the Web community's reliance on them for finding information on the WWW. Table 22.1 shows some of the most often used directories.

Table 22.1 World Wide Web Directory of Services

Directory Name	URL
Yahoo	www.yahoo.com
ElNet Galaxy	galaxy.einet.com
Web Crawler	webcrawler.com
Lycos	lycos.cs.cmu.edu
Whole Internet Catalog	gnn.com/gnn/

continues

Table 22.1 Continued

Directory Name	URL
Harvest	harvest.cs.colorado.edu/Harvest/
InfoSeek	www.infoseek.com

Getting listed on these directory services can be time-consuming. Each has a submission process and listing format you have to adhere to.

These directories can take up to a week to process new entries. Once your listing is added, many will notify you by e-mail. Check your entry to make sure you did not overlook any misspellings, and definitely try out the link to make sure it is pointing to the right Web page. The last thing you want is for users to link to the middle of your content and not understand where they are or how to use your pages.

Netscape has created an advanced HTML feature called **Bulletin** that is used in conjunction with automated programs (called **robots** and **spiders**) that can go out and search the Web for new information. When these programs come across your Web page, they can tell if you made any recent changes to the content from the Bulletin information embedded in your pages. They can then report back to a directory or to users and let them know what's now available. This will be a great way to automate updating your directory listings in the future. For more information about Bulletin, refer to Netscape's home page at **http://www.netscape.com/**.

Submissions master

You could spend hours filling in submissions for each of the directories on the list above. Wouldn't it be great if there was a one-stop Web page that would take your information once and send in properly formatted entries to every directory on the list? There is. The service is called Submit It! It is available at **http://submit-it.permalink.com/submit-it/**. You provide all of your pertinent information into the services form and then choose which directories you want to be listed on. Submit It! then shows you how each format looks before sending it in.

As each directory takes new listing submissions in different ways, sometimes Submit It! sends you to the directory itself, but your information is prefilled in their submission form. Follow their instructions to return to Submit It! and process the next submission. By using this service, you can get through a dozen submissions in the time it may have otherwise taken you to do just a few.

Your ad here

The WWW is just coming into its own as a commercial environment. The market size is growing. Just this year, another three to four million people in the US alone will join the Internet, either through a commercial service like America Online or through an Internet provider. How can you, as an individual or as someone with a small business or Internet information service, get the kind of recognition you can get in the "real world?"

Marketing opportunities are growing on the Internet. The World Wide Web, as a multimedia environment, provides better marketing opportunities than the text-based services, such as Gopher and e-mail. The truth is, the advertising market is still finding its feet, trying to gauge the levels of participation and the costs that companies should pay for different kinds of representation. Basically, there are three ways you can advertise your business or service:

- Post messages in the commercial UseNet forums. These were created so businesses could advertise without creating a backlash against them from the Internet community. The drawback comes from the fact that most users do not choose to read the forums with any regularity.

- Find Web pages that are willing to include a link to your information in return for a similar link form your pages to their own. This kind of small business co-op arrangement makes sense when your audience would be appropriate for their Web content and vice versa.

- Sponsor a popular Web service. Sites like Yahoo are finding corporate sponsorship to be a lucrative opportunity and are willing to jump on that bandwagon.

Of the three, sponsorship is the most visible and probably will give you the best return for your investment. So how do you find Web pages willing to be sponsored? Begin by visiting the Web sites you would associate with your preferred audience. These may be pages related to the information or services you are marketing, or to common services that people use daily on the Web. Look at the various "What's New" directories and online malls.

Some Web services may be willing to barter a month's advertising in exchange for your services. Do research into co-op advertising on the larger and more popular services like Wired Magazine's Hot Wired service. The sites that are open to advertising will most likely have rate sheets that you can use to measure your options and how far your budget will get you.

CAUTION **Advertising for the sake of increasing your business is a good** thing, but don't overlook that increased traffic on your Web pages may result in a much higher bill from your provider. Most charge you by the amount of information that users retrieve from your Web site. The per megabyte rates can vary, so make sure you know how your provider is charging you for your Web service, and plan accordingly.

Choose your Web neighbors

Just as you will want to explore your advertising options on the World Wide Web, you may also want to look into associating yourself and your Web pages with other people and businesses online. Besides trading links with other pages (as discussed above), you can also look to join a "virtual mall" on the Web. These electronic storefronts are a growing way for businesses and services to band together to increase their overall visibility.

The mall association may provide co-op advertising or other advantages beyond your own listing in the mall. These storefronts can vary in price, depending on the size of the mall and the quality of its tenants. A good example of this is the Empire Mall (**http://empire.na.com/**).

Choose your Web associates

Just as there are professional associations in your community that you can belong to, there are also virtual associations that may be valuable for networking (making contacts, not hooking up your computers). One such association that was formed in 1994 is the HTML Writer's Guild, an association of WWW developers and authors. The Guild's purpose is to promote HTML development and encourage a level of professionalism and ethics among its members. For more information about the HTML Writer's Guild, go to **http://www.mindspring.com/guild/**.

Web page upkeep

The point has been made before, but it's important enough to stress again: revise your content! Keep it fresh and interesting. Remove any material that has "expired." A statement like "order before March 31, 1995" looks pretty silly by Christmas of the same year, and it looks like you don't care enough to pay attention to what's on your own Web pages. Add links to new Web sites that are related to your topic. Be current in your field—know what your competitors and colleagues are doing.

If you adapt your content to include new information, events, or news, people will start to rely on you as a source of knowledge, and they will come back to see what else you have for them. Don't let your Web pages sit still and grow stale—like a shark, they need to move forward and change or they will die.

It may seem like this is opening the door on a long road of maintenance and work, but it's all a labor of love. At least, it should be. The World Wide Web is your opportunity to express yourself, to blaze your own trail, and there are no virtual limits to what you can do or how you can touch other people's lives. The Web is a brand-new community, and if we all work at carving our own niches, it will become a community we can be proud of and content being a part of.

23

Designing for Netscape 2.0 and Internet Explorer 2.0

● In this chapter:

- ● **What are the benefits of designing for specific browsers?**

- ● **Frames, fonts, and other Netscape idiosyncrasies**

- ● **What's this Java thing, anyway?**

- ● **Internet Explorer's aggressive additions**

Version 2.0 of Netscape Navigator and version 2.0 of Internet Explorer give you design choices above and beyond other browsers. You can take advantage of them to give your pages more dazzle . . . . ▶

O nly a couple of years ago, all you had to worry about as an HTML author was learning HTML and putting it to use.
But then, near the beginning of 1995, Netscape Navigator first appeared and changed all that. Because Netscape supported several tags and elements that weren't part of official HTML, and some that hadn't even been proposed as standards, writing pages for Netscape was different from writing pages for other browsers.

Isn't HTML supposed to be a standard?

Today, the gap between official HTML and browser-specific HTML has widened further. Netscape Navigator remains the champion of nonstandard HTML, but others have joined the fray. Among them are HotJava, Sun Microsystem's highly regarded browser, and Internet Explorer, Microsoft's entry into the browser game. All of these support proprietary HTML tags, although in HotJava's case the support is for a computer language instead: Java.

The problems of success

Because of its unique coding tags (ALIGN and VSPACE included), Netscape has been blamed for *undemocratizing* the Web. That is, because Netscape makes it possible for authors to create nicer looking pages, they do so. But these pages can't be viewed by non-Netscape users. To an extent, this is certainly true. Many Web sites bear a label stating that the pages have been "enhanced for Netscape," and some sites more or less tell anyone without Netscape to get lost.

But Netscape is only the current culprit. Earlier, the same charges were leveled against NCSA Mosaic, the browser that changed the world. Because Mosaic could display images, images became the core of many Web pages and Lynx users got miffed. Some have even claimed that the Web stopped advancing with the release of

Mosaic because people started designing pages with magazines, rather than computers, in mind.

Netscape 2.0 offers even more enhancements. Soon, most users with graphical access will use it as their browser. Some of the new features are being considered by the Internet Engineering Task Force (IETF) for inclusion in the next version of HTML (3.0), but others, such as **frames**, haven't even made it that far along the path of universal acceptance.

Mosaic's success caused significant problems for the Web and its developers. Netscape's success has done the same. What's important to keep in mind is that not everyone uses these programs and that you have to decide whether or not you'll try to accommodate all users. It's entirely up to you.

Here, you'll take a brief look at designing for version 2.0 of both Netscape Navigator and Internet Explorer. The new HTML possibilities aren't endless, but they're significant. At the very least, you should know about them. And if you want your Web pages to be looked at, you should start designing for them as well.

The benefits and drawbacks of proprietary HTML designs

As soon as you see some of the great pages designed for Netscape 2.0, you'll want to incorporate the new features into your own site. Guaranteed! Before you do, though, keep a few things in mind. They're important if you're hoping to satisfy the largest possible number of readers.

First, if you decide to rely heavily on the new Netscape or Internet Explorer extensions, you should design a separate site to accommodate those who don't use these browsers. Sometimes it's much easier to do it this way than to attempt a design that incorporates all possibilities.

Second, relying on these features might force you to make changes more regularly. Because the features themselves will change (unlike standard HTML), you'll have to keep on top of further enhancements. This isn't a problem if you do all your own work, but if you have people working for you or with you, it could easily demand extra training.

Third, don't expect a pat on the back from everyone out there for your innovative design work. There's still a large contingent of conservative Internet users out there, and they demand adherence to standards—not to someone's well-intentioned whims. If you design for a nonstandard browser, expect to get some mail that tells you exactly what they think.

Here's what's new in Netscape 2

New releases of Netscape always cause excitement among Web developers because they always contain new HTML features. Netscape 2.0 is no exception. Here you'll find frames, targeted windows, font colors, text alignment, and three major enhancements: LiveScript, Java support, and plug-ins.

It's a frame-up!

Probably the most immediately noticeable enhancement in Netscape 2.0 is frames. Frames are basically multiple regions (sub-windows) that display in the same Netscape main window. Figure 23.1 shows frames in action at the site **http://www.ecola.com/ez/frames.htm**.

Fig. 23.1
Ecola's Newsstand uses three frames. The top bar is static, while the left column acts as an interface for the entire site.

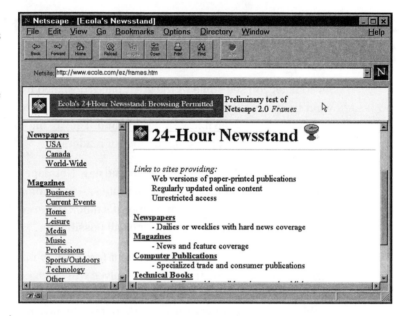

 TIP **The exciting thing about frames is the ability to have one frame** act as an interface with new pages appearing in the main window. As figure 24.1 shows, frames can also be static and can thus display an unchanging logo or other graphic feature.

To create a frame, you use the <FRAMESET></FRAMESET> container, and you must place this before the <BODY> portion of the HTML document (any <BODY> tags will simply be ignored). This encompasses the entire frame area (usually the whole browser window).

Inside the opening <FRAMESET> tag, you can specify the number of rows and columns. The size of the frames can be set according to percentage of the whole, as a pixel size, or as an asterisk (*) telling the row to use the available remaining space.

For example, to create a two-row page with the left row occupying 40% and the right row 60%, type the following:

```
<FRAMESET ROWS="40%,60%">
```

or

```
<FRAMESET ROWS="40%,*">
```

If you wanted a three-row page with the left and middle rows occupying 80 pixels each and the right row taking up the remainder, type the following:

```
<FRAMESET ROWS="80,80,*">
```

 CAUTION **Be careful when creating fixed-pixel sizes. You have no way of** knowing what resolution your readers will be using, and resolution will drastically affect the appearance of your framed pages.

Instead of rows, you can use columns (COLS=). You can also include a FRAMESET within a FRAMESET for a multirow, multicolumn effect. An example of this, taken from the Netscape Web site, is shown in Listing 23.1.

Listing 23.1   A More Complex Frame

```
<FRAMESET COLS="50%,50%">
  <FRAMESET ROWS="50%,50%">
    <FRAME SRC="cell.html">
    <FRAME SRC="cell.html">
  </FRAMESET>
  <FRAMESET ROWS="33%,33%,33%">
    <FRAME SRC="cell.html">
    <FRAME SRC="cell.html">
    <FRAME SRC="cell.html">
  </FRAMESET>
</FRAMESET>
```

This example initially divides the screen into two columns, each taking 50% of the full space. It then divides the left-hand column into two rows of equal size (line two) and the right-hand column into three rows of equal size (line six). The page looks like figure 23.2.

Fig. 23.2
By placing
FRAMESETs inside a
larger FRAMESET, you
can establish a screen
with multiple windows
or **cells**.

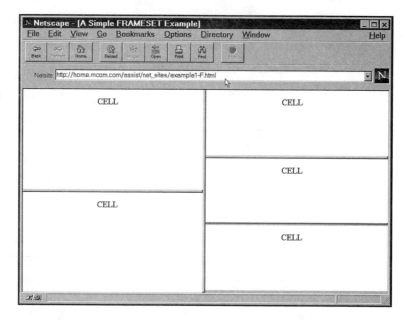

Cool! But what goes inside the frames?

Framesets are just boxes. They don't do anything on their own. But as the code for figure 23.2 shows, once past the <FRAMESET> tags, you begin to specify <FRAME> tags as well. This is where the framing action really happens.

Each frame on the page can be assigned a unique URL (Web address). In other words, you can easily create a two-frame Web page with each frame showing a different URL. In the code for figure 23.2, all five frames point to the same URL, cell.html, but that's not necessary. In the following code, the two rows point to Netscape and Microsoft, respectively.

```
<FRAMESET ROWS=50%,50%>
    <FRAME SRC="http://home.netscape.com/">
    <FRAME SRC="http://www.microsoft.com/">
</FRAMESET>
```

Hardly difficult, is it? Line one simply tells the browser to split the screen into two rows. The top row will contain Netscape's home page, while the bottom will be Microsoft's. The powerful results of this extremely easy coding are shown in figure 23.3.

Fig. 23.3
Each of the frames on this page works independently of the other. This is one way of exploring separate Webs at the same time.

Notice that each of the two frames in figure 23.3 contains a vertical and horizontal scroll bar. Furthermore, the frames are resizable by the user. All they have to do is grab the edges of the frame and drag it to whatever size they wish.

That's great, but sometimes you won't want scrollable or resizable frames. No problem. In the <FRAME> tag, you can include the options SCROLLING and NORESIZE.

<FRAME xxx NORESIZE> prevents the frame from being resized by the user. <FRAME xxx SCROLLING=x> sets the scrolling option. Here, x can be yes, no, or auto. Specifying yes means that scroll bars will *always* be visible for that frame, while no means that they'll *never* be available. The default is auto, which leaves it up to the browser to insert scroll bars as needed.

The problem with frames is that not every browser can show them. In fact, when this was written, only Netscape 2.0 had the capability, and it was an early beta version. You should be sure to provide, therefore, a version of the page for non-frames browsers. How? With <NOFRAME>.

The <NOFRAME></NOFRAME> container lets you include HTML code that will appear if the browser can't recognize the <FRAMESET> tag. You begin the <NOFRAME> portion above the closing </FRAMESET> tag, and in fact, it becomes enclosed within the largest <FRAMESET> container. The <NOFRAME> portion typically begins with the opening <BODY> tag.

The easiest way to incorporate existing pages into frames is to copy the <BODY></BODY> portion of the page inside a <FRAMESET></FRAMESET> container. That way, you don't have to write it all over again.

There's much more to frames, but that's the basics. I'll touch on frames a bit more later. For the full syntactic information, see **http://home.mcom.com/ assist/net_sites/frames.html**.

Setting your targets

Another powerful addition to Netscape 2.0 is targeted windows. Normally, whenever you click a hyperlink, the new Web page replaces the one you were just reading. When you click a hyperlink that's targeted, however, you open a new browser window displaying the destination URL, and the original URL is still available in the original window.

The syntax for targeted windows is as follows:

```
<A HREF="http://xxx.xxxxxx.xxx.html" TARGET="name"></A>
```

As an example, Listing 23.2 shows some simple code that displays nothing but a link on the original page. When clicked, the link brings up my home page in a new window. That's because I set my home page in the link to be a TARGET, as shown in line six.

Listing 23.2   Creating a Target

```
<HTML>
<HEAD>
<TITLE>Targeting Windows</TITLE>
</HEAD>
<BODY>
<A HREF="http://randall.uwaterloo.ca" TARGET="randall">This
will open a new window with my home page</A>
</BODY>
</HTML>
```

Give it a try.

By combining frames with targeted links, you can have one frame act as an interface to the rest of the screen. The original frame will always be available to your readers, and whenever they click a link inside that frame, they'll see the results of the click in the main window.

As an example of this, see the Atlantic Records home page at **http://www.atlantic-records.com/**.

Color your fonts, and spread 'em out over the page

Two useful new controls for your HTML text are available in Netscape 2.0. Font colors let you specify the color of any character, while text alignment lets you align text left, middle, or right.

The font color feature is a new container. The opening tag is <FONT COLOR="#xxxxxx">. The xs represent the color code, which you can see at work in Chapter 21. Place the <FONT COLOR=> tag in front of any character or text string you want to color, then close the container with </FONT>. The string below, for example, would give you a red *H*, a green *T*, a blue *M*, and a black *L*. It would look tacky, but hey… .

```
<FONT COLOR="#FF0000>H</FONT><FONT COLOR="#00FF00">T</FONT>
<FONT COLOR="#0000FF">M</FONT>L
```

The new <DIV ALIGN> container lets you justify text to the left or right margin or in the middle. It's easy. Just place the container around the text you want to justify. <DIV ALIGN="left"></DIV> justifies left, <DIV ALIGN="right"></DIV> justifies right, and <DIV ALIGN="center"></DIV> centers the text. Obviously, the <CENTER></CENTER> container does the same thing as <DIV ALIGN="center">.

Java and LiveScript

It's beyond the scope of this book to get into Java or LiveScript, but I couldn't let you go without at least knowing what they are. Both are programming languages that essentially replace CGI (see Chapter 15) or at least supplement it dramatically. If you've written extensive word processing or database scripts or if you're a programmer, you'll find both of these languages quite easy. If not, expect to take time to learn.

The purpose of Java and LiveScript is to give your Netscape documents a dynamic nature. Java, developed by Sun Microsystems (**http://java.sun.com**) and incorporated into Netscape 2.0, lets you run complete programs inside your HTML documents. LiveScript, developed by Netscape, does the same but is a smaller language and easier to learn (**http://home.mcom.com/comprod/products/navigator/version_2.0/script/script_info/index.html**).

A Java or LiveScript program can make your Web page truly interactive. Clicking the Java link could start an interactive game, for example, in which you challenge your readers to a trivia match or even an Internet quiz. Or you could load a spreadsheet for your employees, allowing them to perform simple calculations. Or you could simply have an animation running, giving your site some needed pizzazz. Java is sophisticated enough to allow a wide variety of possibilities.

And now for Internet Explorer 2.0

Not to be outdone by Netscape, and always seeking a proprietary path in software development, Microsoft Corporation has developed Internet Explorer 2.0 to offer some additional attractive features. Why should this concern you? Because Internet Explorer is being distributed with Windows 95, and as such it promises to challenge Netscape Navigator as the premier browser—at least for the Windows users crowd (and it *is* a crowd).

Give your pages some musical accompaniment

By now, you're used to giving your HTML pages a nice background graphic. Background graphics personalize your work, and they give the reader something nice to look at. Better than the old standard gray—that's for sure.

Well, why not give them some background music as well? They read your pages, they catch a bit of Mozart, they feel cozy, rested, and willing to stay and listen. Or, if you like, hit 'em with a distorted grunge chord and make 'em wish they'd turned off the speakers. Either way, you get their attention.

The <BGSOUND> tag tells Internet Explorer to play an audio file when the page opens. Obviously, you don't want a huge file (painful downloading), but you can get people's attention with a sound or music snippet, and you can **loop** the file (play it repeatedly) as often as you wish. You can use WAV, AU, or MIDI files for this purpose.

To include a background sound, you'll need the following HTML coding:

```
<BGSOUND SRC="xxxxx.yyy" LOOP=n>
BGSOUND SRC="mozart.mid" LOOP=8>
```

On your marquees, get set, go!

Internet Explorer 2.0 tries to make your pages move in several ways, one of which is the scrolling marquee. This is nothing more than a string of text that scrolls by itself across the screen, but the effect is much stronger than, say, the <BLINK> command of earlier HTML. You can draw attention to a particular sentence or phrase, or of course you can overdo the thing entirely and end up with a jumble of moving lines of text.

To create a scrolling marquee, enclose the text inside the <MARQUEE> </MARQUEE> container. For example, the following code causes the string of text "Watch me move!" to move from the right border of the page to the left border and then start over again once it's finished—*ad infinitum.*

```
<MARQUEE>Watch me move!</MARQUEE>
```

You have several options, all of which are specified on the Microsoft pages at **http://www.microsoft.com/windows/ie/ie20html.htm**. Basically, you can set the direction of the scroll, you can have the marquee "bounce" back and forth within the scroll area (i.e., from one side to the other and then back again), you can have it loop a specified number of times, and you can give it a colored background. There's more, but these are the main tags.

Real-time videos

One of the most exciting additions to Internet Explorer's proprietary HTML is the ability to play video files in the .AVI format (the standard Microsoft Windows format). Essentially, these are coded much like graphics files except that because they're video files, they give movement to your pages. Bandwidth issues notwithstanding, these will do a great deal to enhance your reader's Web experience.

The code for incorporating an AVI video file is as follows:

```
<IMG DYNSRC="videofile.avi">
```

Note that this is similar to HTML's calling of graphics files, <IMG SRC>. DYNSRC means dynamic source and is used instead. In practice, though, you should offer both possibilities so that readers without Internet Explorer will see something as well. This would be coded as follows:

```
<IMG DYNSRC="videofile.avi" SRC="graphicfile.gif">
```

Internet Explorer will play the AVI file, while other browsers will display the GIF file.

There aren't many options for the DYNSRC element, but they're important. First, you can specify when the AVI file starts playing. FILEOPEN tells it to begin as soon as the page is retrieved; MOUSEOVER tells it to start playing when the reader moves the cursor over the video image. You can see an example of FILEOPEN at **http://www.microsoft.com/windows/ie/ie20html.htm** and an example of MOUSEOVER at **http://www.microsoft.com/windows/ie/ iedemo.htm**.

The other major option lets you place video controls at the bottom of the video image to let the reader take charge of what displays. The default is to have no controls; to include them, you must use the CONTROLS element:

```
<IMG DYNSRC="videofile.avi" CONTROLS>
```

Backgrounds that don't move

The final major HTML addition within Internet Explorer is the watermark background. These are the same as the background graphics you're used to except that they don't scroll when your readers use the scroll bar. They're quite effective as you can see (again) at **http://www.microsoft.com/ windows/ie/ie20html.htm**.

The code for watermark backgrounds is quite simple: add the BGPROPERTIES=FIXED element to the usual <BODY BACKGROUND> component.

```
<BODY BACKGROUND="mypattern.gif" BGPROPERTIES=FIXED>
```

Enjoy all these additions. But keep in mind that many users won't be able to see them. The best bet, for a while at least, is to include them as options in your Web pages.

Your Editor Is Your Best Friend

● **In this chapter:**

- **The pros and cons of stand-alone editors**

- **Why add on an add-on?**

- **What do you want? What do you need? What's the best Web editing tool for you?**

- **Pass or fail—giving Web editors the grade**

Authoring tools put the building blocks of HTML at your fingertips, allowing you to create sophisticated and accurate Web pages with ease . . . . ❯

As a current WWW designer, you've probably already explored some editing mechanisms and soon realized that the Internet community is bombarded with HTML tools.

Both stand-alone programs and software that act as add-ons to common productivity applications exist for all platforms (most as shareware). This chapter describes the various tools being used by today's HTML authors and helps you select the editor that will satisfy your authoring needs.

Stand-alone editing tools

Stand-alone editors are separate HTML construction programs; that is, they do not require any supplementary applications for functioning. Table 24.1 displays the pros and cons of stand-alone Web editors.

Table 24.1   The pros and cons of stand-alone editors

Advantages	Disadvantages
Maximize interface and workspace with toolbars	Lack of standardization among programs requires users to become familiar with individual software idiosyncrasies
Shareware and freeware programs allow user feedback	Must load document into browser for true display
Low cost (usually under $50)	Constant updating and lack of support for older versions

Add-On editing tools

Add-on Web editors are supplementary programs that function as compliments to existing applications (usually word processing mechanisms). Again, there are both pro and con considerations for incorporating this editing style, as shown in Table 24.2.

Table 24.2 **The pros and cons of add-on editors**

Advantages	Disadvantages
Extension of *familiar* software	Large size—consume disk space and decrease program performance
Document conversion from standard format to HTML makes page translation easy	High cost for word processing or other initial applications (often $200 or more)
Macros and template additions may be modified to add support for new HTML elements	Not easily transportable—add-on remains attached to home program

ASCII editors

When HTML first came to the Internet, the only editors you could get were tagged with standard HTML codes, and these ASCII editors remain the most widespread form of Web creation currently available (see table 24.3). Tagged editors only read information that is complimented with a specific set of regulated codes. Lists of these codes are available in the tag menu of most editors.

Table 24.3 **The pros and cons of ASCII tag editors**

ASCII advantages	ASCII disadvantages
Speedy screen updates	New users often require support material for code manipulation
Most tagged editors supply the middle and end tags requiring users to simply fill in the middle data	Most editors lack syntax checking features
Users may insert custom tags	Editors provide little or no documentation for codes

What-You-See-Is-What-You-Get editors

WYSIWYG stands for **W**hat **Y**ou **S**ee **I**s **W**hat **Y**ou **G**et—an interface that presents your WWW pages without the standard HTML codes. WYSIWYG provides an aesthetic approach to document creation, allowing concrete layout and formatting—in word processing style (see table 24.4).

Table 24.4 The pros and cons of WYSIWYG

WYSIWYG advantages	WYSIWYG disadvantages
Graphic representation provides better page layout	Absorb large amounts of disk space to verify tags, fonts, and display
Built-in syntax checks	Lack most recent tag support
Reduced need for previews and browser verification	Internal interpretation is not always correct

Live Markup

Live Markup boasts the ability to build or edit World Wide Web pages in the actual HTML environment, directly on-screen, without learning or typing any HTML tags. Pull-down, pop-up menus and a toolbar give the user the ability to build or edit World Wide Web pages fast and efficiently in its advanced what-you-see-is-what-you-get format. Most specific HTML commands are contained in simple floating menus that appear when you click your right mouse button—a function that reduces screen clutter and simplifies the Web construction process.

The Pro Version of this versatile Web editor supports viewing of GIF, JPEG, BMP, TGA, PCX, and TIF images directly on-screen. The Pro series is compatible with Microsoft Windows 95 and Microsoft Windows NT complete with "looong" file names in true 32-bit mode. Input and background images are visible directly on your editing screen; Netscape extensions are fully functional; and all HTML 3.0 standards will eventually be implemented.

Exciting updates to the Pro version will include imagemap creation and editing directly on-screen, full table manipulation, and on-screen image resizing. Software Licenses for the full version of <Live Markup> PRO including upgrades until the end of the year, are available at Live Markup's home page: **http://www.digimark.net/mediatech/.**

Web Weaver

Formerly known as SuperEdit, this WYSIWYG Web editor supplies HTML authors with floating element lists, balloon help, and an icon toolbar that supports HTML 2 and some HTML 3 features. Web Weaver's default element lists include Netscape-specific features like BLINK, definable font size, and will even create custom lists of your favorite HTML codes. This *modular* approach to Web construction is very similar to HTML Editor's main interface, but is carried out with greater elegance and harmony among the elements. Web Weaver can be retrieved from **http://www.potsdam.edu/ HTML_Web_Weaver/About_HTML_WW.html.**

BBEdit HTML extensions

Written by Charles Bellver, BBEdit shareware extensions transform this popular Macintosh text editor into a functional HTML editor. Building on BBEdit's strengths as a text editor, HTML extensions support HTML 2 tags and may be customized for HTML 3 and Netscape-specific coding. The program may be downloaded at **http://www.uji.es/bbedit-html-extensions.html**.

Webtor

Webtor supports HTML 2.0 standards and provides users with a syntax checking mechanism that, while configurable and generally very good, is a bit unstable (this is most true with missing tags or extra closing tags). Webtor displays the *structure* of the Web page in basic coded outline format, which is particularly useful for new HTML authors. The Webtor home page is at **http://www.igd.fhg.de/~neuss/webtor/webtor.html**.

HTML Editor

HTML Editor combines coded display with WYSIWYG format, allowing authors to create WWW pages visually—as if using a word processor—while adding the corresponding HTML codes to the completed documents. This editing application exploits a button interface and floating windows to provide HTML 2 support with customizable HTML 3 and Netscape extension options. For added competency, an HTML check program roots out the author's most obvious errors when applying the HTML tags to the on-screen content. HTML Editor's documentation and download link may be accessed at **http://dragon.acadiau.ca:1667/giles/HTML_Editor/ Documentation.html**.

HTML Pro

HTML Pro distinguishes itself from other HTML editors by offering two functional display windows: one that presents the page's HTML tagged format and another that displays the WYSIWYG interpretation of the same page. Users may edit their document from either window, and updates will appear in both documents. All basic HTML elements may be accessed from HTML Pro's Style menu—forms and tables are not yet functional. You can download a copy of HTML pro at **ftp://ftp.leo.org/pub/comp/platforms/ macintosh/communication/tcp/www/authoring/html-pro-108.sit**.

HTML.edit

Virtually all of HTML.edit's editing power may be accessed through the program's floating toolbars. This interface design is highlighted by the program's logical but jarring file management methods. HTML.edit divides files into two categories with title and headings in one area and the document's body in another. Because most users neglect the title header of a Web page under construction, this interface separates the elements to simplify the file.

HTML.edit is a fairly typical World Wide Web page editor, providing support for all the usual HTML tags including forms, tables, and preview command that launches a specified browser directly from the toolbar. You can download a copy of HTML.edit from **ftp://ftp.leo.org/pub/comp/platforms/ macintosh/communication/tcp/www/authoring/html-edit-112.sit**.

HotDog

The brainchild of Sausage Software, a newcomer to the HTML tools arena, HotDog is a **code-only** editor that aims to replace all other HTML Web construction programs. This editor provides HTML 2 and HTML 3 standards as well as Netscape 1.1's nonstandard HTML extensions, pull-down menu options for nearly every conceivable HTML component, and color definition options. HotDog even converts existing HTML documents to plain text files by stripping out the HTML characters from Web pages and leaving the text layout intact.

The HotDog Web editor is customizable, allowing you to create document templates and define special boilerplate HTML strings. The program's toolbar supports context-sensitive help (leave the mouse over a button for a few seconds and a message pops up describing its function), and the editor provides "Handy Hints" upon startup that may be disabled when you become familiar with the software. Most importantly, the HotDog Web editor has been designed with Windows 95 features (for the most advanced user), but remains fully compatible with Windows 3.1 in order to accommodate a larger audience.

TIP **When you first fire up HotDog, a few important features may go** unnoticed. For example, the row of tabs along the bottom of the window (which they call the Document Bar) lets you open more than one document at a time and switch between them with ease. HotDog even comes with a simple File Manager for locating HTML documents and automating relative links to them.

HotDog Pro, a professional version of the HotDog editor provides additional document management and customizing options, unlimited file sizes, a spell checker, and some WYSIWYG editing features. Both programs may be accessed from the Sausage Software site at **http://www.sausage.com/**.

SoftQuad HoTMetaL

SoftQuad is famous for HoTMetaL's built-in HTML validation, a feature requiring codes that conform to the current Level standard. This is a great option for beginners who are still learning what can go where. Unfortunately, this is a draw-back for users who are creating Web pages specifically for Netscape audiences and intend to use Netscape's nonstandard extensions. HoTMetaL is also available in UNIX format and in a professional (commercial) version. Freeware versions of each are available at **http://www.sq.com/**.

HTMLed

Another code-only Windows utility, HTMLed provides pull-down menus and permanent toolbars that contain the primary functions of Level 2 HTML coding. Written by I-Net Training & Consulting, HTMLed provides even the most timid beginner with a clean, straightforward interface and workspace.

 TIP **HTMLed's button bar displays a mixture of icons and text to make** document creation a clear and simple process. For example, the new document button is represented by an icon of a blank page, but to add a heading, you access a button labeled "heading."

The HTMLed applications do not adhere to Microsoft's recommended conventions, but any deviations from the norm are for the sake of clarity and ease of use. Unfortunately, simplicity has a price. The editor does not provide support for HTML 3 elements (even those in common usage, such as forms and tables) or Netscape's HTML extensions.

Thankfully, HTMLed does allow you to create a custom toolbar to add HTML 3 and Netscape extensions, preventing users from looking elsewhere to fulfill their editing needs. HTMLed can be downloaded from **ftp:// ftp.cica.indiana.edu/pub/pc/win3/util/htmed.zip**.

HTML Writer

Another fairly generic HTML editing program is the stand-alone HTML Writer. Though it supports the usual suite of HTML elements, including forms, it does not handle tables. The most commonly accessible HTML tags are readily available from the program's toolbar, and users may define templates so you don't have to retype common Web page layouts. But perhaps the most impressive feature of HTML Writer is its ability to drag and drop highlighted text. More information about HTML Writer is available at **http://lal.cs.byu.edu/people/nosack/index.html**.

Internet Assistant

Internet Assistant is an HTML template and formatting stylesheet in the guise of a word processor. The trick to Internet Assistant is that you may never have to leave Microsoft Word to accomplish all of your HTML creation, previewing, and Web browsing functions. The browsing capability is provided by a custom implementation of BookLink's (now America Online's) InternetWorks stand-alone browser.

IA orders all of its editing options in pull-down menus and icon-based toolbars. The software supports all HTML 2 and some common HTML 3 features, such as forms. IA also manages your HTML assets (image files and information links) with detailed dialog boxes and property sheets. Its WYSIWYG feature allows you to visualize content as you create it, a feature more common with add-ons than with stand-alone editors. See **http:// www.microsoft.com/** for more information.

25

Make Mine Multimedia

● **In this chapter:**

- **Making your images transparent (this is a good thing)**

- **Little utilities for creating big imagemaps**

- **Tools for making lots of noise**

Creating imagemaps, transparent images, and other media files can be time consuming and difficult. But some of the shareware and freeware utilities that are available on the Net can make your life a lot easier . . . . ❯

I nevitably, while you're designing a Web page, you'll most likely want to add complex graphics to it. Whether it's a transparent image or an imagemap, there are software tools available to help you along. This chapter isn't meant to tell you how to work with images, but rather what tools you have at your disposal for working with them.

Fortunately, there are some good tools for both Macintosh and Windows that take away most of the headaches. Some of these programs are simple and often quick and dirty, but they do their jobs as advertised.

Making see-through images that look great in all browsers

One of the greatest things about the Internet is that it is a cross-platform network that brings together all users. However, this means that there are lots of different pieces of software being used to access the Net. Web browsers are a good example of this. Even though there are a few browsers that seem to be gaining large shares of the market, there will always be the browsers that work on obscure operating systems and early versions of browser software that users haven't bothered upgrading.

You can't possibly design your pages so that they will look perfect in every browser, but there are some steps you can take that will make your images seem like they were custom designed for each individual browser. One thing you can do is make your images transparent. Transparent images not only look better in most instances, they also do a lot to bridge the browser gap.

What's a transparent image?

On some graphically intensive Web pages, you'll see a picture that seems to blend in very well with the background. That is a transparent image. (Actually, it's a transparent **background** to the image.) What it basically does is let the Web browser determine what the background color for that image should be. As a result, a transparent image will appear to "float" above the background. Because the background color of the image is used when making transparent pictures, the background should be a solid color.

So, no matter what browser the user is running, the image will float on the browser's background color. There are a number of tools for both Windows and the Macintosh that can help users make transparent images. The important thing to remember is that only images that have a definite, distinguishable background will work.

Lview Pro

There are image viewing programs and then there are image editing programs. Lview Pro is a program that straddles the two. It is a great image viewer because it loads in all of the most popular image formats and handles them really well. It also offers very simple image editing features, such as editing colors and simple cut-and-paste functionality.

Once an image is loaded you can change the colors of the image with a variety of mechanisms. Additionally, an image can be rotated, cropped, or have text added to it. If you want, you can drag-and-drop a group of files and view them through Lview Pro as a slide show. You can make a contact sheet out of all of them, print them out, or convert them all to JPEG files. You can even preview pictures or do screen captures. Because of all this picture-manipulation functionality, Lview Pro can easily generate transparent images.

To make a transparent GIF with Lview Pro, do the following:

1 Load the image by choosing File, Open.

2 Select the Options menu title and then Background Color selection.

3 A window will pop up displaying a number of square, colored palettes.

4 Find the background color from the window and select it. Then click OK.

5 Now save the file as a GIF89a picture.

You can download the latest copy of Lview Pro from **http://world.std.com/ ˜mmedia/lviewp.html**. The program is shareware, and the registration fee is $30.00.

Paint Shop Pro

Transparent GIFs rely on having only one color as the background to work properly. But what happens if you have more than one color for the background (like in a digitized picture)? You have to get a paint program and touch it up. Paint Shop Pro is a Windows-based shareware program that will let you do these things with a wide range of picture formats.

With Paint Shop Pro, you can alter images with various brushes and change colors with exact precision. You can easily convert a background that has many different colors into one solid color with the use of the fill function. Additionally, transparent GIFs can be made directly by changing the background color of the image. Obviously the particular color should be chosen carefully so that the image looks correct on people's browsers. User-definable brushes, picture rotation, and color coding are all part of this fantastic package. Though this program might be of little use to you if you have an image with a solid color background, it is highly recommended if you don't (see fig. 25.1).

Fig. 25.1
Paint Shop Pro is a potent image editing program for Windows users.

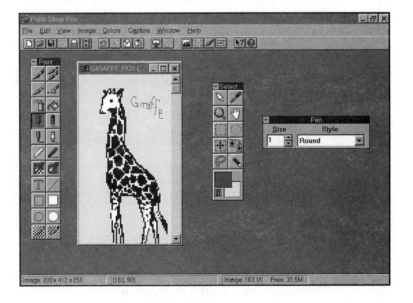

Paint Shop Pro is shareware, and must be registered after 30 days for $75 US. You can get the latest trial version of Paint Shop Pro from most of the big Windows software FTP sites, but the following smaller site is much less busy and easier to get into: **ftp://pluto.cc.umr.edu/pub/windows/**.

Transparency

A very quick and dirty program available for the Macintosh is Transparency. It can only read in GIF files, but as the name implies, it makes them transparent. To specify which color is the background color, click inside the image and hold down the mouse button. The image's palette will show up along with a button on top titled None. If you see an *X* in the color palette, the color the *X* is on represents the current background color. Select the color you want to be the background color, and let go of the mouse button. If you don't want any color to be the background color, select None. Finally, save the picture as a GIF89a file and the next time it's accessed, the picture's background color will match the browser's.

Transparency is only available for the Macintosh, and can be downloaded from **ftp://ftp.med.cornell.edu/pub/aarong/transparency/transparency10.sit.hqx**.

Graphic converter

There are few programs on any platform that are "must haves," but Graphic Converter is such a program. It can load in over 50 different file formats and allow you to modify them as you like. It offers color manipulation, cut and paste, image rotation, and image resizing.

In addition to all these features, you can draw primitive objects (rectangles, ellipses, and text) onto the image. Batch image conversion with any of Graphic Converter's supported formats into almost two dozen formats is possible. It also provides the easiest method for making transparent GIFs under the Picture menu, Colors submenu, and Transparent GIF Color option. Simply put, you're shown the image's color palette, you select a color, and check the Transparent button. You'll see the effect of choosing that color on the right-hand side of the window.

Graphic Converter is also only available for the Macintosh, and is available for download from **http://www.sonoma.edu/Software/graphic-converter-207.hqx**.

Tools for making imagemaps

More and more Web sites are using imagemaps as their whole home page, or at least as their navigational tool. People remember images easily and get used to using a visual navigational tool quite quickly. Perhaps the reason that imagemaps are becoming so standard is that they are becoming increasingly easy to create. This is due to the useful tools that have become available for both Windows and Macintosh.

MapEdit

Windows users will be able to use MapEdit. When you first start it, you must specify a map file name and a GIF (image) file. After loading in the image, you use the Tools menu to create polygons, circles, and rectangles. You must right-click the mouse to signify that you're done creating a region. You must specify the URL that the region links to and optionally put in some comments. When you're done creating regions, simply save the file. MapEdit will create the map file under the name you specified at the beginning.

MapEdit is a very simple and no-nonsense program offering no shortcuts for region creation, like WebMap. However, it does make up for this shortcoming by letting you nest the clickable regions. Also, it comes with the useful ability to test and edit the imagemap regions, so you can see which regions get activated where.

You can download a copy of MapEdit from **http://sunsite.unc.edu/pub/ packages/infosystems/www/tools/mapedit/**. The cost to register MapEdit is $25.

WebMap

Macintosh users won't be left out in the cold for imagemap editing programs. There's an adequate one available called WebMap, a commercially available product, to make imagemaps quickly. You can load GIF or PICT images and then draw rectangles, circles, ellipses, polygons, or dots as clickable regions on them. Once you've created each region, you specify the URL it will point to and optionally put a comment in for yourself. Be advised that you can't put a smaller clickable region within a larger one.

After you've created all the clickable areas you want, you simply save the file. In addition to saving the picture, it will also create an .M file, which is what

MacHTTP needs for imagemaps. To create a map file useable for other HTTP daemons, choose File, Export As Text. You will be able to create your choice of an NCSA or CERN-compatible map file.

WebMap can be downloaded from **http://www.City.net/cnx/software/ webmap.html**.

Tools for creating sound

There are a number of tools that allow you to listen to audio files after you've downloaded them from the Internet. However, not too many people know how to go about actually making and editing their own noise. There are some applications available that can really help you get started. You can either use preexisting digital sound files or, if you have a microphone, create your own from scratch. The questions are: What do you do with them, and how do you edit them?

RealAudio Server, Player, and Encoder

It used to be that using audio clips on a Web page was something you only did in moderation. The reason was that audio compression was still not very good, and, therefore, audio files were huge and took a long time to download. With most audio files, you have to download them and then fire up an audio player to listen. However, a company called RealAudio has come up with some software that allows Internet users to listen to audio files as they are being downloaded.

This means that instead of sitting in front of your monitor waiting patiently for a file to download, you can sit back and listen as it downloads. And, if you missed something, you can play the file over again because it is saved to your hard drive. You can also pause, stop, and rewind the file.

Not only does RealAudio distribute RealAudio Player with versions for Windows and the Mac, it also distributes RealAudio Encoder, which compresses digital audio files that are in WAV, PCM, or AU formats, and converts them to RealAudio format. The resulting .RA files can be played with the RealAudio Player and delivered through the Internet using the RealAudio Server.

You can't just put a RealAudio file on your Web site and expect it to work properly. You need to have the RealAudio Server running in order to deliver .RA files in real-time format. RealAudio Server is quite expensive for personal use (over $1,000), so the company has made available the RealAudio Personal Server. You can't serve nearly as much audio with the Personal Server, but at $99 it's much less expensive

These tools can all be accessed from the RealAudio home page at **http://www.realaudio.com/**.

Wham

Wham is a nifty little sound file editor for Windows that gives the user lots of control over individual bits of sound. Using Wham, you can speed up, slow down, and reverse entire sound files or just parts of them. You can also change the volume of the sound file or part of the sound file, and you can manipulate the sound resolution of your file (see fig. 25.2).

You can download a copy of Wham from **http://www.prism.uvsq.fr/public/wos/multimedia/wham133.zip**. Wham is shareware, and the author of the program requests a donation of $20 to $30 be sent if you continue to use the program.

Fig. 25.2
You can use your mouse to select the part of a sound that you want to edit when you use the Wham audio program.

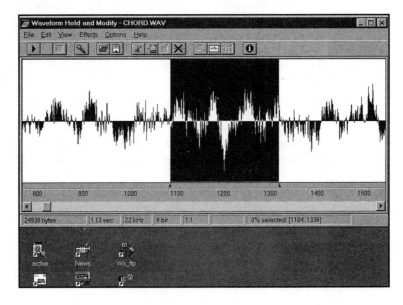

GoldWave

Wham is a neat little program, but GoldWave is really a step up. Not only does it have all of the editing features that you can find in Wham, but it also includes the ability to convert files between mono and stereo sound and to add tremolo effects. You can also designate specific cue points in a sound file, so that you can get back to those specific points later.

The most impressive feature of the GoldWave program, though, is the ability of users to separately edit the channels of stereo sound. There are also numerous predefined filters and the ability to add fade-ins, fade-outs, echoes, and other interesting effects (see fig. 25.3).

You can download a copy of GoldWave from **http://www.cs.mun.ca/~chris3/goldwave/release.html**. This program is shareware, and registration costs $25.00.

Fig. 25.3
GoldWave is a robust sound file editor that enables users to take advantage of numerous predefined effects.

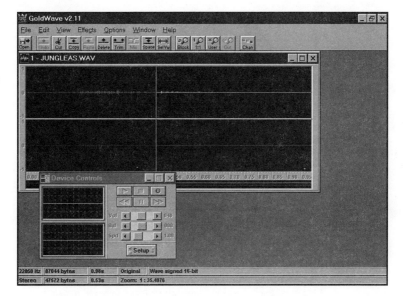

HTML Elements Reference

This appendix presents the HTML 2.0 elements by their appropriate usage in Web documents. HTML 3.0 elements are included and noted if they're supported by any available Web clients. Netscape extensions are also included and noted as such (including the version of Netscape that is required for compatibility).

The standard format of an entry is as follows:

ELEMENT

Element description

Container or empty element?

Syntax of usage

Attributes

Attribute description

Syntax of usage

Attribute option and option description

Usage

Legal uses of current element

The following is an example:

P

Inserts a paragraph break at the current point in the document, beginning with the next line of text or inline graphic against the left margin two lines beneath the current text.

Empty element, requiring no closing tag.

Syntax: <P>

Attributes

ALIGN   HTML 3.0 revision of P element, using it as a container and applying alignment to all of the content within the container.

              Syntax: <P ALIGN=center> ... </P>

Usage

Body section—stand-alone and within lists, preformatted text and forms containers.

Whole Document Elements

BODY

Defines the body section in an HTML document.

Container element, requires </BODY> closing tag.

Attributes

BACKGROUND   Netscape 1.1 extension to the standard HTML, specifying a graphic image to be used for the background of the current document.

              Syntax: <BODY BACKGROUND=*URL*> (where *URL* is a graphic URL)

BGCOLOR   Netscape 1.1 extension specifying a color to be used for the current document.

              Syntax: <BODY BGCOLOR=*value*> (where *value* is a color notation)

              Color notation: "xyz" (where x is the value for the red color component, y is the value for the green color component, and z is the value for the blue color component; values range from 0–9)

TEXT   Netscape 1.1 extension specifying a color to be used for the body content text.

              Syntax: <BODY TEXT=*value*> (where *value* is a color notation)

              Color notation: "xyz" (where x is the value for the red color component, y is the value for the green color component, and z is the value for the blue color component; values range from 0–9)

LINK   Netscape 1.1 extension specifying a color to be used for body content hyperlinks.

Syntax: <BODY LINK=value> (where value is a color notation)

Color notation: "$xyz" (where x is the value for the red color component, y is the value for the green color component, and z is the value for the blue color component; values range from 0–9)

VLINK   Netscape 1.1 extension specifying a color to be used for visited body content hyperlinks.

Syntax: <BODY VLINK=value> (where value is a color notation)

Color notation: "$xyz" (where x is the value for the red color component, y is the value for the green color component, and z is the value for the blue color component; values range from 0–9)

ALINK   Netscape 1.1 extension specifying a color to be used for active body content hyperlinks.

Syntax: <BODY ALINK=value> (where value is a color notation)

Color notation: "$xyz" (where x is the value for the red color component, y is the value for the green color component, and z is the value for the blue color component; values range from 0–9)

Usage

Enclose all HTML content that is a part of the document's body data that is to be displayed by Web clients, including text, inline images and hyperlink anchors.

Comment Coding

Nonstandard HTML container for inserting hidden comments in HTML documents, which are not displayed in Web viewers.

Container element, requiring closing tag.

Syntax: <!—...—>

Attributes
None

Usage
Any document section and in containers if required.

HEAD

Defines the head section in an HTML document.

Container element, requiring </HEAD> closing tag.

Attributes
None

Usage
Encloses all HTML content that isn't a part of the body data in a document, including the document's title and link relationships.

HTML

Defines the HTML content in a document on a Web server.

Container element, requiring </HTML> closing tag.

Syntax: <HTML>...</HTML>

Attributes
None

Usage
Encloses all content in a document that should be recognized as HTML by Internet applications (such as Web viewers).

Head Section Elements

BASE

Indicates the URL of the current document. This helps Web viewers process relative hypertext links within the document.

Empty element, requiring no closing tag.

Syntax: <BASE HREF=*URL*> (where *URL* is specific for the current document)

Attributes

None

Usage

Head section only, not within containers.

ISINDEX

Indicates that the current Web page can be searched with the Web client's search feature. Requires server-side index search capabilities.

Empty element, requiring no closing tag.

Syntax: <ISINDEX>

Attributes

PROMPT   Netscape 1.0 extension, customizes text message in search dialog box or window

Syntax: <ISINDEX PROMPT="*value*"> (where *value* is the new text message)

Usage

Head section only, not within containers. Requires the server-side capability to service searches.

LINK

Establishes a relationship between the current document and another document. Can be used more than once to define multiple relationships.

Empty element, requiring no closing tag.

Syntax: <LINK *attribute* HREF=*URL*> (where *attribute* is the applicable relationship, and *URL* is the other party in the relationship)

Attributes

REL   Defines the relationship between the current document and the URL.

Syntax: <LINK REL=*relationship* HREF=*URL*> (where *relationship* is the type of relationship being defined)

Options:

PRECEDE	The current document precedes the resource in the *URL* value
PREV	The *URL* value resource precedes the current document
USEINDEX	The *URL* document is a related index used in searches in the current document
USEGLOSSARY	The *URL* document is an index used for glossary queries in the current document
ANNOTATION	The *URL* document provides secondary information (such as margin notes) for the current document
REPLY	The *URL* document provides primary information for the current document
PRECEDES	Defines the ordered relationship between the two documents, where the current document comes before the *URL* document
SUBDOCUMENT	Defines the hierarchical relationship between two documents, where the current document is higher than the *URL* document
PRESENT	States that whenever the current document is retrieved, the *URL* document must be retrieved as well (but not vice versa)
SEARCH	States that when the *URL* document is accessed, a search is carried out on it before its content is retrieved
SUPERSEDES	The *URL* document is a previous version of the current document
HISTORY	The *URL* document contains a documented history of the versions of the current document
MADE	The *URL* value is the e-mail address of the creator of the current document

    OWNS The *URL* value defines the owner of the current document

   INCLUDES The current document includes (as a grouping) the *URL* value

 REV Defined the relation between the URL and the current document (the reverse relationship of REL)

    Syntax: <LINK REV=*relationship* HREF=*URL*> (where *relationship* is the type of relationship being defined)

    Options: Use the same as with REL, but reverse the defined relationships

Usage

Head section only, not within containers.

NEXTID

Indicates the nextID value to use for link name.

Empty element, not requiring a closing tag.

Syntax: <NEXTID=*value*> (where *value* is a unique number)

Attributes

None

Usage

Head section only, not within containers.

TITLE

Indicates the document's title, which is displayed in Web viewers but not in the body of the document text.

Container element, requiring </TITLE> closing tag.

Syntax: <TITLE>...</TITLE>

Attributes

None

Usage

Head section only, not within containers.

Body Section Elements

A

Indicates a document anchor, used to create links to other resources or to define a location that can be linked to.

Container element, requiring </A> closing tag.

Options:

Creating a hyperlink to a WWW resource:

Syntax: <A HREF= "*URL*">...</A> (where *URL* describes a valid WWW resource)

Attributes: None

Usage: Body section, stand-alone or within text, form, and table containers. Text between the anchor tags is clickable and will appear in the viewer's currently defined link color. Clicking the link text activates the link and accesses the specified Web resource.

Defining a named anchor location:

Syntax: <A name="*value*">...</A> (where *value* is a unique anchor name for the current document)

Attributes: None

Usage: Body section, stand-alone or within text, form, and table containers. Text between the anchor tags is not highlighted or clickable.

Creating a hyperlink to a named anchor:

Syntax: <A HREF= "*URL#value*">...</A> (where *URL* describes a valid WWW document and *value* is a named anchor within that document)

Attributes: None

Usage: Body section, stand-alone or within text, form, and table containers. Text between the anchor tags is clickable and will appear in the viewer's currently defined link color. Clicking the link text activates the link and accesses the specified location in the specified Web page.

Creating a hyperlink to a named anchor in the same document:

Syntax: <A HREF= "#*value*">...</A> (where *value* is a named anchor within the same document)

Attributes: None

Usage: Body section, stand-alone or within text, form, and table containers. Text between the anchor tags is clickable and will appear in the viewer's currently defined link color. Clicking the link text activates the link and accesses the specified location in the same Web page.

ADDRESS

Defines the address of the document author and is displayed in Web viewers.

Container element, requiring </ADDRESS> closing tag.

Syntax: <ADDRESS>...</ADDRESS>

Attributes
None

Usage
Body or form sections, stand-alone or within containers.

B

Formats the container text as bold text. Requires HTML break elements for text breaks. Can be combined with active HTML style elements.

Container element, requiring </B> closing tag.

Syntax: <B>...</B>

Attributes
None

Usage
Body section, stand-alone, and within list and form containers.

BASEFONT

Defines the default document text size to a value from 1–7 (3 is the common default). Requires Netscape support. Affects relative FONT element use.

Empty element, does not require a closing tag.

Syntax: <BASEFONT SIZE=*n*> (where *n* is a font size value from 1–7)

Attributes
None

Usage
Body section, stand-alone, and within list and form containers.

BLINK

Makes the container text blink on and off in the WWW client window. Requires Netscape support. Can be combined with active HTML style elements.

Container element, requiring </BLINK> closing tag.

Syntax: <BLINK>...</BLINK>

Attributes
None

Usage
Body section, stand-alone, and within list and form containers. Support is very limited and the element is unpopular with readers. Use sparingly.

BLOCKQUOTE

Defines the container text as a quotation from another source, using the viewer's current text settings. Retains all natural line and paragraph breaks in the text and indents both right and left margins. Can contain active HTML style elements.

Container element, requiring </BLOCKQUOTE> closing tag.

Syntax: <BLOCKQUOTE>...</BLOCKQUOTE>

Attributes
None

Usage
Body section, stand-alone, and within list and form containers.

BR

Inserts a line break at the current point in the document, beginning with the next line of text or inline graphic against the left margin one line beneath the current text.

Empty element, requiring no closing tag.

Syntax:

Attributes

CLEAR   Netscape 1.0 extension, defining where the content can begin the next line in the document.

Syntax: <BR CLEAR=*value*> (where *value* is a valid option)

Options:

LEFT   The content can continue on the next available line whose left margin is clear

RIGHT   The content can continue on the next available line whose right margin is clear

ALL   The content can continue on the next available line where both margins are clear

Usage

Body section—stand-alone and within lists, preformatted text and form containers.

CENTER

Aligns the container text relative to the current container. Requires Netscape 1.0 support. Can be combined with active HTML style elements.

Container element, requiring </CENTER> closing tag.

Syntax: <CENTER>...</CENTER>

Attributes

None

Usage

Body section, stand-alone, and within list and form containers. Will be superseded by HTML 3.0's ALIGN attribute to the P and H elements.

CITE

Defines the container text as a text citation, using the viewer's current text settings. Requires HTML break elements for text breaks. Can be combined with active HTML style elements.

Container element, requiring </CITE> closing tag.

Syntax: <CITE>...</CITE>

Attributes
None

Usage
Body section, stand-alone, and within list and form containers.

CODE

Defines the container text as computer code text, using the viewer's current text settings. Requires HTML break elements for text breaks. Can be combined with active HTML style elements.

Container element, requiring </CODE> closing tag.

Syntax: <CODE>...</CODE>

Attributes
None

Usage
Body section, stand-alone, and within list and form containers.

DD

Formats subsequent body text as a text definition. Provides additional space when it is superseded by a new element. Can contain active HTML elements.

Empty element, does not require a closing tag

Syntax: <DD>

Attributes
None

Usage
Body section, a component of definition lists (DL), generally following a definition term (DT).

DFN

Defines the container text as definition text, using the viewer's current text settings. Requires HTML break elements for text breaks. Can be combined with active HTML style elements.

Container element, requiring </DFN> closing tag.

Syntax: <DFN>...</DFN>

Attributes
None

Usage
Body section, stand-alone, and within list and form containers. Support by current Web viewers is inconsistent (not recommended for use).

DIR

Formats the container text as a file directory list. Contains list items (LI). Can contain active HTML elements. Intended to format text in compressed columns, but viewer support is rare.

Container element, requiring </DIR> closing tag.

Syntax: <DIR>...</DIR>

Attributes
None

Usage
Body section, stand-alone, or within other list, form, and table containers.

DL

Formats the container text as a definition list. Contains definition term (DT) and definition text (DD). Provides a double-spaced closing text break.

Container element, requiring </DL> closing tag.

Syntax: <DL>...</DL>

Attributes
None

Usage
Body section, stand-alone, or within other list, form, and table containers.

DT

Formats subsequent body text as a definition term. Provides additional space after the term. Can contain active HTML elements.

Empty element, does not require a closing tag

Syntax: <DT>

Attributes

None

Usage

Body section, a component of definition lists (DL).

EM

Defines the container text as emphasized, using the viewer's current text settings. Requires HTML break elements for text breaks. Can be combined with active HTML style elements.

Container element, requiring </EM> closing tag.

Syntax: <EM>...</EM>

Attributes

None

Usage

Body section, stand-alone, and within list and form containers.

FONT

Formats the container text to the specific or relative font size indicated. Requires Netscape support. Does not affect the use of any other HTML elements.

Container element, requiring </FONT> closing tag.

Syntax: <FONT SIZE=*value*>...</FONT> (where *value* is an absolute or relative font size)

Attributes

None

Usage

Options:

> *Absolute font size.* Font will be displayed at a specific size ranging from 1–7 (one being the smallest font and seven the largest)

> Syntax example: <FONT SIZE=5>...</FONT>

> *Relative font size.* Font will be displayed at a size relative (using the plus and minus symbols) to the current base font, which is normally a size 3.

> Syntax example: <FONT SIZE=–2>...</FONT>

Usage

Body section, stand-alone, and within list and form containers.

H*n*

Defines the container text as a heading, using the viewer's current text settings. Requires HTML break elements for text breaks. Can be combined with active HTML style elements.

Container element, requiring </H*n*> closing tag.

Syntax: <H*n*>...</H*n*> (where *n* corresponds to the heading level)

Level values of 1–6 are valid and each will have unique text definitions; in general, the lower the level number, the larger and more prominent the display text will be.

Attributes

ALIGN   HTML 3.0 revision of H element, applying on-screen alignment to all of the content within the container.

> Syntax: <H*n*ALIGN=*value*>...</H*n*> (where *value* is a valid alignment option and *n* corresponds to the heading level)

> Options:

>> *LEFT*   The content is aligned against the left text margin

>> *RIGHT*   The content is aligned against the right text margin

>> *CENTER*   The content is centered between the left and right text margins

Usage

Body section, stand-alone, and within list and form containers. Headings define logical relationships; for example, H2 is a subheading of H1 and a superheading of H3. Alignment options are relative to the current container.

HR

Displays a horizontal rule in the WWW client window. The rule fills the current container from the left to the right margins. Does not affect other HTML elements in use.

Empty element, does not require a closing tag.

Syntax: <HR>

Attributes

WIDTH   Netscape 1.0 extension, defines the actual or window percentage length of the horizontal rule

Syntax: <HR WIDTH=*value*> (where *value* is a pixel measurement or a percentage, as in 50 percent)

SIZE   Netscape 1.0 extension, defines the height or thickness of the horizontal rule

Syntax: <HR SIZE=*n*> (where *n* is a pixel measurement)

NOSHADE   Netscape 1.0 extension, displays the rule as a solid black line with no drop shadow

Syntax: <HR NOSHADE>

ALIGN   Netscape 1.0 extension, aligns the horizontal rule relative to the current container

Syntax: <HR ALIGN=*value*> (where *value* is a valid alignment option)

Options:

         LEFT   The rule is aligned against the left text margin

         RIGHT   The rule is aligned against the right text margin

CENTER   The rule is centered between the left and right margins

Usage

Body section, stand-alone, and within text containers.

I

Formats the container text as italicized text. Requires HTML break elements for text breaks. Can be combined with active HTML style elements.

Container element, requiring </I> closing tag.

Syntax: <I>...</I>

Attributes

None

Usage

Body section, stand-alone, and within list and form containers.

IMG

Displays inline images and image maps in the document body.

Empty element, does not require a closing tag.

Syntax: <IMG SRC="*URL*"> (where *URL* describes a valid graphic image file)

Attributes

SRC   Defines the source of the associated image file

ALT   Defines a text string to be displayed by a WWW client if inline graphic support is not available.

Syntax: <IMG SRC="*URL*" ALT"*value*"> (where *URL* is a valid graphic file and *value* is a text message)

ISMAP   Defines the inline image as an image map.

Syntax: <IMG SRC="*URL*" ISMAP> (where *URL* is a valid graphic file)

ALIGN   Applies a specific alignment to text on the same line as the current inline graphic.

Syntax: <IMG SRC="*URL*" ALIGN=*value*> (where *URL* is a valid graphic file and *value* is a valid alignment option)

Options:

TOP	Align the top of the image with the line's text
MIDDLE	Align the middle of the image with the line's text
BOTTOM	Align the bottom of the image with the line's text (default)
LEFT	Netscape 1.0 extension, aligns the graphic along the left-hand margin and allows text to flow beside the image
RIGHT	Netscape 1.0 extension, aligns the graphic along the right-hand margin and allows the text to flow beside the image
TEXTTOP	Netscape 1.0 extension, aligns the top of the image with the top of the tallest text on the line
ABSMIDDLE	Netscape 1.0 extension, aligns the middle of the image with the middle of the line's text
BASELINE	Netscape 1.0 extension, aligns the bottom of the image with the baseline of the line's text
ABSBOTTOM	Netscape 1.0 extension, aligns the bottom of the image with the bottom of the line's text

HSPACE   Netscape 1.0 extension, defines the space along the horizontal edges of an inline graphics between the graphic and the adjacent text.

Syntax: <IMG SRC="*URL*" HSPACE=*n*> (where *URL* is a valid graphic file and *n* is the measurement of the blank space in pixels)

Usage: Often used in conjunction with VSPACE.

VSPACE   Netscape 1.0 extension, defines the space along the vertical edges of an inline graphic between the graphic and the adjacent text

Syntax: <IMG SRC="*URL*" VSPACE=*n*> (where *URL* is a valid graphic file and *n* is the measurement of the blank space in pixels)

Usage: Often used in conjunction with HSPACE.

WIDTH   Netscape 1.0 extension, defines the width of the inline image for the convenience of the WWW client; used with HEIGHT

HEIGHT   Netscape 1.0 extension, defines the height of the inline image for the convenience of the WWW client; used with WIDTH

Syntax: <IMG SRC="*URL*" WIDTH=*n1* HEIGHT=*n2*> (where *URL* is a valid graphic file, *n1* is the measurement of the width of the image in pixels, and *n2* is the measurement of the height of the image in pixels)

Usage: The WIDTH and HEIGHT values can be purposefully different than the image's actual measurements to force the image to "scale" to the new dimensions.

BORDER   Netscape 1.0 extension, determines the size of the client-provided border for an inline image.

Syntax: <IMG SRC="*URL*" BORDER=*n*> (where *URL* is a valid graphic file and *n* is the thickness of the border in pixels)

LOWSRC   Netscape 1.0 extension, defines a "low resolution" version of the inline image to be displayed at initial retrieval of the document, before the primary image is retrieved.

Syntax: <IMG SRC="*URL1*" LOWRSC="*URL2*"> (where *URL1* is a valid graphic file and *URL2* is a valid low resolution substitution for *URL1*)

Usage
Body or form sections, stand-alone, or within containers.

KBD

Defines the container text as keyboard input text, using the viewer's current text settings. Requires HTML break elements for text breaks. Can be combined with active HTML style elements.

Container element, requiring </KBD> closing tag.

Syntax: <KBD>...</KBD>

Attributes
None

Usage
Body section, stand-alone, and within list and form containers.

LI

Defines a new item in a list.

Empty element, does not require a closing tag.

Syntax: <LI>...

Attributes

TYPE   Netscape 1.0 extension, defines the current list type (regardless of the list container)

     Syntax: <LI TYPE=value> (where value is a valid type option)

     Options:

CIRCLE	Defines the unordered list marker type as filled circles
SQUARE	Defines the unordered list marker type as filled squares
DISC	Defines the unordered list marker type as unfilled circles
A	Defines the ordered list numbering characters as uppercase letters
a	Defines the ordered list numbering characters as lowercase letters
I	Defines the ordered list numbering characters as uppercase Roman numerals
i	Defines the ordered list numbering characters as lowercase Roman numerals

    1   Defines the ordered list numbering characters as numbers (default)

VALUE   Netscape 1.0 extension, defines the new beginning sequential value for the container's current and subsequent list items

    Syntax: <LI VALUE=*n*> (where *n* is a sequential value)

Usage

Body section, in ordered lists (OL) and unordered lists (UL)

LISTING

Defines the container text as a computer text list, using the viewer's current text settings. Retains all natural line and paragraph breaks in the text. Does not recognize internal HTML style elements.

Container element, requiring </LISTING> closing tag.

Syntax: <LISTING>...</LISTING>

Attributes

None

Usage

Body section, stand-alone, and within list and form containers. This element is deprecated and support by current Web viewers is inconsistent (not recommended for use).

MENU

Formats the container text as a menu list. Contains list items (LI). Can contain active HTML elements.

Container element, requiring </MENU> closing tag.

Syntax: <MENU>...</MENU>

Attributes

None

Usage

Body section, stand-alone, or within other list, form, and table containers.

NOBR

Prevents the container text from wrapping in the viewer window. Requires Netscape 1.0 support. Can be combined with active HTML style elements.

Container element, requiring </NOBR> closing tag.

Syntax: <NOBR>...</NOBR>

Attributes

None

Usage

Body section, stand-alone, and within list and form containers.

OL

Formats the container text as an ordered list. Sequentially numbers each enclosed list item (LI). Requires HTML break elements for text breaks. Can contain active HTML style elements.

Container element, requiring </OL> closing tag.

Syntax: <OL>...</OL>

Attributes

TYPE   Netscape 1.0 extension, defines the marker type for items in the contained list

       Syntax: <UL TYPE=*value*> (where *value* is a valid marker option)

       Options:

           A   Defines the numbering characters as uppercase letters

           a   Defines the numbering characters as lowercase letters

           I   Defines the numbering characters as uppercase Roman numerals

           i   Defines the numbering characters as lowercase Roman numerals

           1   Defines the numbering characters as numbers (default)

START   Netscape 1.0 extension, defines the starting sequential value for the container's list items

Syntax: <OL START=n> (where n is the starting value for the listed items)

Usage

Body section, stand-alone and within other containers. Uses the LI element to identify list items.

P

Inserts a paragraph break at the current point in the document, beginning the next line of text or inline graphic against the left margin two lines beneath the current text.

Empty element, requiring no closing tag.

Syntax: <P>

Attributes

ALIGN   HTML 3.0 revision of P element, using it as a container and applying alignment to all of the content within the container.

Syntax: <P ALIGN=*value*> ... </P> (where *value* is a valid option)

Options:

LEFT	The content is aligned against the left text margin
RIGHT	The content is aligned against the right text margin
CENTER	The content is centered between the left and right text margins

Usage

Body section—stand-alone and within lists, preformatted text and forms containers. ALIGN values are relative to the current container.

PLAINTEXT

Defines the subsequent text as unformatted text, using the viewer's current text settings. Retains all natural line and paragraph breaks in the text. Does not recognize internal HTML style elements.

Empty element, requiring no closing tag.

Syntax: <PLAINTEXT>

Attributes

None

Usage

Body section, stand-alone. This element has no closing tag, and all subsequent content (including HTML elements) is displayed as plain text. This element is deprecated and support by current Web viewers is *very* inconsistent (not recommended for use).

PRE

Defines the container content as preformatted and is displayed with the viewer's current text settings (usually a standard proportional font). Retains all natural line and paragraph breaks within the text. Can contain active HTML style elements.

Container element, requiring </PRE> closing tag.

Syntax: <PRE>...</PRE>

Attributes

WIDTH   Defines the width of a preformatted text container, in characters.

Syntax: <PRE WIDTH=n>...</PRE> (where n is the number of characters per line)

Usage

Body section, stand-alone and within lists and form containers.

S

Formats the container text with strikeouts. Requires HTML break elements for text breaks. Can be combined with active HTML style elements.

Container element, requiring </S> closing tag.

Syntax: <S>...</S>

Attributes

None

Usage

Body section, stand-alone and within list and form containers. Support by current Web viewers is rare (will become more common with the adoption of HTML 3.0).

SAMP

Defines the container text as sample output text, using the viewer's current text settings. Requires HTML break elements for text breaks. Can be combined with active HTML style elements.

Container element, requiring </SAMP> closing tag.

Syntax: <SAMP>...</SAMP>

Attributes
None

Usage
Body section, stand-alone and within list and form containers.

STRONG

Defines the container text as strongly emphasized, using the viewer's current text settings. Requires HTML break elements for text breaks. Can be combined with active HTML style elements.

Container element, requiring </STRONG> closing tag.

Syntax: <STRONG>...</STRONG>

Attributes
None

Usage
Body section, stand-alone and within list and form containers.

TT

Formats the container text as typewriter-style text (monospaced font). Requires HTML break elements for text breaks. Can be combined with active HTML style elements.

Container element, requiring </TT> closing tag.

Syntax: <TT>...</TT>

Attributes
None

Usage
Body section, stand-alone and within list and form containers.

U

Formats the container text as underlined text. Requires HTML break elements for text breaks. Can be combined with active HTML style elements.

Container element, requiring </U> closing tag.

Syntax: <U>...</U>

Attributes

None

Usage

Body section, stand-alone and within list and form containers. Support by current Web viewers is inconsistent (will become more common with the adoption of HTML 3.0).

UL

Formats the container text as an unordered list. Mark each enclosed list item (LI) with a viewer-defined bullet. Requires HTML break elements for text breaks. Can contain active HTML style elements.

Container element, requiring </UL> closing tag.

Syntax: <UL>...</UL>

Attributes

TYPE   Netscape 1.0 extension, defines the marker type for items in the contained list

Syntax: <UL TYPE=*value*> (where *value* is a valid marker option)

Options:

CIRCLE   Defines the marker type as filled circles

SQUARE   Defines the marker type as filled squares

DISC   Defines the marker type as unfilled circles

Usage

Body section, stand-alone and within other containers. Uses the LI element to identify list items.

VAR

Defines the container text as a text variable, using the viewer's current text settings. Requires HTML break elements for text breaks. Can be combined with active HTML style elements.

Container element, requiring </VAR> closing tag.

Syntax: <VAR>...</VAR>

Attributes
None

Usage
Body section, stand-alone and within list and form containers.

WBR

Indicates a possible break point in the text. Requires Netscape 1.0 support. Is often used with the NOBR container elements.

Empty element, does not require a closing tag.

Syntax: <WBR>

Attributes
None

Usage
Body section, stand-alone and within list and form containers.

XMP

Defines the container text as a prefromatted text example, using the viewer's current text settings. Retains all natural line and paragraph breaks in the text. Does not recognize internal HTML style elements.

Container element, requiring </XMP> closing tag.

Syntax: <XMP>…</XMP>

Attributes
None

Usage
Body section, stand-alone and within list and form containers. This element is deprecated and support by current Web viewers is inconsistent (not recommended for use).

Table Elements (HTML 3.0 features)

CAPTION

Defines the table's caption text. Can contain active HTML elements.

Container element, requiring the </CAPTION> closing tag

Syntax: <CAPTION>…</CAPTION>

Attributes
ALIGN   Defines the alignment of the caption text with the table

Syntax: <CAPTION ALIGN=value> (where value is a valid alignment option)

Options:

TOP   Aligns caption above the table

Syntax: <CAPTION ALIGN=TOP>

BOTTOM   Aligns caption below the table

Syntax: <CAPTION ALIGN=BOTTOM>

Usage
Body section, within table containers only.

TABLE

Defines the container text as a table. Contains rows (TR), cells (TD), headers (TH), and captions (CAPTION). Can contain active HTML elements, including forms.

Container element, requiring </TABLE> closing tag.

Syntax: <TABLE>...</TABLE>

Attributes

BORDER   Defines the line weight of the border around the table cells.

Syntax: <TABLE BORDER=n> (where n is a number representing the chosen line weight)

Usage: If no border attribute is included, table will display cells without borders.

CELLSPACING   Netscape 1.1 extension, defines horizontal spacing between adjacent cells.

Syntax: <TABLE CELLSPACING=n> (where n is the number of pixels between adjacent cells)

CELLPADDING   Netscape 1.1 extension, defines vertical spacing between adjacent cells.

Syntax: <TABLE CELLPADDING=n> (where n is the number of pixels between adjacent cells)

WIDTH   Netscape 1.1 extension, defines width of table cells in pixels or as a percentage of the container's width.

Syntax: <TABLE WIDTH=*value*> (where *value* is the number of pixels or the percentage, expressed as n percent, of the width of the individual cells)

Usage

Body section, stand-alone or within other list and form containers.

TD

Defines the text in individual table cells. Supports active HTML elements.

Container element, requiring </TD> closing tag

Syntax: <TD>...</TD>

Attributes

ALIGN   Defines the text's horizontal alignment within the specific table cell

Syntax: <TD ALIGN=*value*> (where *value* is a valid alignment option)

Options:

LEFT	Aligns the text with the cell's left edge
RIGHT	Aligns the text with the cell's right edge
CENTER	Centers the text in the cell

VALIGN   Defines the text's vertical alignment within the specific cell

Options:

TOP	Aligns the header text with the top of the cell
MIDDLE	Aligns the header text with the middle of the cell
BOTTOM	Aligns the header text with the bottom of the cell

NOWRAP   Instructs the viewer not to wrap the text within the table cell

Syntax: <TD NOWRAP>

COLSPAN   Instructs the viewer to span the specified number of table columns

Syntax: <TD COLSPAN=*n*> (where *n* is a number of table columns to span)

ROWSPAN   Instructs the viewer to span the specified table rows

Syntax: <TD ROWSPAN=n> (where n is the number of table rows to span)

WIDTH   Netscape 1.1 extension, defines the width of the specific table cell

Syntax: <TD WIDTH=*value*> (where *value* is either the number of pixels or the percentage, expressed as n percent, of the width of the table header)

Usage
Body section, within table row containers only.

TH

Defines header text in a table. Does not support additional HTML elements.

Container element, requiring </TH> closing tag

Syntax: <TH>…</TH>

Attributes
ALIGN   Defines the horizontal alignment of the header text within the table cell

Syntax: <TH ALIGN=*value*> (where *value* is a valid alignment option)

Options:

LEFT   Aligns the header text with the cell's left edge

RIGHT   Aligns the header text with the cell's right edge

CENTER   Centers the header text in the cell

VALIGN   Defines the vertical alignment of the header text within the cell

Options:

TOP   Aligns the header text with the top of the cell

	MIDDLE	Aligns the header text with the middle of the cell
	BOTTOM	Aligns the header text with the bottom of the cell

NOWRAP   Instructs the viewer not to wrap the header text within the table cell

Syntax: <TH NOWRAP>

COLSPAN   Instructs the viewer to span the specified number of table columns

Syntax: <TH COLSPAN=*n*> (where *n* is a number of table columns to span)

ROWSPAN   Instructs the viewer to span the specified table rows

Syntax: <TH ROWSPAN=*n*> (where *n* is the number of table rows to span)

WIDTH   Netscape 1.1 extension, defines the width of the table header cell within the table

Syntax: <TH WIDTH=*value*> (where *value* is either the number of pixels or the percentage, expressed as *n* percent, of the width of the table header)

Usage
Body section, within table containers only.

TR

Defines a row within a table

Container element, requiring </TR> closing tag

Syntax: <TR>...</TR>

Attributes
ALIGN   Defines the horizontal alignment of the text within the table row

Syntax: <TR ALIGN=*value*> (where *value* is a valid alignment option)

Options:

LEFT	Aligns text to the left edge in the row's cells
RIGHT	Aligns text to the right edge in the row's cells
CENTER	Centers text in the row's cells

VALIGN   Defines the vertical alignment of the text within the row's cells

Options:

TOP	Aligns the text with the top of the row's cells
MIDDLE	Aligns the text with the middle of the row's cells
BOTTOM	Aligns the text with the bottom of the row's cells

Usage
Body section, within table containers only.

Form Elements (HTML 3.0 features)

FORM

Defines the container text as a form. Contains input fields (INPUT), selection lists (SELECT) and input boxes (TEXTAREA). Can contain active HTML elements.

Container element, requiring </FORM> closing tag.

Syntax: <FORM>...</FORM>

Attributes
ACTION   Defines the program that will process the current form.

METHOD   Defines the procedure for passing information to the ACTION URL

Syntax: <FORM ACTION="*URL*" METHOD=*value*> (where *URL* is a valid Web resource and *value* is a valid method option)

Options:

GET	Program retrieves data from current document
POST	Web page sends the data to the processing program

Usage

Body section, stand-alone or within list or table containers.

INPUT

Defines an input field where the user may enter information on the form.

Empty element, does not require a closing tag.

Syntax: <INPUT>

Attributes

TYPE   Defines the format of input data

Syntax: <INPUT TYPE=value> (where value is a valid type option)

Options:

TEXT	Define input type as character data
PASSWORD	Define input type as character data
CHECKBOX	Define input type as a checkbox
RADIO	Define input type as a radio button
SUBMIT	Define input type as a submit form data button
RESET	Define input type as a reset form data button

NAME   Establishes the symbolic name for this input field

Syntax: <INPUT NAME=*value*> (where *value* is a text name)

Usage: Required for all INPUT types except SUBMIT and RESET.

CHECKED   Indicates that this input field is checked by default

Syntax: <INPUT CHECKED>

SIZE   Defines the physical size of the input field

Options:

For single-line input fields

Syntax: <INPUT SIZE=n> (where n is the number of charac-ters for the field)

For multiline input fields

Syntax: <INPUT SIZE=x,y> (where x is the number of characters per line and y is the number of lines in the input field)

MAXLENGTH   Establishes the maximum number of characters of input that can be entered into an input field

Syntax: <INPUT MAXLENGTH=n> (where n is the number of characters allowed in the input field)

Usage
Body section, form container only.

OPTION

Defines a selection item in a selection list; does not support HTML elements.

Empty element, does not require a closing tag.

Syntax: <OPTION>...

Attributes
SELECTED   Indicates the selection list option that is selected by default

Syntax: <OPTION SELECTED>

Usage
Body section, form container, within a SELECT list only.

SELECT

Defines a list of options that can be selected from a pull-down list in the current form; can contain active HTML elements.

Container element, requires </SELECT> closing tag.

Syntax: <SELECT>...</SELECT>

Attributes

NAME   Establishes the symbolic name for this selection list

Syntax: <SELECT NAME=*value*> (where *value* is a text name)

SIZE   Defines the number of options or choices that will be available in the selection list

Syntax: <SELECT SIZE=*n*> (where *n* is the number of available selections)

MULTIPLE   Indicates that multiple selections are allowed from the selection list

Syntax: <SELECT MULTIPLE>

Usage
Body section, form container only.

TEXTAREA

Defines a multiline input field; does not support HTML elements.

Container element, requires </TEXTAREA> closing tag

Syntax: <TEXTAREA>...</TEXTAREA>

Note: Default text to be displayed in the input field is filled between the tags.

Attributes

NAME   Establishes the symbolic name for this selection list

Syntax: <TEXTAREA NAME=*value*> (where *value* is a text name)

ROWS   Defines the number of rows the input field will display

Syntax: <TEXTAREA ROWS=*n*> (where *n* is the number of input field rows visible)

COLS   Defines the width (in characters) of the text input area

Syntax: <TEXTAREA COLS=*n*> (where *n* is the number of columns or characters of the input field's width)

Usage: Regularly combined with ROWS to specify the text input field's display dimensions.

Usage

Body section, within a form container only.

HTML 2.0 Entities

Note: These escape sequences must be entered in lowercase.

Accented Characters

Æ   for uppercase AE diphthong (ligature)

Á for uppercase A, acute accent

Â   for uppercase A, circumflex accent

À for uppercase A, grave accent

Å   for uppercase A, ring

Ã   for uppercase A, tilde

Ä   for uppercase A, dieresis or umlaut mark

Ç for uppercase C, cedilla

Ð   for uppercase Eth, Icelandic

É for uppercase E, acute accent

Ê   for uppercase E, circumflex accent

È for uppercase E, grave accent

Ë   for uppercase E, dieresis or umlaut mark

Í   for uppercase I, acute accent

Î   for uppercase I, circumflex accent

Ì   for uppercase I, grave accent

Ï   for uppercase I, dieresis or umlaut mark

Ñ   for uppercase N, tilde

Ó for uppercase O, acute accent

Ô   for uppercase O, circumflex accent

Ò   for uppercase O, grave accent

Ø   for uppercase O, slash

Õ   for uppercase O, tilde

Ö   for uppercase O, dieresis or umlaut mark

Þ   for uppercase THORN, Icelandic

Ú   for uppercase U, acute accent

Û   for uppercase U, circumflex accent

Ù   for uppercase U, grave accent

Ü   for uppercase U, dieresis or umlaut mark

Ý   for uppercase Y, acute accent

á   for lowercase a, acute accent

â   for lowercase a, circumflex accent

æ   for lowercase ae diphthong (ligature)

à   for lowercase a, grave accent

å   for lowercase a, ring

ã   for lowercase a, tilde

ä   for lowercase a, dieresis or umlaut mark

ç   for lowercase c, cedilla

é   for lowercase e, acute accent

ê   for lowercase e, circumflex accent

è   for lowercase e, grave accent

ð   for lowercase eth, Icelandic

ë   for lowercase e, dieresis or umlaut mark

í   for lowercase i, acute accent

î   for lowercase i, circumflex accent

ì   for lowercase i, grave accent

ï   for lowercase i, dieresis or umlaut mark

ñ   for lowercase n, tilde

ó for lowercase o, acute accent

ô   for lowercase o, circumflex accent

ò for lowercase o, grave accent

ø for lowercase o, slash

õ for lowercase o, tilde

ö   for lowercase o, dieresis or umlaut mark

ß   for lowercase sharp s, German (sz ligature)

þ   for lowercase thorn, Icelandic

ú for lowercase u, acute accent

û   for lowercase u, circumflex accent

ù for lowercase u, grave accent

ü   for lowercase u, dieresis or umlaut mark

ý for lowercase y, acute accent

ÿ   for lowercase y, dieresis or umlaut mark

ASCII Characters

&#*n*;   (where *n* is the specified ASCII code)

Reserved HTML Characters

<   for < character

>   for > character

&   for & character

"   for " character

®   Netscape 1.0 extension, for registered trademark symbol

©   Netscape 1.0 extension, for copyright symbol

WWW Bibliography

The following bibliographical references are all available over the World Wide Web; they constitute the majority of the information available regarding HTML and the standards process (as well as references to topics, such as Perl, UseNet, and the WWW itself). Some of these documents will change location over time because the Web isn't a fixed environment. If you have trouble finding a specific document listed here, use a Web searching facility (such as Web Search) to see whether the document is maintained elsewhere.

The quality of the information in these documents varies as does the quality of any data on the Internet. Consider the source before you take the accuracy of any information for granted. Many documents also include links to other documents on this list. In this manner, the WWW lives up to its reputation as a sort of spider's web or maze, and it's very easy to find yourself back where you started after a long, convoluted search.

HTML Documentation

http://www.utirc.utoronto.ca/HTMLdocs/NewHTML/htmlindex.html

Dr. Ian Graham, University of Toronto

World Wide Web Frequently Asked Questions

http://sunsite.unc.edu/boutell/faq/www_faq.html

Thomas Boutell

A Beginner's Guide to HTML

http://www.ncsa.uiuc.edu/General/Internet/WWW/HTMLPrimer.html

National Center for Supercomputing Applications (pubs@ncsa.uiuc.edu)

HTML Quick Reference

http://kuhttp.cc.ukans.edu/lynx_help/HTML_quick.html

Michael Grobe, The University of Kansas

Composing Good HTML

http://www.willamette.edu/html-composition/strict-html.html

James "Eric" Tilton (jtilton@willamette.edu)

HyperText Markup Language (HTML)

http://info.cern.ch/hypertext/WWW/MarkUp/MarkUp.html

Daniel W. Connolly, World-Wide Web Consortium (W3C) in the Laboratory for Computer Science, MIT

HyperText Markup Language Specification Version 3.0

http://www.hpl.hp.co.uk/people/dsr/html/CoverPage.html

Dave Raggett, W3C

A Beginner's Guide to URLs

http://www.ncsa.uiuc.edu/demoweb/url-primer.html

Marc Anderssen (mosaic@ncsa.uiuc.edu)

Crash Course on Writing Documents for the Web

http://www.pcweek.ziff.com/~eamonn/crash_course.html

Eamonn Sullivan, PC Week

Elements of HTML Style

http://bookweb.cwis.uci.edu:8042/Staff/StyleGuide.html

J.K. Cohen, UC Irvine (jkcohen@uci.edu)

Hypertext Terms

http://info.cern.ch/hypertext/WWW/Terms.html

The Common Gateway Interface

http://hoohoo.ncsa.uiuc.edu/cgi/

Rob McCool, NCSA (robm@ncsa.uiuc.edu)

Style Guide for Online Hypertext

http://info.cern.ch/hypertext/WWW/Provider/Style/Overview.html

Tim Berns-Lee, W3C (timbl@w3.org)

Entering the World Wide Web: A Guide to Cyberspace

http://www.eit.com/web/www.guide/

Kevin Hughes, Enterprise Integration Technologies

A Basic HTML Style Guide

http://guinan.gsfc.nasa.gov/Style.html

Alan Richmond, NASA GSFC

IETF HyperText Markup Language (HTML) Working Group

ftp://www.ics.uci.edu/pub/ietf/html/index.html

The HTML 3.0 Hypertext Document Format

http://www.w3.org/hypertext/WWW/Arena/tour/start.html

Daniel W. Connolly's Welcome Page

http://www.w3.org/hypertext/WWW/People/Connolly/

Daniel W. Connolly

The WWW Virtual Library

http://info.cern.ch/hypertext/DataSources/bySubject/Overview2.html

vlib@mail.w3.org

SGML (Standard Generalized Markup Language)

http://nearnet.gnn.com/wic/comput.39.html

The World Wide Web

http://www.w3.org/hypertext/WWW/TheProject.html

Tim Berns-Lee, W3C (timbl@w3.org)

Authoring WWW Documents: Overview

http://rsd.gsfc.nasa.gov/users/delabeau/talk/

Jeff de La Beaujardière (delabeau@camille.gsfc.nasa.gov)

HTML Writers Guild

http://ezinfo.ucs.indiana.edu/~awooldri/www-writers.html

awooldri@indiana.edu

The Web Developer's Journal

http://www.awa.com/nct/software/eleclead.html

NCT Web Magazine
Markland Communities, Inc.

WAIS, A Sketch of an Overview

Jeff Kellem, Beyond Dreams (**composer@Beyond.Dreams.ORG**)

World Wide Web Primer

http://www.vuw.ac.nz/~gnat/ideas/www-primer.html

Nathan Torkington

The Internet Index

http://www.openmarket.com/info/internet-index/current.html

Win Treese (treese@OpenMarket.com)

HTML Documents: A Mosaic Tutorial

http://fire.clarkson.edu/doc/html/htut.html

Wm. Dennis Horn, Clarkson University

How to Create High-Impact Documents

http://home.mcom.com/home/services_docs/impact_docs/
creating-high-impact-docs.html

Netscape Communications Corporation

Bad Style Page

http://www.earth.com/bad-style/

Tony Sanders, (sanders@bsdi.com)

The Web Communications Comprehensive Guide to Publishing on the Web

http://www.webcom.com/html/

Web Communications (support@webcom.com)

WebTechs and HTML

http://www.hal.com/~markg/WebTechs/

Mark Gaither, HaL Computer Systems (markg@hal.com)

SGML

http://info.cern.ch/hypertext/WWW/MarkUp/SGML.html

Tim Berns-Lee, W3C (timbl@w3.org)

Perl FAQ

http://www.cis.ohio-state.edu/hypertext/faq/usenet/perl-faq/top.html

Stephen P. Potter and Tom Christiansen (perlfaq@perl.com)

PERL—Practical Extraction and Report Language

http://www-cgi.cs.cmu.edu/cgi-bin/perl-man

Larry Wall (lwall@netlabs.com)

University of Florida's Perl Archive

http://www.cis.ufl.edu/perl/

Steve Potter, Varimetrix Corporation (spp@vx.com)

Action Index

General HTML

continues

Advanced HTML

Special HTML tips and tricks

continues

When you need to...	Look here...
Design lists for optimum effect	P. 230
Use hyperlinks for maximum benefit	P. 235
Design to help the user navigate	P. 235
Control font sizes	P. 236
Maximize your use of graphic elements	P. 241
Determine the size of graphic images	P. 243
Work with various resolutions	P. 244
Make your graphics transparent	P. 246
Work with graphics of text elements	P. 247
Design buttons for easy navigation	P. 249
Animate graphics in your Web site	P. 252
Use pull animation techniques	P. 253
Use server-push animation techniques	P. 255
Update graphics using the META element	P. 254
Work with CGI to animate pages	P. 255
Design pages with video components	P. 260
Practice working with text enhancements	P. 264
Make sure your Web site works by testing	P. 267
Design pages using Netscape 2.0 enhancements	P. 281
Design pages using Internet Explorer 2.0 enhancements	P. 288
Work with Netscape frames	P. 282
Set HTML clicks to target pages	P. 286
Use font colors	P. 287
Work with background audio	P. 288

When you need to...	Look here...
Design scrolling marquees	P. 289
Work with built-in video files	P. 289

Other HTML issues

When you need to...	Look here...
Advertise your site on the Web	P. 275
Develop a plan for maintaining and updating	P. 277
Announce your site in Web indexes	P. 272
Determine where to advertise	P. 276
Choose an HTML editor	p. 21
Find graphics and multimedia tools	P. 302

Index

PLUG YOURSELF INTO...

The Macmillan USA Information SuperLibrary (tm)

See the new SuperLibrary Newsletter

sams net

SAMS PUBLISHING

Hayden Books

que

New Riders

BradyGAMES

ADOBE PRESS

que E&T

THE MACMILLAN INFORMATION SUPERLIBRARY™

Free information and vast computer resources from the world's leading computer book publisher—online!

FIND THE BOOKS THAT ARE RIGHT FOR YOU!

A complete online catalog, plus sample chapters and tables of contents!

- **STAY INFORMED** with the latest computer industry news through our online newsletter, press releases, and customized Information SuperLibrary Reports.

- **GET FAST ANSWERS** to your questions about QUE books.

- **VISIT** our online bookstore for the latest information and editions!

- **COMMUNICATE** with our expert authors through e-mail and conferences.

- **DOWNLOAD SOFTWARE** from the immense Macmillan Computer Publishing library:
    - Source code, shareware, freeware, and demos

- **DISCOVER HOT SPOTS** on other parts of the Internet.

- **WIN BOOKS** in ongoing contests and giveaways!

TO PLUG INTO QUE:

WORLD WIDE WEB: **http://www.mcp.com/que**

FTP: ftp.mcp.com

Complete and Return this Card
for a *FREE* Computer Book Catalog

Thank you for purchasing this book! You have purchased a superior computer book written expressly for your needs. To continue to provide the kind of up-to-date, pertinent coverage you've come to expect from us, we need to hear from you. Please take a minute to complete and return this self-addressed, postage-paid form. In return, we'll send you a free catalog of all our computer books on topics ranging from word processing to programming and the internet.

Mr. ☐ Mrs. ☐ Ms. ☐ Dr. ☐

Name (first) [ ] (M.I.) ☐ (last) [ ]

Address [ ]

City [ ] State [ ] Zip [ ]

Phone [ ] Fax [ ]

Company Name [ ]

E-mail address [ ]

1. Please check at least (3) influencing factors for purchasing this book.

Front or back cover information on book .... ☐
Special approach to the content .... ☐
Completeness of content .... ☐
Author's reputation .... ☐
Publisher's reputation .... ☐
Book cover design or layout .... ☐
Index or table of contents of book .... ☐
Price of book .... ☐
Special effects, graphics, illustrations .... ☐
Other (Please specify): _____ ☐

2. How did you first learn about this book?

Saw in Macmillan Computer Publishing catalog .... ☐
Recommended by store personnel .... ☐
Saw the book on bookshelf at store .... ☐
Recommended by a friend .... ☐
Received advertisement in the mail .... ☐
Saw an advertisement in: _____ ☐
Read book review in: _____ ☐
Other (Please specify): _____ ☐

3. How many computer books have you purchased in the last six months?

This book only .... ☐   3 to 5 books .... ☐
2 books .... ☐   More than 5 .... ☐

4. Where did you purchase this book?

Bookstore .... ☐
Computer Store .... ☐
Consumer Electronics Store .... ☐
Department Store .... ☐
Office Club .... ☐
Warehouse Club .... ☐
Mail Order .... ☐
Direct from Publisher .... ☐
Internet site .... ☐
Other (Please specify): _____ ☐

5. How long have you been using a computer?

☐ Less than 6 months   ☐ 6 months to a year
☐ 1 to 3 years   ☐ More than 3 years

6. What is your level of experience with personal computers and with the subject of this book?

	With PCs	With subject of book
New	☐	☐
Casual	☐	☐
Accomplished	☐	☐
Expert	☐	☐

Source Code ISBN: 0-7897-0622-9

7. Which of the following best describes your job title?

- Administrative Assistant ☐
- Coordinator ☐
- Manager/Supervisor ☐
- Director ☐
- Vice President ☐
- President/CEO/COO ☐
- Lawyer/Doctor/Medical Professional ☐
- Teacher/Educator/Trainer ☐
- Engineer/Technician ☐
- Consultant ☐
- Not employed/Student/Retired ☐
- Other (Please specify): _____ ☐

8. Which of the following best describes the area of the company your job title falls under?

- Accounting ☐
- Engineering ☐
- Manufacturing ☐
- Operations ☐
- Marketing ☐
- Sales ☐
- Other (Please specify): _____ ☐

9. What is your age?

- Under 20 ☐
- 21-29 ☐
- 30-39 ☐
- 40-49 ☐
- 50-59 ☐
- 60-over ☐

10. Are you:

- Male ☐
- Female ☐

11. Which computer publications do you read regularly? (Please list)

_____
_____
_____
_____
_____
_____
_____
_____
_____

Comments: _____
_____
_____

Fold here and scotch-tape to mail.